Blake's Milton Designs:
The Dynamics of Meaning

J. M. Q. Davies

LOCUST HILL PRESS
West Cornwall, CT
1993

Library of Congress Cataloging-in-Publication Data

Davies, J. M. Q.
  Blake's Milton designs : the dynamics of meaning / J.M.Q. Davies.
  347p.   cm. – (Locust Hill literary studies ; no. 7)
  Includes bibliographical references and index.
  ISBN 0-933951-40-X : $40.00
  1. Blake, William, 1757–1827--Themes, motives. 2. Blake, William,
  1757–1827--Criticism and interpretation. 3. Milton, John,
  1608–1674--Illustrations. I. Title II. Series.
  ND 1942.B55D39   1992
  759.2--dc20   92-32678
                                                                      CIP

Printed on acid-free, 250-year-life paper
Manufactured in the United States of America

For
Poh Pheng
Ashley *and* Graham

Contents

Illustrations

The Paradise Lost *Designs*

Illustrations

The Nativity Ode *Designs*

The L'Allegro and Il Penseroso *Designs*

Illustrations

Preface

Blake's Milton illustrations have attracted a good deal of attention over the last two decades, but discussion has been characterized less by progressively deepening understanding than by disagreement. Not only minute particulars or individual designs but entire sequences have elicited diametrically opposed interpretations, and only a general consensus has emerged that they are in some measure critical of Milton. This is hardly surprising perhaps, considering the formidable range of hermeneutic variables the Blake Milton perplex brings into play. How we construe Blake's pictorial commentaries is inevitably affected by how radical we consider Milton to be in the seventeenth-century context, by whether we are disposed to see Blake as more concerned with commending his precursor's visionary insights or with exposing his doctrinal errors, by the degree to which we regard Blake as anticipating our postmodern assumptions, and so on.

The difficulty of being moderately confident that we are responding to what Blake intended to convey is compounded by the fact that we are dealing with sequentially arranged pictorial images, which are often richly suggestive in relation to tradition. Moreover, in the case of only one of the five—or, counting duplicate versions, eight—completed sequences have brief descriptive notes in Blake's hand survived to assist interpretation. Consequently, the line between legitimate inference and inadvertent allegoresis—or even wholesale deconstruction—can be a fine one. Yet no one who contemplates the large, resplendent set of illustrations to *Paradise Lost* in the Boston Museum of Fine Arts, or the small but highly finished *L'Allegro and Il Penseroso* series in the Pierpont Morgan Library, can doubt that Blake put a great deal of thought and care into these compositions.

For these reasons, the essay form in which three of the following chapters first appeared has been retained: they are intended as *essais* in the provisional exploratory sense implied in Montaigne's original use of the term. They differ from much previous commentary in arguing that these sequences are very tightly organized internally, and that Blake's departures from his texts are often imaginatively audacious. A summary discussion of the Blake Milton relationship and some of the methodological assumptions of this study are presented in the introduction to provide access for a wider readership. But the analyses of individual sequences are substantially self-contained and may be consulted directly for what they have to contribute. Some of the readings proposed may turn out to be overinterpretations, and it seems likely that the *Paradise Lost* and *Paradise Regained* designs in particular may look rather different when Blake's illustrations to the Bible have been more fully studied. Yet Blake is almost never dull, and his simplest lyrics, aphorisms, and marginal comments have an astonishing power to stir the imagination. There seems no intrinsic reason, therefore, to suppose that he would have responded to Milton with less humor, or less imaginative vigor, when he came to illustrate his poems than he had done in *The Marriage of Heaven and Hell* and *Milton*.

Grateful acknowledgment is due to the Killam Foundation for initial sponsorship of this research, to the *Durham University Journal*, the *Journal of the Australasian Universities Language and Literature Association*, and Locust Hill Press which published earlier versions of some of the material, and to the University of Melbourne and the Northern Territory University for assistance with the cost of illustrations. These are reproduced courtesy of the following holding institutions: the Boston Museum of Fine Arts; the British Library; the British Museum; the Fitzwilliam Museum; the Fogg Art Museum, Harvard University; the Frick Collection; the Houghton Library, Harvard University; the Huntington Library and Art Galleries; the Library of Congress; the Manchester City Art Gallery; the Pierpont Morgan Library; the Museum of Art, Rhode Island School of Design; the National Gallery, Washington; the National Gallery of Victoria; the National Library of Australia; Petworth House; the Princeton University Library; the State Library of Victoria; the Tate Gallery; the University of Illinois Library; the Victoria and Albert Museum; the Whitworth Art Gallery; and the Yale Center for British Art. *Fortuna gratias*, I owe a personal debt to John E. Grant, who supervised my doctoral thesis and has continued to be unstintingly generous with his time and "damn bracing" in his criticism; to my former colleague Edward J. Rose, whose ranging conversations led me to perceive some of Blake's infinite particulars; to Geoffrey M. Down for expert assistance with the prints; to Robert F. Gleckner for practical help along the way; to Margaret Hood and Harold Davies for their meticulous perusal of the manuscript; and above all to Michael J. Tolley, whose acuity and skepticism have repeatedly forced me to rethink. I hold none of them responsible for the shortcomings of these essays.

Abbreviations

1. Works by Blake

AllR	*All Religions Are One*
Am	*America*
DesC	*Descriptive Catalogue*
EG	*The Everlasting Gospel*
Eur	*Europe*
FR	*The French Revolution*
FZ	*The Four Zoas*
GP	*The Gates of Paradise*
J	*Jerusalem*
MHH	*The Marriage of Heaven and Hell*
Mil	*Milton*
NNR	*There Is No Natural Religion*
SE	*Songs of Experience*
SI	*Songs of Innocence*
SoL	*The Song of Los*
Ur	*The Book of Urizen*
VDA	*Visions of the Daughters of Albion*
VLJ	*A Vision of the Last Judgment*

2. Secondary Works and Editions

B	Martin Butlin, *The Paintings and Drawings of William Blake* (New Haven: Yale Univ. Press, 1981), Vol. II
BR	G. E. Bentley, Jr., *Blake Records* (Oxford: Clarendon Press, 1969)
E	David V. Erdman, ed., *The Complete Poetry and Prose of William Blake* (New York: Doubleday, 1982)
H & P	Francis Haskell and Nicholas Penny, *Taste and the Antique* (New Haven: Yale Univ. Press, 1981)
IB	David V. Erdman, *The Illuminated Blake* (New York: Doubleday, 1974)
P	Marcia Pointon, *Milton and English Art* (Toronto: Univ. of Toronto Press, 1970)

Introduction:
The Blake Milton Perplex

Blake's ongoing dialogue with Milton has served as the basis for an entire theory of intertextuality, as an archetypal paradigm of the struggle of all major poets to transcend the influence of their precursors and find their own artistic voice.[1] Yet it is hard to think of any literary relationship which generates a comparable sense that the issues engaged are, in Blake's memorable phrase, "the extent of the human mind" (E 544). Around 1810, during a period of crisis brought on by setbacks, a sense of professional isolation, and aspersions of madness, Blake defiantly referred to himself as a "Mental Prince" (E 580). And the scope of his achievement is no doubt primarily a correlative of his high intuitive intelligence—a kind of inspired common sense that he admired in Christ and referred to variously as the poetic genius or the divine gift of imagination that made every honest man potentially a prophet. It also has to do with his formidable powers of assimilation and association—his syncretist ability to see and expostulate against a common denominator of error in thinkers as diverse as

> this Newtonian Phantasm
> This Voltaire & Rousseau: this Hume & Gibbon & Bolingbroke
> This Natural Religion! this impossible absurdity!
>   (*Mil* 40.11–13, E 141)

But the imaginative range and comprehensiveness which make Blake's work perhaps the closest thing we have to a *summa* for the post-Enlightenment era are also partly attributable to his complex response to the challenge of Milton's encyclopedic poems, to the fact that we are dealing with a giant standing upon giant shoulders.

Aside from the Bible, no other cultural edifice played a more seminal part in Blake's creative development than Milton, and when he declared that

> I must Create a System, or be enslav'd by another Mans
> I will not Reason & Compare: my business is to Create,
>   (*J* 10.20–21, E 153)

1

one system he undoubtedly had very much in mind was the system of "Miltons Religion" (*Mil* 22.39, E 117). His imaginative involvement with his precursor was at once aesthetic, political, religious, and personal. The Romantic era may have been, as Schiller believed, an age characterized by reflective self-consciousness—only Goethe among his contemporaries seemed to him to have retained the artistic spontaneity of Homer.[2] But it was a period too in which the momentous events that inspired Blake to write *The French Revolution* (1789), *America* (1793), and *Europe* (1794) called for models of heroic poetry such as Milton provided. Moreover, as a republican who in the 1780s had associated with Paine, Holcroft, Godwin, Wollstonecraft, and other radicals at the bookseller Joseph Johnson's "weekly dinners," Blake was further drawn to the prophetic Milton, the champion of Christian liberty in an earlier revolutionary age.[3] At the same time he was also heir to the skepticism of the Enlightenment: "Voltaire," he remarked to the diarist Crabb Robinson, "was commissioned by God to expose" the Bible in its "natural sense."[4] And he could see that as a compendium of traditional Christian doctrine *Paradise Lost*, with its immense prestige, had become something of a "Covering Cherub" (*Mil* 9.50, E 104), an obstacle to man's perception of the simple Christian truths he thought of as the Everlasting Gospel. Blake's personal sympathies were undoubtedly more broadly democratic than Milton's, but temperamentally the two poets were not dissimilar in their high sense of the artist's calling, their idealism and industry, their unwillingness to mince words or suffer fools gladly, and their dedication to the task of rousing their fellow Englishmen to a perception of the infinite as each conceived it.[5] When Blake quotes Moses' prayer, "Would to God that all the Lord's people were Prophets. Numbers XI. ch. 29v." (E 96) as the epigraph to *Milton*, a prayer Milton had also reiterated in *Areopagitica*, it is partly in acknowledgment that Milton had indeed been animated by the spirit of true prophecy, despite his doctrinal errors.[6] Something of the total imaginative involvement which is characteristic of Blake's relationship with Milton is suggested by the amusing episode reported by Gilchrist, and usually retold to illustrate Blake's eccentricity and simplicity of character:

> At the end of the little garden in Hercules Buildings there was a summer-house. Mr Butts calling one day found Mr and Mrs Blake sitting in this summer-house, freed from "those troublesome disguises" which have prevailed since the Fall. "Come in!" cried

Blake; "it's only Adam and Eve, you know!" Husband and wife had been reciting passages from *Paradise Lost*, in character, and the garden of Hercules Buildings had to represent the Garden of Eden: a little to the scandal of wondering neighbours, on more than one occasion.[7]

Furthermore, when this anecdote is taken as an emblem of Milton's vital presence not only in Blake's imaginative life but also in the culture, it helps account for the urgency with which he sought to expose what he regarded as the "False Tongue" (*Mil* 2.10, E 96) of Milton's Christian doctrine.[8]

Blake's most direct engagement with Milton's conceptual errors occurs in *The Marriage of Heaven and Hell* (1790), in *Milton* (1804–16), and in his sequences of watercolor illustrations to *Comus* (1801, c. 1816), *Paradise Lost* (1807, 1808), the *Nativity Ode* (1809, c. 1816), *L'Allegro and Il Penseroso* (c. 1816), and *Paradise Regained* (c. 1816–25). However, the persistent presence of Milton's influence in Blake's work, from the early Ossianic fragment "Samson" (1783) on, means that hermeneutic clues to the exact meaning of these designs are often oblique and can come from virtually anywhere in his poetic and pictorial canon. It is probable, for instance, that *L'Allegro* and *Il Penseroso*, immensely popular during the eighteenth century, had some influence on the *Songs of Innocence and of Experience* (1794), advertised in the subtitle as "Shewing the Two Contrary States of the Human Soul" (E 7). But when Blake comes to illustrate Milton's companion poems twenty years later (Figs. 55–66), he seems to take him to task precisely for his failure to recognize that Mirth and Melancholy are contraries, wittily introducing Milton himself five times as *Il Penseroso* dressed in somber Puritan garb, as against twice as *L'Allegro*—a good instance of his holistic way of thinking about his precursor.[9] Milton is also Blake's point of departure in *Europe*, where an allusion to the *Nativity Ode* serves to ironize the ensuing chronicle of the woes of fallen history since Christ's advent:

> The deep of winter came;
> What time the secret child,
> Descended thro' the orient gates of the eternal day:
> War ceas'd, & all the troops like shadows fled to their abodes.
>
> (*Eur* 3.1–4, E 61)

The bleakness of Blake's vision of the Christian era in this prophecy—presided over on the frontispiece (Fig. 82) by Milton's Creator with his twin compasses—provides a possible explanation for the fact that in the fifth *Nativity Ode* design Moloch worship seems very much alive.[10] What we may in fact be witnessing is not the "Flight of Moloch" (Figs. 51–52), but his reinstatement by the departing scarlet bat-winged Satan overhead.

But the work of Milton's that is most pervasively present as a shaping influence on Blake during the decade between 1790 and 1800 when he resided at 13 Hercules Buildings, Lambeth, is, of course, *Paradise Lost*. As England's outstanding Protestant epic, which dramatized the central myth of Western Christendom in scenes of great sublimity and pastoral beauty, it not only summarized much that he regarded as retrogressive socially, but was also richly suggestive as a model for new mythopoeic poetry in an age reduced by the successive "unveilings" of comparative mythographers to "Single vision & Newtons sleep" (E 722).[11] Some of Blake's most fundamental objections to Milton's religion are raised by "The voice of the Devil" on plate 4 of the *Marriage*, a work centrally concerned with the education of a prophet.

> All Bibles or sacred codes have been the causes of the following Errors.
> 1. That Man has two real existing principles Viz: A Body & a Soul.
> 2. That Energy, calld Evil, is alone from the Body, & that Reason calld Good, is alone from the Soul.
> 3. That God will torment Man in Eternity for following his Energies
> But the following Contraries to these are True
> 1. Man has no Body distinct from his Soul for that calld Body is a portion of Soul discernd by the five Senses, the chief inlets of Soul in this age.
> 2. Energy is the only life and is from the Body and Reason is the bound or outward circumference of Energy
> 3. Energy is Eternal Delight
>
> (*MHH* 4, E 34)

A point not always appreciated in this passage is that the first three propositions constitute not the contraries of the second three but, in Blake's later terminology, their negations.[12] Blake refined but never abandoned his belief that "Without Contraries is no progression" and that "Attraction and Repulsion, Reason and Energy, Love and Hate" are as "necessary to Human existence" (*MHH* 3, E 34) as the expansion and contraction of the human heart. And these principles inform pictures as widely separated in time as the mirror images of Urizen (Fig. 83) and Orc (Fig. 84) on plates 8 and 10 of *America* (1793), and the reunion of Jerusalem and Albion (Fig. 85) on the penultimate plate of *Jerusalem* (c. 1820). They are particularly important to an understanding of the *Paradise Lost* designs, where there are grounds for suspecting that Adam and Eve are allegorized as Reason and Sense, or the Soul and Body as they appear personified in some of Blake's roughly contemporaneous illustrations to Robert Blair's *The Grave* (1808).[13]

There seems to be a more oblique relationship between the Milton sequences and the great passage in the *Marriage* that interprets God's expulsion of Satan as a parable of the repression of desire by reason, equates Satan as desire with the true Messiah, and concludes that

> in Milton, the Father is Destiny, the Son, a Ratio of the five
> senses, & the Holy-ghost, Vacuum!
> Note. The reason Milton wrote in fetters when he wrote of Angels
> & God, and at liberty when of Devils & Hell, is because he was a
> true Poet and of the Devils party without knowing it.
>
> (*MHH* 5, E 35)

The wittily irreverent inversions on this plate are deliberately and self-consciously polemical, as is clear from Blake's marginal note in his copy of Swedenborg's *Heaven and Hell* (trans. 1784): "Thus Fools quote Shakespeare . . . You might as well quote Satans blasphemies from Milton & give them as Miltons Opinions" (E 601).[14] Later they were modified considerably, as Blake expanded his sketch of a rebellious Jesus in the *Marriage* (E 43) into a more comprehensive symbol of imagination, brotherhood, and love, and came to associate Satan more generally with error and with selfhood in a sense quite compatible with Milton's portrayal of him. He also came to recognize that any of the four Zoas or living principles could in fallen man become Satanic, though in Milton and the culture of the Enlightenment it was the dominance of reason that tended to destroy man's psychic equilibrium. A striking example of the kind of hermeneutic dilemmas this evolving symbolism generates occurs in the two opening infernal scenes in the *Paradise Lost* designs. Both depict a naked heroic Satan with arms raised in defiance, but in "Satan Arousing the Rebel Angels" (Figs. 19–20) he appears hemmed in by billowing clouds like Urizen on *America* 8, while in "Satan, Sin and Death: Satan Comes to the Gates of Hell" (Figs. 21–22) these iconographic clues seem to be contradicted by Satan's intimate association with the flames behind him, which imply an analogy with Orc as he appears on *America* 10. Such puzzles bring home the importance of the general methodological point made by E. H. Gombrich, that the pictorial symbol "only acquires its specific meaning in a given context."[15]

5

Blake's reshaping of the mythic world of *Paradise Lost*, which many still regarded as referring to historical events, into a radical "new system" based on the premise that "All deities reside in the human breast" (*MHH* 11, E 38) proceeded of course concurrently with these ideological polemics, and the note of irreverence toward Milton in the *Marriage* is often sounded in the Lambeth prophecies.[16] His Creation myth in *The Book of Urizen* (1794), for instance, not only caricatures Milton's Mosaic God outrageously but parodies all the qualities arousing dread in Milton's poem that Burke regarded as quintessentially sublime—obscurity, power, infinity, "Vacuity, Darkness, Solitude and Silence."[17] In *The Book of Ahania* (1795), where Urizen's confrontation with his son Fuzon echoes Milton's Hell Gate scene, one also suspects the modifying influence of pictorial renderings such as those by Hogarth (P 80) and James Barry (Fig. 92).[18] But it is in *The Four Zoas* (c. 1796–1807) that the comprehensiveness of Blake's deconstruction of the Christian archetypes of *Paradise Lost* comes into full view. The apocalyptic symbolism of Blake's first full-scale epic and its division into nine "Nights" reflect the influence of Young's *Night Thoughts*, for which during 1796 and 1797 he produced 537 exuberantly beautiful watercolor illustrations—several of them containing Miltonic allusions.[19] But the focus on man's fall and redemption, the quarrels between the Zoas and their female Emanations, the interstellar voyages of Urizen, the central symbol of the Tree of Mystery, and the elevated rhetoric of this great unfinished poem are all Miltonic in inspiration, and bear directly or indirectly on interpretation of the Milton illustrations. Blake's psychological myth of the fall of "Albion the Ancient Man" (*FZ* 2, E 300) as a "fall into Division & . . . Resurrection to Unity" (*FZ* 4.1, E 301), for instance, appears to function as a structuring principle in both the *Comus* and the *Paradise Lost* designs, while the norm of spousal harmony which the poem takes over from the *Marriage* seems to inform all the Milton sequences to some degree.[20]

Collectively these echoes indicate an ongoing engagement with Milton's poetry throughout the 1790s, and support the manuscript evidence that Blake had probably completed a first draft of *The Four Zoas* before he moved to Felpham in 1800, to embark on his "Three years Herculean Labour" (E 572) under the patronage of William Hayley.[21] But if, as his letters suggest, Blake learned more from Hayley as a literary entrepreneur than as a Miltonist, Hayley's promotion of his material welfare and his "Polite Disapprobation" (E 730) and unconscious "admiration join'd with envy" (*Mil* 12.7, E

105) of his creative work undoubtedly forced him to take stock.[22] For *Milton*, a record of Blake's "Spiritual Acts" (E 728) during this period, though not etched until around 1809, is a more self-conscious work in Schiller's sense than *The Four Zoas*, and displays less of the lyrical spontaneity that links the earlier poem with the *Night Thoughts* illustrations. Like the *Marriage* it is partly about the education of a prophet, and Blake himself in his capacity as Bard of Albion is in this respect the ultimate subject of the poem. Indeed, it might be described as a sustained meditation on the influence of Milton on Blake's thought and art during the previous decade. The complexities of this reflexive work raise the question of whether in the Milton sequences we should not expect comparable subtleties of thought. Doctrinally, too, there is a high degree of consistency between the *Marriage* and this more detailed exploration of the errors of Milton's religion. The dynamic nature of the principle of contraries is clarified by the notion of negations or errors, which must be incessantly cast off. And its operation is extended to the religious plane of Milton and the Churches through a subversive analogy with the traditional categories of the Reprobate, the Redeemed, and the Elect, in which

> the Elect cannot be Redeemed, but Created continually
> By Offering & Atonement in the cruelties of Moral Law.
> (*Mil* 5.11–12, E 98)

Earlier in the *Songs* Blake had observed sardonically that "Pity would be no more, / If we did not make somebody Poor" (E 27), and he objected to the doctrine of election on the analogous grounds that it was based on the Puritans' besetting sin, self-righteousness and the exclusion or sacrifice of others, and placed a premium on justice rather than forgiveness.

The dualistic assumptions outlined in the *Marriage*, which Milton and traditional Christian doctrine inherited from Plato, are also more fully and dramatically explored in *Milton* in terms of their effects on Milton's personal life.[23] The idea of making Milton the protagonist of an apocalyptic epic may have evolved out of the *Night Thoughts* project, since Young as narrator is a constant presence in his poem. But it could equally have been inspired by the personal note in Milton's work, both in his invocations in *Paradise Lost* and in his prose, where the self-righteousness that Blake objected to is more apparent.[24] Dr. Johnson's remark about Milton's "Turkish contempt for females" may also at some stage have influenced Blake's view of his precursor's shortcomings.[25] But he goes beyond this to suggest a causal connection between Milton's troubled domestic life and his inability to come to terms with the affective side of his own being, and he sees this as symptomatic of the repressive legacy of Puritanism. The limits to Milton's ability to transcend the assumptions of his age are ably summarized by Peter Malekin:

> Milton's counter-thrusting instincts for repressive authority and religious individualism were maintained in uneasy equilibrium by his refusal to question the ultimate presuppositions behind his religion and the Puritan system; final intellectual freedom was not within his reach—such questions he viewed as sacrilege. The hierarchy of the Puritan family, with the rational male at its head, was internalized in Milton's distrust of the heart. . . . Reason for Milton is, at least theoretically, synonymous with intelligence or understanding and, as Raphael says in [*Paradise Lost*] Book V, lines 486–90, intelligence ranges from the intuitive mind of the angels to the discursive ratiocination that is the dominant mode of thinking among humans. In practice, however, he tends to reduce reason to reasoning. . . . The heart Milton tends to equate with the passionate emotion and he allows no place for the higher perceptive intelligence of intuitive feeling. In fact, he does not think of feeling as intelligent at all, seeing it simply as something to be controlled by reason; this is a great loss to his perceptions of life, since the intelligence of the heart is ultimately unitive, whereas ratiocination by its very nature is restricted to duality.[26]

It is these unresolved dualities in Milton that prompt Blake to introduce him with wry humor at the beginning of *Milton*, "pondring the intricate mazes of Providence / Unhappy tho in heav'n" (*Mil* 2.17–18, E 96). And whatever its relation to Blake's frustrations under Hayley's patronage, the dramatic function of the Bard's Song, with its devil's party account of "Satan [as] Urizen" (*Mil* 10.1, E 104) attempting to usurp Imagination's role, is to reveal to Milton his own shortcomings:[27]

> And Milton said, I go to Eternal Death. The Nations still
> Follow after the detestable Gods of Priam; in pomp
> Of warlike selfhood, contradicting and blaspheming.
> When will the Resurrection come; to deliver the sleeping body
> From corruptibility: O when Lord Jesus wilt thou come?
> Tarry no longer; for my soul lies at the gates of death.
> I will arise and look forth for the morning of the grave.
> I will go down to the sepulcher to see if morning breaks!
> I will go down to self annihilation and eternal death,

Lest the Last Judgment come & find me unannihilate
And I be siez'd & giv'n into the hands of my own Selfhood
The Lamb of God is seen thro' mists & shadows, hov'ring
Over the sepulchers in clouds of Jehovah & winds of Elohim
A disk of blood, distant; & heav'ns & earths roll dark between
What do I here before the Judgment? without my Emanation?
With the daughters of memory, & not with the daughters of
    inspiration?
I in my Selfhood am that Satan: I am that Evil One!
He is my Spectre!

                                    (*Mil* 14.14–31, E 108)

Milton's subsequent descent through the "Mundane Shell" (*Mil* 17.19, E 110) onto Blake's left foot, and struggle to subdue his Urizenic Specter, culminate in a vision of Satan as the God of Justice and Atonement he had worshipped (*Mil* 38.50f, E 139), and of the Whore as the system of "Moral Virtue" (*Mil* 40.21, E 142) he had promulgated. And it is his consequent resolve to cast off all the past errors of religion and philosophy that Blake regarded as "Not Human" (*Mil* 41.1, E 142) in propensity which opens the way for the marriage of true contraries—his spousal reunion with his "Six-fold Emanation" (*Mil* 2.19, E 96) Ololon, representing "those three females whom his Wives, & those three whom his Daughters / Had represented and contain'd" (*Mil* 17.1–2, E 110). As the poem closes, they literally become one in Christ who, no longer "distant" and obscured by the "clouds of Jehovah & winds of Elohim," is manifest as the selfless love uniting them, and with a shriek Ololon's virginity flees like Noah's dove into the abyss. Blake himself, who like St. John of Revelation is at once witness, author, and transmitter of these visions, collapses momentarily by his wife Catherine's side in awe at Milton's "Spiritual Acts." But as the lark ascends, his creative energies revive, replenished by the spirit of prophecy in a Milton no longer fettered by doctrinal errors, inspiring him "To go forth to the Great Harvest & Vintage of the Nations" (*Mil* 43, E 144).[28]

Milton is thus Blake's most comprehensive commentary on Milton, his legacy and influence, and as the watermarks in the four extant copies indicate (E 806), he was still occupied with it between 1808 and 1816, the years to which most of the Milton illustrations probably belong. And it provides a correspondingly rich repository of thematic parallels and iconographic clues—ranging from the presence of Milton himself in the *L'Allegro and Il Penseroso*, and perhaps also in the later *Comus* series, to the spousal suggestiveness of the Judgment scene in the *Paradise Lost* designs (Figs. 37–38), where Christ's medial position between Adam and Eve and his conciliatory gesture seem to invoke the formula used by Perugino, Raphael, Dürer, and others in their depictions of the *Marriage of the Virgin*.[29] The parallel between Milton's wrestling with his Specter on the shores of the Arnon and Christ's confrontation with Satan in the wilderness in the *Paradise Regained* designs is particularly striking, and tends to endorse Harold Bloom's suspicion that Milton's brief epic may have provided the chief model for Blake's poem.[30] One of the iconographic features of this series which suggests that Blake's intentions are subversive is the fact that Satan is portrayed with the full beard traditionally associated with the Father.[31] Equally suggestive, however, in view of the austerely masculine tenor of *Paradise Regained*, is the frequency with which female figures are introduced. As Northrop Frye has astutely observed, "there is no emanation in Milton; no Beatrice or Miranda;" woman in his mature work is always seen as temptress.[32]

Given the general consistency of Blake's attitude to Milton's system of beliefs in the *Marriage* and *Milton*, it seems reasonable to assume, as commentary has tended to, that there is also a measure of conceptual consistency underlying the Milton illustrations. This seems likely even though they were done over a number of years and vary considerably in size, style, and finish.[33] At the same time, in the case of the *Comus*, *Paradise Lost*, and *Nativity Ode* series, which exist in two versions, there are differences in iconographic detail that imply a certain amount of rethinking and refinement on Blake's part. In the larger and more resplendent set to *Paradise Lost* in the Boston Museum of Fine Arts, for instance, which is dated 1808, only a year later than the Huntington set, "Satan Spying on Adam and Eve, and Raphael's Descent into Paradise" (Fig. 27) is replaced by "Adam and Eve Asleep" (Fig. 28), showing Satan as a toad close at the ear of Eve. Perhaps the most dramatic evidence of rethinking, however, occurs in the *Nativity Ode* series, where the iconographic discrepancies in the fourth design raise the possibility of a fundamental shift in Blake's interpretation of Milton's hymn. In the first version of "The Overthrow of Apollo and the Pagan Gods" (Fig. 49), the statue of Apollo seems curiously alive and is depicted in the moment of his triumph over Python. Only in the second version (Fig. 50) does he seem genuinely statuesque and frozen, more in line with Milton's text.

But there are other variables affecting interpretation upon which there is little consensus, and concerning which it is as well for commentary to articulate its critical assumptions. One is the nature and extent of Blake's indebtedness in these sequences to various iconographic traditions. There have been several extended studies of their relation to commercial Milton illustration, to which Medina, Cheron, Hayman, Mortimer, Richter, Burney, Stothard, Fuseli, and Westall were among the chief contributors.[34] And perhaps the most challenging hypothesis to emerge has been Joseph A. Wittreich, Jr.'s contention that Blake's designs are more celebratory than critical, and seek to retrieve Milton from the misrepresentations of past pictorial commentary.[35] There seems little doubt that the formulae developed and subjects chosen by earlier artists from *Paradise Lost*, by far the most frequently and profusely illustrated of Milton's poems, did influence Blake's *Paradise Lost* designs to some degree, particularly in the opening infernal scenes. Indeed, Blake is generally less innovative in his choice of subjects from the poem than some of his contemporaries, notably Westall, and Fuseli in his *Milton Gallery* series.[36] But as Anthony Blunt, Jean H. Hagstrum, Janet A. Warner, and others have demonstrated, Blake is the supreme eclectic when it comes to sources, and in the *Paradise Lost* series echoes and modulations of *topoi* developed by the great Renaissance masters in the main tradition of devotional art are at least as frequent as motifs adapted from other Milton illustrators.[37] In the case of the *Paradise Regained* designs, it is hard to detect any significant trace of the comparatively uninspired tradition of commercial illustration of the poem, whereas figures from Raphael and Michelangelo (available to Blake through engravings) and *pathos* formulae associated with Christ's Passion are used repeatedly.[38] So the vexing question of whether such borrowings are merely formal or carry iconographic implications occurs with corresponding frequency in these late designs.

A second factor affecting interpretation pertains to the degree of importance placed on the fact that Blake's Milton illustrations are pictorial narratives arranged in sequence. In a study that focuses principally on *Thel*, *Urizen*, and *Jerusalem*, W. J. T. Mitchell contends that "although Blake considers himself in some sense to be a 'history painter,' it is clear that he has little interest in attempting to construct his compositions as narrative texts."[39] The case is a little different with Blake's illustrations of the work of others, however, since he was constrained by the sequential unfolding of the text, which in the case of the Gray and *Night Thoughts* projects was inserted in offset windows forming the nucleus of each illustration.[40] That all the Milton sequences, with the doubtful exception of the *Nativity Ode* series, follow the narrative order of the poems suggests that Blake may have exploited this as an alternative mode of control over meaning to that afforded in the illuminated books by his own poems.

If in contemplating the Milton illustrations we adopt what may be termed the footnote hypothesis, and assume that Blake's primary concern is to illuminate Milton's poems, then we will find our imagination moving in a predominantly "vertical" direction between text and individual designs, observing him use details of attitude and gesture to highlight Milton's visionary insight here or to comment ironically on his doctrinal blindness there.[41] But in matters as momentous as the Fall of Man or the Divine Humanity of Christ, it is not hard to imagine Blake's being roused to a bolder and more comprehensive visionary counterstatement in his illustrations than can be accommodated by this hypothesis. And if we take seriously his contention that "when a Work has Unity it is as much in a Part as in the Whole, the Torso is as much a Unity as the Laocoön" (E 269), then we would expect the internal orchestration of the particulars, the "horizontal" progressions and relationships as they unfold in narrative sequence, to be at least as crucial to interpretation as their "vertical" relation to the text. In the 1808 set of *Paradise Lost* designs, for instance, the hypothesis that Blake may be interpreting the Fall in terms of his own rather than Milton's system is supported visually by the way Adam and Eve draw farther apart in successive designs (Figs. 26, 28, 30, 36), suggesting their gradual fall into division. And internal analogues and contrasts, such as that between Sin in medial position in the Hell Gate scene (Fig. 22) and Eve in the corresponding position in the Sylvan Lodge (Fig. 30), become potentially important determinants of meaning.

General analogues and precedents for Blake's internally coherent pictorial narratives are more common than specific models. Many of the works that influenced him throughout his life unfold sequentially—Michelangelo's Old Testament scenes on the Sistine Chapel ceiling, for instance, or Raphael's *Cartoons* (then at Hampton Court) depicting the lives of St. Peter and St. Paul, or Dürer's *Passion* sequences and splendid designs of the Apocalypse.[42] Single-leaf prints on biblical subjects frequently included several incidents in order to give the main outline of the story, as in the case of an engraving of *The Creation of Eve* after Ghiberti (Fig. 86). Commemorative history painting in English public buildings—as exemplified by the work of Rubens, Thornhill, Louis Laguerre, and others—also often had a significant narrative component.[43] Some of the major contemporary ventures in book illustration, such as Boydell's *Shakespeare Gallery* (1803) or Boyer's edition of Hume's *History of England* (1806), tended to focus on moments of high drama. But others, like Flaxman's illustrations to the *Iliad* and *Odyssey* (1793) and the *Divine Comedy* (1793/1807), follow the line of narrative quite closely. And in an age given to drawing analogies between the Sister Arts, we find that even the lesser genres, such as the conversation pictures explored by Ronald Paulson, or the comic works of Rowlandson, or the political cartoons on which Blake drew occasionally, are all apt to tell or at least imply a story.[44]

But the closest model for Blake's minutely orchestrated Milton illustrations is arguably provided by the engraved sequences of Hogarth. The two artists are not often considered together, since Hogarth is essentially an observer of the empirical world, whereas Blake as an idealist is committed to seeing through, not with, the natural eye. But if Blake is unlikely to have been sympathetic to Hogarth's endorsement of the ruling-class morality of virtues and vices, he would nonetheless have recognized him as a man in touch with the people and sympathetic to their misery, and may well have responded to the subversive aspects of his art.[45] Hogarth had done much, moreover, to elevate the status of engraving in England, and Blake had high praise for him as one whose powers of invention equalled his facility in execution, using him to illustrate his own conviction that "Ideas cannot be Given but in their minutely Appropriate Words nor Can a Design be made without its minutely Appropriate Execution" (E 576). It is true that specific connections with Hogarth are not common in Blake's pictorial canon, and that Hogarth's major sequences are generically different from the Milton illustrations in that, despite the many suggestive parallels with Fielding's novels, they are not directly constrained by a literary text.[46] It is rather in the choreography—the presentation of characters in dynamic and iconographically significant relation to each other, and to details of setting in a dramatically unfolding continuum—that the significant parallel would seem to lie. Few artists can conform more closely than Hogarth to the principles implied in Blake's entreaty that

the Spectator . . . attend to the Hands & Feet to the Lineaments of the Countenances; they are all descriptive of Character & not a line is drawn without intention & that most discriminate & particular. As Poetry admits not a Letter that is Insignificant so

> Painting admits not a Grain of Sand or a Blade of Grass
> Insignificant, much less an Insignificant Blur or Mark.
>
> (*VLJ* 83, E 560)

Two further variables affecting interpretation of these designs
need to be mentioned. One has to do with reading pictures rather
than words. A pertinent discussion is provided by Gombrich in
Symbolic Images, where he challenges the assumption that during
the Middle Ages and Renaissance symbols were "a kind of code
with a one-to-one relationship between sign and significance," by
drawing attention to the Neoplatonic tradition in which "the symbol is seen as the mysterious language of the divine."[47] Expanding
on St. Thomas Aquinas's observation that "truth can be manifested
in two ways: by things or by words," Gombrich argues that "images apparently occupy a curious position somewhere between the
statements of language, which are intended to convey a meaning,
and the things of nature, to which we only can give a meaning" (p.
2). Contrary to deconstructionist theory, Gombrich maintains that
language "is a social institution that has evolved along lines of
utility" (p. 166) and whose meanings are inherently relatively stable,
whereas "the limit of significance . . . is much more open in the case
of symbolic images" (p. 95):

> The symbol that presents to us a revelation cannot be said to have
> one identifiable meaning assigned to its distinctive features. All
> its aspects are felt to be charged with a plenitude of meanings that
> can never be exhaustively learned, but must be found in the very
> process of contemplation it is designed to engender.   (p. 159)

This principle was operative, Gombrich contends, even in figures
like Cesare Ripa, usually considered a codifier of pictorial imagery,
but "the Age of Reason dismissed the mysterious image as an
absurdity" (p. 182), and it was left to the German Romantic philosophers of art, followed by Coleridge, to "invest the word symbol
with a new aura of mystery" (p. 183), and to distinguish between
symbolism and allegory.

In Blake, of course, the term mystery tends to have negative
associations with the interdictions of the Judeo-Christian deity. But
as regards obscurity in art, he concurred with "the wisest of the
Ancients" in considering "what is not too Explicit as the fittest for
Instruction because it rouzes the faculties to act" (E 702). And his
insistence on the difference between "Fable or Allegory [which] is
Formd by the Daughters of Memory" and "Vision" (E 554) reflects

his concern to stimulate the kind of complex contemplative response which Gombrich regards as characteristic more of the way we react to symbolic images than to words. Commenting on the iconography of *The Book of Urizen*, Mitchell remarks on "a maddening omnidirectional ambiguity" which seems "more like a Rorschach test than a pictorial statement," and concludes that "this is precisely what Blake intends" (pp. 145–46). And more recently Robert F. Gleckner has argued that in his picture *The Characters in Spenser's Faerie Queene* (B 879) Blake uses iconographic ambiguity as a means to foster true vision by frustrating one-to-one allegorical interpretation.[48] In the case of the Milton sequences, the effect of Blake's strategy of minute fidelity to, combined with intermittent deviance from, the letter of Milton's texts is to present us with a series of pictorial images which often have precisely the kind of suggestive power and hermeneutic open-endedness that Gombrich talks about. How are we to tell whether the analogy between Sin in medial position between Satan and Death before Hell Gate (Fig. 22), and Eve between Adam and Raphael in the Sylvan Lodge (Fig. 30) in the 1808 *Paradise Lost* series, is to be construed as a parallel or as a contrast? Should the aureole surrounding Christ on the pinnacle in the *Paradise Regained* designs (Fig. 76) be read as a token of his victory over Satan and his recognition of his own divinity in a sense compatible with Milton's own intentions? Is its phallic suggestiveness deliberate, a sign that Blake may be subverting Milton's vision of a celibate Christ, or would such a reading constitute a post-Freudian projection, an instance of what Paulson calls "one of the pitfalls of hermeneutics in graphic art," the "failure to limit the possible range of meanings when different images . . . are equally evoked"?[49]

Such puzzles are of course part of the wider question of the extent to which Blake's system itself eschews closure in a postmodern sense, an issue which is related to the debate in recent literary theory about the limits of pluralism.[50] Because Blake seems closer to us than Milton on such fundamentals as the origin of all religions, or the dangers of repression and guilt, it is easy to regard him as more of a Nietzschean relativist than is perhaps the case.[51] Clearly there is a perspectivist dimension to Blake's thought, most forcefully expressed perhaps in his proverbs undermining belief in sacred codes or urging imaginative self-transcendence, such as:

One Law for the Lion & Ox is oppression   (E 44)

or:

> How do you know but ev'ry Bird that cuts the airy way,
> Is an immense world of delight, clos'd to your senses five?
>
> (E 35)

Perspectivism is also one of the implications of his vortex symbolism, as articulated in the great passage in *Milton* explaining Milton's descent from Eternity into the sea of Time and Space:

> The nature of infinity is this: That every thing has its
> Own Vortex and when once a traveller thro Eternity
> Has passd that Vortex, he perceives it roll backward behind
> His path, into a globe itself infolding, like a sun:
> Or like a moon, or like a universe of starry majesty,
> While he keeps onwards in his wondrous journey on the earth
> Or like a human form, a friend with whom he livd benevolent.
> As the eye of man views both the east & west encompassing
> Its vortex; and the north & south, with all their starry host;
> Also the rising sun & setting moon he views surrounding
> His corn-fields and his valleys of five hundred acres square.
> Thus is the earth one infinite plane, and not as apparent
> To the weak traveller confin'd beneath the moony shade.
> Thus is the heaven a vortex passd already, and the earth
> A vortex not yet pass'd by the traveller thro' Eternity.
>
> (*Mil* 15.21–35, E 109)

And a degree of ethical relativism could certainly be inferred from Blake's emphasis on change, from his doctrine of forgiveness, and from his vision of the Last Judgment as concerned not with virtues and vices but with truth and error, concepts which target states while absolving individuals.

Despite this, however, terms like ambivalence, relativism, and indeterminacy seem at odds with the downrightness of Blake's artistic personality, his contempt for "doubt which is Self Contradiction" (E 512), and the ardor which he brought to his vatic role as Bard of Albion. Moreover, proverbs such as

> A fool sees not the same tree that a wise man sees   (E 35)

assume that such a distinction can be made, and the principle of rejecting error and embracing truth presupposes that truth can indeed be recognized and pursued through "Mental Fight" (E 95). Despite shifts in emphasis in Blake's epics from Orc to Los and from the Zoas to Christ, the priority of spiritual values over the values of Caesar is never in doubt. In his iconography, too, as Warner, David V. Erdman, and others have amply demonstrated, he with considerable consistency uses soaring, dancing, or awakening figures, verdant settings, and open skies redemptively, and constricted figures, barren settings, and louring or starry skies negatively.[52] All of this suggests that Blake's libertarianism coexisted with an equally firm persuasion that "In Equivocal Worlds Up & Down are Equivocal" (E 650).

What seems to determine the "bound or outward circumference" (E 34), as it were, of Blake's perspectivism are two assumptions he shared with many of the moral philosophers of the eighteenth century: that there are universal principles analogous to Newton's laws governing human behavior, and that a moral sense is innate in man. Debate on these issues had been fueled by the subversive ideas of Thomas Hobbes, who, as Basil Willey points out, "had challenged all the fundamentals of [Christian] civilization: he had turned sovereignty into arbitrary power; denied free will, the soul and natural goodness of heart; and made his Leviathan the arbiter of morality, religion and even truth itself."[53] Among the many voices raised in protest against Hobbes, Cudworth the Cambridge Platonist opposed his ethical relativism with the argument that moral truths, like the truths of geometry, were eternal and immutable.[54] Shaftesbury and Hume responded to his vision of man as motivated solely by self-interest by insisting on man's capacity for disinterested benevolence, and on the primacy of feeling over reason in the ethical response, while Rousseau denied that man is savage in his natural state and attributed his moral corruption to civilization.[55] But all of them argued or assumed that universal principles governing ethical behavior can be found. The impulse is essentially analogous to that of the eighteenth-century mythographers in their search for an underlying principle uniting all mythologies.

Because of Blake's known hostility to Deism and the empiricism of "Bacon, Newton [&] Locke" (E 251), and his reiterated assertion that "To generalize is to be an Idiot" (E 630), it is easy to overlook the fact that he is nevertheless still very much of the eighteenth century in assuming it is possible to generalize about human nature. What circumscribes Blake's perspectivism is his belief in the common yet divine humanity of all mankind, whether "heathen, turk or jew" (E 13). At the very outset of his prophetic career he announces that *All Religions Are One*, and proceeds to lay down as a fundamental principle that "As all men are alike in outward form, so (and with the same infinite variety) all are alike in the Poetic Genius" (E 1). And later, in his *Descriptive Catalogue*, he emphasizes that the same human types recur in every age, drawing specific parallels between the deities of Classical Antiquity and Chaucer's Canterbury Pilgrims (E 532). The imagination is thus the common factor that unites all men and accounts for the parallels between different religions. Moreover, as his conviction that "the voice of honest indignation is the voice of God" (E 38) implies, it is the divine gift of imagination, which replaces the divine gift of reason in Milton's system, that allows man to recognize "Self Evident Truth" (E 624) when confronted with it. The connection with Blake's Christology is made clear in the passage in *Milton* where the Bard vouches for his prophetic Song by asserting

> I am inspired! I know it is Truth! for I Sing
> According to the inspiration of the Poetic Genius
> Who is the eternal all-protecting Divine Humanity
> To whom be Glory & Power & Dominion Evermore Amen.
>
> (*Mil* 13.51–14.3, E 108)

Christ becomes a symbol of love, truth, and imagination for Blake, not for sectarian reasons, but because he exemplified these qualities to a supreme degree, and because Blake happened to have been born into a Christian culture.

How intimately Blake's ethics and his demystified humanist religious position are bound up with his artistic credo can be clearly seen in the passage toward the end of the *Descriptive Catalogue* extolling the linear and fulminating against the painterly traditions in art:

> The great and golden rule of art, as well as of life, is this: That the more distinct, sharp and wiry the bounding line, the more perfect the work of art; and the less keen and sharp, the greater is the evidence of weak imitation, plagiarism, and bungling. Great inventors, in all ages, knew this: Protogenes and Apelles knew each other by this line. Rafael and Michael Angelo, and Albert Durer, are known by this and this alone. The want of this determinate and bounding form evidences the want of idea in the artist's mind, and the pretence of the plagiary in all its branches. How do we distinguish the oak from the beech, the horse from the ox, but by the bounding outline? How do we distinguish one face or countenance from another, but by the bounding line and its infinite inflexions and movements? What is it that builds a house and plants a garden, but the definite and determinate? What is it that distinguishes honesty from knavery, but the hard and wiry line of rectitude and certainty in the actions and intentions. Leave out this line and you leave out life itself; all is chaos again, and the line of the almighty must be drawn out upon it before man or

beast can exist. Talk no more then of Correggio, or Rembrandt, or
any other of those plagiaries of Venice or Flanders.   (E 550)

There is no trace here of the dissociation between truth and beauty
which was to occur with the advent of Aestheticism. Blake may
thus be seen as a sort of intellectual Janus figure, anticipating the
kind of transvaluation of values we associate with the modern era,
yet in some respects still firmly rooted in eighteenth-century assumptions, while also reviving a religious mode of perception
which antedated the Enlightenment. His system, with its un-Miltonic
insistence on forgiveness, is flexible enough to accommodate change
and individual liberty, yet is committed to the American and French
revolutionary ideals of the brotherhood of man, and is unequivocal
in maintaining that a return of Adam into Paradise is possible if we
do not remain "blind to all the simple rules of life" (FZ 92.33, E 364).

Notes

1   See Harold Bloom, *The Anxiety of Influence: A Theory of Poetry* (New
     York: Oxford Univ. Press, 1973).

2   See Friedrich Schiller, *On the Naive and Sentimental in Literature*, trans.
     H. Watanabe-O'Kelly (Manchester: Carcanet New Press, 1981), pp.
     10f.

3   See Alexander Gilchrist, *Life of William Blake* (London: Dent, 1942), p.
     79.

4   Edith J. Morley, ed., *Henry Crabb Robinson on Books and Their Writers*
     (London: Dent, 1938), I.333; see Florence Sandler, "The Iconoclastic
     Enterprise: Blake's Critique of 'Milton's Religion,'" *Blake Studies*, 5
     (1972), 13–57.

5   Christopher Hill in *Milton and the English Revolution* (London: Faber &
     Faber, 1977), the most comprehensive study of the parallels between
     Milton's thought and that of his radical sectarian contemporaries,
     notes his increasing disillusionment with the people, "the confidence
     of *Areopagitica* contrast[ing] sadly with Messiah's denunciation of the
     people in *Paradise Regained*" (p. 256). "It is difficult," he concludes, "to
     make a final assessment of Milton's attitude towards 'the people,' or
     even to be sure what he meant by the word" (p. 186). Considering
     Milton's radicalism from Blake's perspective, Jackie Di Salvo in *War of
     Titans* (Pittsburgh: Univ. of Pittsburgh Press, 1983), p. 41, writes that
     "Blake's experience of working-class conditions led him beyond
     Milton's analysis. The fact that by Blake's time Puritanism had passed
     out of the camp of the devils into that of the ruling angels, where it
     became part of their artillery against the laborers, urged a thorough
     revaluation of the Miltonic vision."

6   See Merritt Y. Hughes, ed., *John Milton: Complete Poetry and Major Prose* (New York: Odyssey, 1957), p. 744. Quotations from Milton's poems are from this edition, except in the penultimate chapter, where Blake's handwritten excerpts from *L'Allegro* and *Il Penseroso* accompanying his designs have been followed.

7   G. E. Bentley, Jr., *Blake Records* (Oxford: Clarendon Press, 1969), p. 54.

8   See R. D. Havens, *The Influence of Milton on English Poetry* (Cambridge: Harvard Univ. Press, 1922), pp. 3–43; and Paul A. Cantor, *Creature and Creator: Myth-making and English Romanticism* (Cambridge: Cambridge Univ. Press, 1984), pp. 1–25.

9   Milton is mentioned by name only once in Blake's notes (E 683) to "The Sun at His Eastern Gate" (Fig. 57) in the *L'Allegro* series, but he probably also intended the dreaming "Youthful Poet" in the sixth design (Fig. 60) to be identified with Milton.

10 See *Paradise Lost*, VII.225. J. T. Smith in his early biographical sketch described the *Ancient of Days* as one of Blake's favorite designs, and made the connection with Milton that Blake seems also to have had in mind, even though it is the Son who in Milton is the Creator of the natural world (BR 470).

11 For the recurrence of the concept of "unveiling" in the mythographers, see Frank E. Manuel, *The Eighteenth Century Confronts the Gods* (Cambridge: Harvard Univ. Press, 1959), p. viii.

12 In the first three propositions, which are specifically described as errors, each of the traditional binary terms negates the other, whereas in the second three they are revealed as dynamically interdependent contraries. The ambiguity arises from the phrase "Contraries *to these*," but the context surely makes Blake's meaning plain.

13 See S. Foster Damon, *Blake's Grave* (Providence: Brown Univ. Press, 1963), pls. IV, V, VI, X, XI, and Figs. 96–97 below. Subsequent references to the series are numbered as in this edition.

14 For a further discussion of this passage, see Bloom, "Dialectic of *The Marriage of Heaven and Hell*" in *Ringers in the Tower* (Chicago: Univ. of Chicago Press, 1971), pp. 55–62.

15 E. H. Gombrich, *Symbolic Images* (London: Phaidon, 1972), p. 16.

16 The title of Jacob Bryant's *A New System; or An Analysis of Ancient Mythology* (London, 1774–76), on the plates to which Blake worked as James Basire's apprentice, articulates the system-building impetus of eighteenth-century mythographers more generally. See Manuel, pp. 272–80.

17 See Edmund Burke, *A Philosophical Enquiry into the Origin of Our Ideas of the Sublime and Beautiful*, ed. J. T. Boulton (London: Routledge, 1958), pp. 57f.; 71f.

18 See Marcia R. Pointon, *Milton and English Art* (Toronto: Univ. of Toronto Press, 1970), pp. 57–59, 102.

19 See John E. Grant, Edward J. Rose, Michael J. Tolley, and David V. Erdman, eds., *William Blake's Designs for Edward Young's Night Thoughts* (Oxford: Clarendon Press, 1980), pls. 119, 244, 261, 296, 297, 304, 305, 338, 339, 416, 451, 452, 508, 537. Subsequent references to individual designs in the series follow the standard numbering in this edition.

20 See Stephen C. Behrendt, *The Moment of Explosion* (Lincoln: Univ. of Nebraska Press, 1983), pp. 145f.

21 See David V. Erdman, ed., *The Complete Poetry and Prose of William Blake* (New York: Anchor, 1982), pp. 816–18.

22 For opposing views on the extent of Hayley's influence on Blake's intellectual development, see Joseph A. Wittreich, Jr., "Domes of Mental Pleasure: Blake's Epics and Hayley's Epic Theory," *Studies in Philology*, 4 (1971), 101–19; and Judith Wardle, "Satan not having the Science of Wrath, but only of Pity," *Studies in Romanticism*, 13 (1974), 147–54.

23 See Irene Samuel, *Milton and Plato* (Ithaca: Cornell Univ. Press, 1947), pp. 69–79.

24 See Hughes, pp. 690f., 817f. Hayley owned Birche's 1753 edition of Milton's prose; see *A Catalogue of the Very Valuable and Extensive Library of the Late William Hayley, Esq.* in A. N. L. Munby, ed., *Poets and Men of Letters: Sale Catalogues of Libraries of Eminent Persons* (London: Mansell, 1971), II.150.

25 See Mona Wilson, ed., *Johnson: Prose and Poetry* (London: Hart-Davis, 1957), p. 829.

26 Peter Malekin, *Liberty and Love: English Literature and Society 1640–88* (London: Hutchinson, 1981), p. 158.

27 For an influential reading of the Bard's Song as topical allegory, see Damon, *William Blake: His Philosophy and Symbols* (1924; Gloucester: Peter Smith, 1958), pp. 168–82. This approach has been challenged recently, however, by John Howard, who in *Blake's Milton: A Study in the Selfhood* (Cranbury: Associated Univ. Presses, 1976), p. 87, argues that "the essence of the narrative is not topical allegory. Entirely too much remains unexplored. . . . Indeed, it is a cynical irony to view Blake as quietly sitting in judgment on Hayley . . . in a mean and unforgiving way that suggests the very selfhood Blake takes to task."

28 See Howard, pp. 180f., for an excellent detailed analysis of the poem.

29 Raphael's and Perugino's versions are compared in John Pope-Hennessy, *Raphael* (London: Phaidon, 1970), pp. 85–86 and figs. 73–74.

For Dürer's version, see Erwin Panofsky, *The Life and Art of Albrecht Dürer* (1943; Princeton: Princeton Univ. Press, 1955), p. 103 and pl. 143.

30 Bloom, *Blake's Apocalypse: A Study in Poetic Argument* (Ithaca: Cornell Univ. Press, 1970), pp. 362–63, 366.

31 See Wittreich, *Angel of Apocalypse: Blake's Idea of Milton* (Madison: Univ. of Wisconsin Press, 1975), p. 133, where it is suggested that "through a 'radical' contraction [Blake] allows us to see Milton's Satan and Milton's God 'compacted into one.'"

32 Northrop Frye, *Fearful Symmetry* (Princeton: Princeton Univ. Press, 1947), p. 352.

33 See Martin Butlin, *The Paintings and Drawings of William Blake* (New Haven: Yale Univ. Press, 1981), I.373–404.

34 See Morse Peckham, "Blake, Milton, and Edward Burney," *Princeton University Library Chronicle*, 11 (1950), 107–26; Pointon, pp. 1–90; Behrendt, pp. 89–127; and Albert C. Labriola and Edward Sichi, Jr., eds., *Milton's Legacy in the Arts* (University Park: Pennsylvania State Univ. Press, 1988), pp. 1–93.

35 Wittreich, *Angel of Apocalypse*, pp. 75–146.

36 See Gert Schiff, *Johann Heinrich Füsslis Milton-Galerie* (Zurich: Fretz & Wasmuth, 1964), pp. 141–52; and Pointon, pp. 119–21.

37 Anthony Blunt, *The Art of William Blake* (New York: Columbia Univ. Press, 1959), p. 32; Jean H. Hagstrum, *William Blake Poet and Painter* (Chicago: Univ. of Chicago Press, 1964), pp. 23–71; and Janet A. Warner, *Blake and the Language of Art* (Kingston: McGill-Queen's Univ. Press, 1982), pp. 69–82.

38 For a discussion of Blake's use of *pathos* formulae, see Bo Lindberg, *William Blake's Illustrations to the Book of Job* (Åbo: Åbo Akademi, 1973), pp. 113–21.

39 W. J. T. Mitchell, *Blake's Composite Art* (Princeton: Princeton Univ. Press, 1978), p. 25.

40 See Irene Tayler, *Blake's Illustrations to the Poems of Gray* (Princeton: Princeton Univ. Press, 1971), pp. 20–22. Subsequent references to the Gray designs are to this edition.

41 See my review of Bette C. Werner, *Blake's Vision of the Poetry of Milton: Illustrations to Six Poems* (Lewisburg: Bucknell Univ. Press, 1986) in *Philological Quarterly*, 68 (1989), 280–82.

42 See Charles Seymour, Jr., *Michelangelo: The Sistine Chapel Ceiling* (New York: Norton, 1972); Jenijoy La Belle, "Michelangelo's Sistine Frescoes and Blake's 1795 Color-Print Drawings: A Study in Structural Relationships," *Blake: An Illustrated Quarterly*, 54 (1980), 66–84; John

Shearman, *Raphael's Cartoons* (London: Phaidon, 1972); and Panofsky, pls. 186–93.

43 See Ronald Paulson, *Emblem and Expression* (London: Thames & Hudson, 1975), pp. 12–18.

44 Paulson, pp. 121–36; see Alexander S. Gourlay, "'Idolatry or Politics': Blake's Chaucer, the Gods of Priam, and the Powers of 1809" in Stephen Clark and David Worrall, eds., *Historicizing Blake* (London: Macmillan, 1992).

45 See Paulson, *Book and Painting: Shakespeare, Milton and the Bible* (Knoxville: Univ. of Tennessee Press, 1982), pp. 68–87.

46 This is not, of course, the case with Hogarth's early work illustrating *Hudibras* and *The Beggar's Opera*, discussed in Paulson, *Hogarth: His Life, Art and Times*, abridged ed. (New Haven: Yale Univ. Press, 1974), pp. 52–84. For Blake's engraving of one of the *Beggar's Opera* series, see Roger R. Easson and Robert N. Essick, eds., *William Blake: Book Illustrator* (Memphis: American Blake Foundation, 1979), Vol. 2, XXXIV. pl. 1A. See further Robert E. Moore, *Hogarth's Literary Relationships* (Minneapolis: Univ. of Minneapolis Press, 1948); and Peter van de Vogd, *Henry Fielding and William Hogarth: The Correspondences of the Arts* (Amsterdam: Rodopi, 1981).

47 Gombrich, p. 13.

48 Robert F. Gleckner, *Blake and Spenser* (Baltimore: Johns Hopkins Univ. Press, 1985), pp. 117–57.

49 Paulson, *Emblem and Expression*, p. 8.

50 See, for example, Wayne C. Booth, "Preserving the Exemplar: or, How Not to Dig Our Own Graves," and M. H. Abrams, "The Deconstructive Angel" in the special issue on the limits of pluralism of *Critical Inquiry*, 3 (1977), 407–23 and 425–47; and more recently the articles on pluralism and its discontents in *Critical Inquiry*, 12 (1986), 467–596.

51 "What compels us," writes Nietzsche, "to assume there exists any essential antithesis between 'true' and 'false'? Is it not enough to suppose grades of apparentness and as it were lighter and darker shades and tones of appearance—different *valeurs*, to speak in the language of painters? Why could the world *which is of any concern to us*—not be a fiction? And he who then objects: 'but to the fiction there belongs an author?'—could he not be met with the round retort: *why*? Does this 'belongs' perhaps not also belong to the fiction?" *Beyond Good and Evil*, trans. R. J. Hollingdale (Harmondsworth: Penguin, 1973), p. 47. For the influence of Nietzsche's radical skepticism on recent literary theory, see, for example, J. Hillis Miller, "Stevens' Rock and Criticism as Cure, II," *Georgia Review*, 30 (1976), 330–48.

52   See Warner, "Blake's Use of Gesture" in Erdman and Grant, eds., *Blake's Visionary Forms Dramatic* (Princeton: Princeton Univ. Press, 1970), pp. 174–95; and Erdman, *The Illuminated Blake* (New York: Doubleday, 1974).

53   Basil Willey, *The English Moralists* (London: Chatto & Windus, 1964), p. 167.

54   See Ralph Cudworth, *A Treatise Concerning Eternal and Immutable Morality* in J. B. Schneewind, ed., *Moral Philosophy from Montaigne to Kant* (Cambridge: Cambridge Univ. Press, 1990), I.275f.

55   See the Earl of Shaftesbury, *An Inquiry Concerning Virtue or Merit* in Schneewind, II.483f.; David Hume, *An Enquiry Concerning the Principles of Morals* in Schneewind, II.545f.; and Jean-Jacques Rousseau, *Discourse on the Origin and Foundations of Inequality Among Men* in Schneewind, II.605f.

"Attempting to be More than Man we Become Less": The *Comus* Designs

Blake's first and larger (approx.. 22 x 18 cm.) set of *Comus* illustrations, now in the Huntington Library, was painted in Felpham for the Rev. Joseph Thomas late in 1801, at a time when Blake's correspondence reveals his growing frustration with the amount of routine work his patron and corporeal friend Hayley seemed to be putting in his way.[1] The smaller (approx. 15 x 12 cm.), highly finished set for Thomas Butts, now in the Boston Museum of Fine Arts, has on stylistic grounds been grouped by Martin Butlin with the Huntington *Nativity Ode* designs and dated around 1815.[2] It appears therefore to emanate from a more serene period in Blake's life, when he had completed the first two copies of *Milton* and his "more consolidated & extended work" *Jerusalem* (3, E 145) was in progress.[3] Despite the lapse in time and difference in size and style, there is an overall resemblance between the two sets, and no new subjects are introduced in revision as is the case with the *Paradise Lost* designs (see Figs. 27–28). At the same time, small iconographic discrepancies suggest shifts in emphasis or attempts at clarification, which sometimes provide clues to the direction of Blake's thought. It should also be remembered, however, that he may not have had access to Thomas's designs at Epsom, and worked the Butts set up from drawings such as have survived for the *Nativity Ode* (B 728, 730–31) or *Job* designs (B 758f.).

There is a consensus among scholars that Blake is critical of Milton in both these *Comus* sequences, but opinion is divided as to whether they expose the limitations of his precursor's doctrines by presenting a redemptive counterstatement, or simply by highlighting their negative effects. In her important essay on the earlier set, Irene Tayler contends that the Lady overcomes her sexual fears in the shape of Comus and his crew, "escape[s] being Thel and readies herself to become Oothoon, to pluck that glowing flower of sweet delight."[4] And Pamela Dunbar, who in discussing both sets also touches upon Neoplatonism, reaches similar conclusions.[5] The opposite view is taken by Stephen C. Behrendt, who argues that

"Blake subverts the masque by his literal fidelity to it," portraying the Lady as paralyzed throughout by fear, incapable of choice and dependent upon higher beings, unable to recognize Comus and the Spirit as necessary contraries.[6] And pursuing further the reasons for Blake's negative portrayal, Dennis M. Welch proposes that as in *Milton* he is here critical of his mentor's Calvinist doctrine of election.[7] Warner suggests that the "passivity of the Lady in designs where others are moving with dance-like energy indicates constancy on her part rather than paralysis."[8] And most recently Bette C. Werner has urged that in the first series "Blake registers his disagreements with Milton's didacticism," whereas in the second he "discovers a clear strain of authentic vision in Milton's theme of the soul's testing in experience."[9]

Each of these positions tends to emphasize some particulars at the expense of others, and a number of curious features, such as the resemblance of the disguised Comus in the Boston series to Milton himself, have yet to be explained. The ensuing horizontal reading is an attempt to resolve some of these perplexities by showing how the gestures, attitudes, and interaction of the characters in Blake's pictorial commentary are interrelated as minutely and dynamically as they are in the major sequences of Hogarth. While Tayler's interpretation remains the most persuasive, more needs to be said about Blake's presentation of Comus and the Attendant Spirit as true and false spiritual guides and their effect upon the Lady and her Brothers. Particularly fascinating is the unexpected and amusing way in which he appears to turn Comus against his creator, cleverly revealing his two faces as the two faces of Milton's Puritanism. Also at issue is the status of the Lady's experience in the wood: is not Blake's deconstructed vision of Milton's fable closer perhaps in spirit to *Visions of the Daughters of Albion* than to *The Book of Thel?*

Because of the high degree of compression involved in translating Milton's symbolic action into purely visual terms, and in organizing it into eight dynamically interrelated scenes, one is perhaps more conscious of the overall progress of Blake's lost travelers from darkness, separation, and bondage to freedom, reunion, and light than one would be in a performance of the stately masque itself. And the headlong descent of Comus and his crew in the first design (Figs. 3–4) supports the hypothesis that Blake thought of their journey as a fall into division and resurrection to unity, a descent into the night side of the mind analogous to those depicted on the title page of *Milton* (IB 217) and the frontispiece to *Jerusalem* (IB 280). In the Boston version, moreover, the way the attention of all the figures, including the Lady, is focused on the cup at the highest point in the design signals more clearly than in the Huntington version that it will be important in the ensuing mental contest. In both sequences the Lady then moves from limited freedom in the second design (Figs. 5–6), where she turns away from the hovering Attendant Spirit and begins to follow Comus, to consequent absolute subjection to him in the Magic Banquet scene (Figs. 11–12). Comus now stands before the Lady undisguised, his wand in Tayler's words "held over her head in a kind of phallic dominion" (p. 243). A complicating factor in the Boston version, however, is that the angle at which Comus holds his wand is accentuated somewhat, so that arm and wand now recall the twin compasses of Urizen (Fig. 82). The impression given in the Huntington version, moreover—that Comus might at the same time be *withholding* the goblet from the Lady—is also enhanced in the later version, where he now points with his wand to an alternative closed vessel that the dwarfish attendant with the skull-like head has just brought in.

A regenerative countermovement is initiated in both sets in the fourth design (Figs. 9–10), where the Spirit disguised as Thyrsis appears between the Brothers, who are now both armed, and shows them not, as in Milton, the "unsightly root" (629) of haemony but its "bright golden flow'r" (633). And one of the puzzles here is why the quite unequivocal *snipping* gesture he makes with his left hand in the Huntington design, which suggests that he is exhorting the Brothers to pluck this flower of sweet delight, should have been eliminated in the revised version. This regenerative moment leads directly to the expulsion of Comus and the liberation of the Lady from her fears in the sixth design (Figs. 13–14), where the Brothers seize the cup but do not, as in Milton, cast it to the ground. Their reunion is then formalized and the Lady's release completed under the auspices of Sabrina in the seventh design (Figs. 15–16), and in the last design (Figs. 17–18) the siblings are restored to their parental home by the departing Spirit, who resumes his heavenly form. The auspicious implications of this transformation, of the rising sun, and of the un-Miltonic humble cottage are, as Tayler intimates (p. 248), qualified in the Huntington series by the inquisitorial note in the reception of the Lady. But this may reflect only upon the parents, and it is eliminated in the later series where she is greeted with concern rather than suspicion. Moreover, the addition of a rainbow above Sabrina suggests that in the course of revision Blake came to think of the entire action as a descent from Generation in the wood to the Ulro of Comus' windowless vault-like hall, and a return through Beulah to unity in "eternity's sun rise" (E 470).

The Lady and her Brothers are the subjects of this spiritual pilgrimage, and if we are to enter Blake's images "on the Fiery Chariot of [our] Contemplative Thought" (*VLJ* 82, E 560) more deeply, and understand how precisely they are orchestrated to reveal the evils of Milton's "sage / And serious doctrine of Virginity" (786–87), as a manifestation of his Puritan belief in Christian liberty through restraint and discipline, we should begin with a preliminary reconsideration of their relationship. Tayler (p. 243) is surely right that Blake would have seen a causal connection between the Lady's fears and her separation from her male companions. But since Blake assimilated ideas and symbols from his early work into the later polysemous prophecies, and since Milton's protagonists are themselves little more than allegorical abstractions, he is likely to have thought of the Lady and her Brothers not just as children lost and found, but simultaneously as (respectively) reason and energy, soul and body, and thus as facets of archetypal fallen man. This hypothesis would be consistent with the Lady's predominant passivity and with the Brothers' progress from lassitude, doubt, and self-division to vigorous activity. It would also help to explain why the Brothers are not differentiated consistently in either sequence, and why, beginning with the sixth design, where they are reunited with the Lady, they are grouped and act together as one man.[10]

Tayler's interpretation (pp. 245f.) of the Brothers' resumption and deployment of their swords in phallic terms is equally plausible, and it does not necessarily conflict with her view of Comus as exercising phallic dominion over the Lady. Blake believed that "Every Thing has its Vermin" (*J* 1, E 144), and in line with biblical tradition he often used the same motif both *in bono* and *in malo*, as medievalists might say. But then, in order to accommodate Sabrina, who in Milton effects the Lady's physical release, Tayler is obliged to conclude that in "The Brothers Driving Out Comus" (Fig. 13) they release her from her *mental* fears. One would, however, expect such enlightenment to come about through an increase in sensual enjoyment. And it would be quite consistent with the iconographic progressions Tayler traces, and with Blake's use of multivalent images elsewhere, to see this also as a symbolic "moment of desire" (*VDA* 7.3, E 50), in which the Brothers respond to Thyrsis' urging them to pluck the flower and, acting as one man, take possession of the cup of life, and to interpret the Sabrina scene as one in which the event is solemnized and ratified. The myths of Classical Antiquity abound in unions between siblings, and an important precedent occurs in the Song of Songs (4.10, 4.12), where the beloved is addressed as "my sister, my spouse." Such symbolism would be no more elliptical than in the case of "The Little Girl Lost" and "The Little Girl Found" from the *Songs* (E 20–22), which are interestingly related to the *Comus* series because little Lyca's initiation leads not to the expulsion of the beasts but to the discovery that they were after all benign. And though the hypothesis must be tested against all the particulars in context, it would certainly square with the parallel Dunbar (p. 33) notes between the reception of the Lady in the last Huntington design and that of the heroine in "A Little Girl Lost" (*SE*, E 29), who *does* have an innocent experience.

If Blake recognized a mark of true vision in the siblings' separation and reunion, albeit one understood imperfectly by Milton, he must have been equally delighted with Milton's use of pastoral convention to present Comus, whom the Lady takes to be a "gentle Shepherd" (271; see 307, 330), and Thyrsis as true and false types of Christ the Good Shepherd. One of the preoccupations which underlie both poets' entire prophetic enterprise is the *difficulty* of distinguishing between truth and error, of detecting and exposing Satan's wiles. But while Blake often recognized the spirit of true prophecy in his precursor, he also believed that reason in Milton had become demonic and usurped the voice of God. Malekin writes that "the energetic but sternly repressive virtue of Puritanism may be admirable, but it is also narrow, hugely afraid of the more sensuous aspects of human nature, not tolerant of fundamental disagreement and open to no humour but that of scorn and derision."[11] However, despite Comus' Bacchic parentage and hedonism, Behrendt's suggestion (pp. 76, 86) that he and Thyrsis represent Dionysian and Apollonian contraries rejected by the Lady is problematic, since from Blake's point of view as well as Milton's, Comus also has his unattractive side. Indeed, in this votary of Cotytto's conviction that "'Tis only daylight that makes Sin" (126), his hypocrisy, his tyranny, and his degradation of the "human count'nance, / Th'express resemblance of the gods . . . / Into some brutish form" (68–70), Blake could hardly have failed to recognize all the disastrous consequences of Milton's Puritan faith in liberty through restraint that he had sought to reveal from the *Songs of Experience* on. And it is these unattractive qualities rather than his exuberance as courtly lover, urging the Lady not to "let slip time" lest her beauty "like a neglected rose" should "wither[s] on the stalk" (773–74), that seem to be emphasized in both these sequences.

As in Milton, Comus and the Spirit are polarized as the absolute negation of each other, one leading the lost travelers astray, the other returning them to their true home. But the very different implications this had for Blake begin to emerge when one thinks of Comus as a divisive spirit, who seeks to keep the Lady and her Brothers as contraries apart, and Thyrsis as the spirit who unites them. The key to understanding how Blake uses Milton's figures to express his own reservations about Milton and the "black cloud" (*Mil* 15.50, E 110) of Puritan tradition seems, however, to lie in his presentation of Comus' two faces. Both he and the Attendant Spirit appear in different guises, but having invited us to consider them together by giving them similar hats, Blake manages through a series of deftly handled visual contrasts to suggest that the Spirit is nonetheless a constant guide, whereas the protean Comus is quite other than he seems. In both series the disguised Comus is a stooping figure dressed in black, who approaches the Lady (Figs. 5–6) and gazes at the Brothers under their "green mantling vine" (294; Figs. 7–8) with hypocritical humility, hat in hand; on the other hand, Thyrsis instructing the Brothers (Figs. 9–10) and opposite Sabrina (Figs. 15–16) is an upright figure who doffs his hat to no man. Comus conceals his rod, which points toward the earth, while Thyrsis reveals a flower and gestures toward heaven. Comus appears now old (Figs. 5, 8), now young (Figs. 6, 7), suggesting his association with the fallen world of mutability. Thyrsis is in eternal youth. Above all, Comus seems to be a friend but in the Banquet scene reveals himself a tyrant, like Satan/Hayley who in the Bard's Song in *Milton* is accused of "Seeming a brother, being a tyrant" (7.22, E 100) to Palamabron/Blake. In *Jerusalem* Blake was to associate corporeal and spiritual friendship with true and false prophecy more closely.

Evidently Blake wished to emphasize this tranformation because it is much more dramatic than in the case of the Attendant Spirit, who in both sets is recognizably the same figure throughout, his hat modulating into a halo in the Boston series to underline the point. And if Comus is more than simply the embodiment of the Lady's fears, we must consider that Blake may have intended his two starkly contrasted guises as a kinetic and causally related vision of Milton's repressive doctrine and its consequences. For despite his polemical early proclamation that "The lust of the goat is the bounty of God" (*MHH* 8, E 36), Blake was as horrified by lust and depravity as Milton, but he perceived its causes and its cure quite differently. And by highlighting Comus' metamorphosis from seeming friend who hides his rod from the Lady, into manifest tyrant flaunting it in phallic dominion over her, Blake seems to be hinting that Milton's idealistic emphasis on chastity is *itself* the "Spiritual Cause" (*Mil* 26.44, E 124) of the aggressive bestiality in Comus and his crew that Milton believed it could contain. "Attempting to be more than Man We become less," as he succinctly expressed this insight in *The Four Zoas* (135.21, E 403). Blake's splendid fourth illustration in the *Paradise Lost* series (Figs. 25–26) reflects a lively appreciation of Milton's vision of Adam and Eve "Imparadis't in one another's arms" (IV.506). But *Milton* leaves no doubt that he also perceived this innocent vision was for Milton constrained by reason, and Adam and Eve's sensual lapsarian relations lustful. As Malekin perceptively observes, Milton's Puritan view of the hierarchical relationship between the sexes was "flawed by his undervaluing of the female and of the feminine side of his own nature" (p. 159). When the Lady says defiantly to Comus that though he may hold her body spell-bound, "Thou canst not touch the freedom of my mind" (663), she expresses the moral and psychological priorities of Milton and his age. But closer scrutiny of the designs as a dynamic continuum tends to support the hypothesis that Blake's central aim is to expose this dualistic error, by proclaiming that the mind cannot be free while the bodily and affective side of man remains frozen in virginity.

As in the title page to the *Songs* (IB 42), which invokes the Fall and the Expulsion, and to the *Marriage* (IB 98), where the embracing couple point the way for the "return of Adam into Paradise" (*MHH* 3, E 4), Blake manages to introduce several of his main ideas into "Comus with His Revellers" (Figs. 3–4), so that in each set, though with different emphases, it functions as a sort of pictorial preface. In the Huntington version the notion of a fall into division suggested by the revelers' descent is endorsed by the Lady's position at the lowest point in the design, and by the way Comus, placed immediately above her in the traditional position of dominion, comes, as Tayler (p. 242) notices, between her and the Attendant Spirit. Sitting alone and root-bound by her virgin fears, by this vision of sex as bestial, she is an earlier type of "Mary at Her Distaff" (Fig. 70) lamenting Jesus' absence in the *Paradise Regained* designs. The smiling, naked Comus is superficially an attractive figure as he is in Milton, and resembles several dancing fauns and Bacchic revellers engraved from classical sources that Blake is likely to have known.[12] But as Warner (pp. 151f.) reminds us, dancing is not always used *in bono* in Blake's iconography, and here no musical instruments are present, as they are in the redemptive contexts of *Milton* 18 (IB 234) or *Job* 21 (B 717), and there is a heedlessness about Comus and his crew that links them with the figures in the dance of death on *Night Thoughts* 205. There is also a one-sidedness about Comus' hedonism in the masque—a consequence of the fundamental dualism at the heart of Milton's Puritan beliefs— which Blake was later to find fault with in Mirth and her companions (Fig. 55) in the *L'Allegro and Il Penseroso* series. Indeed, the facial resemblance of Mirth to Comus in this first design suggests that he may have thought of Milton's tempter and his earlier portrayal of him when delineating her. The close connection with Blake's frontispiece illustration to J. T. Stanley's version of G. A. Bürger's *Leonora*, published in 1796, is also ominous.[13] Not only does Comus look like Death the Tyrant and act out his role as Covering Cherub, but his "Ounce, or Tiger, Hog" (71) and other canine follower link arms like the moonlit revelers dancing the dance of death, in demonic parody of the jubilant angels on *Night Thoughts* 341 and *Job* 14 (B 710). The inscription to the frontispiece, describing how "Death affecting Forms least like himself / . . . Lay'd by his Horrors, and put on his Smiles / . . . And then, he dropt his Mask," is also suggestive in relation to the idea of Comus' two faces.

In the more elliptical Boston version the Spirit is now "viewless" (93) and his gesture of abhorrence has been transferred to the Lady, who here sits beneath a more rounded embankment which, on analogy with the "cranial cave" on the frontispiece to *Visions of the Daughters of Albion* (IB 125), may be taken as suggestive of the internal nature of this vision. She seems more spiritually awake in this prefatory design than in the earlier series: her gesture, which anticipates that of "Christ Refusing the Banquet Offered by Satan" (Fig. 72) in the *Paradise Regained* designs, and the direction of her gaze suggest that she is horrified specifically by the spell that, as J. Karl Franson notices, Comus is in the act of casting with his wand upon the cup.[14] Its exalted and focal position—the minotaur even shields his eyes to gaze at it like the traveler seen from behind on *Night Thoughts* 11—is consistent with the notion that this is the cup of life on which Milton's doctrine cast its "spells of law" (*VDA* 5.22, E 49). The more schematic line of the revelers' descent, which Blake has elongated the leading figure considerably to emphasize, divides the composition more clearly than in the Huntington version into two right-angled triangles. We know from Robert N. Essick's analysis that the triangular configurations in Blake's 1795 color print of *Newton* (B 394) are thematically related to Newton's rationalist vision of the universe.[15] And since the motif recurs in the shape of the vine-covered rock in the third design (Figs. 7–8), what Blake seems to be implying here is that Urizen's Puritan severities lie behind the excessive, bestial hedonism of Comus and his crew. The stars are of course providential guides in Milton's masque, as the Elder Brother's "Unmuffle ye faint stars . . ." (331 et seq.) makes clear. And Blake too sometimes used them *in bono*, as in *Night Thoughts* 450 where a humanized female star attempts to guide a male lost traveler. But here their significance is more probably Urizenic, since they are later dispelled by the returning sun.

Behrendt (p. 70) maintains that the Lady is incapable of choice, but in fact there are two quite carefully counterpointed moments of choice in these designs. One occurs in the second design, where the Lady encounters and decides to follow Comus (Figs. 5–6), precipitating her enthralment in the Banquet scene; the other occurs in the fourth design, where the Brothers resolve to follow Thyrsis' counsel, which leads to her release. In Milton the Lady is alone when she is approached by Comus, like Eve in the temptation scene of *Paradise Lost*. But Blake makes clear that she is still free to choose by introducing the Attendant Spirit and placing her between him and Comus in the position of Hercules at the Crossroads between Virtue and Pleasure. As Erwin Panofsky has shown, Raphael, Carracci, Rubens, Poussin, Reynolds, Thornhill, and many less illustrious painters contributed to this pictorial tradition.[16] And in the eighteenth century it had received wide intellectual currency through Shaftesbury's discussion of it in his *Characteristics*.[17] The extent of the formula's domestication is revealed by Paulson in his discussion of the first plate of Hogarth's *Harlot's Progress*, where Mary Hackabout is depicted between Mother Needham and an indifferent clergyman—an important precedent for Blake's use of it with a female protagonist.[18] There are few absolute constants in the tradition, but the engraving by Johann Sadeler (Fig. 87)—whom Blake mentions with approval (E 574)—after Friedrich Sustris is typical in that *Virtus* appears barefoot, veiled, and fully clad on Hercules' right, and urges him to embark on the steep and stony path leading toward the distant peak on which Pegasus has landed, while *Voluptas* on his left is shown unveiled, in revealing dishabille, adorned with pearls and peacock fan and wearing sandals, and seeks to lure the hero down the flowery path leading to eventual shipwreck on

Fortune's stormy seas. Virtue frequently appears with Minerva's spear and helmet or even, as in Rubens, fully clad in armor, but sometimes her rigors are suggested by a rod or pilgrim's staff.[19] The transience of Pleasure's gifts is consistently symbolized by flowers, which she sometimes offers to the hero, as in Battoni or in Raphael's *Dream of Scipio*, owned in Blake's day by Sir Thomas Lawrence; the deceptive nature of her gifts is suggested by small emblematic masks.[20]

In the second *Comus* illustration we find these traditional components rearranged suggestively. Particularly pertinent to our tentative interpretation of Comus' two faces is that Comus appears on the Lady's right, the side traditionally reserved for Virtue because of its biblical association with redemption. Like Virtue he too is austerely clad and carries a rod—indeed, with his rod and sable weeds and plodding gait and sage and serious look, he seems a marvellous caricature of Puritan virtue. Yet unlike the taskmistress of traditional iconography and very like her rival, he is quite other than he seems. The winged and airy Spirit by contrast appears on the Lady's left, and he is lightly clad in semi-diaphanous white robes which recall the traditional garb of Pleasure. Strictly, moreover, he has been included in this scene without Miltonic authority, and he is shown bearing aloft the flower haemony as he departs much earlier than this magic talisman is mentioned in the masque. These particulars seem to imply that the Spirit is intended at this point to represent a redemptive vision of Pleasure.

The gesture of the Lady standing dressed in white between them expresses her uncertainty, but she inclines her head toward Comus, with whom she is united within the cranial cave of the two arching trees, and she is divided from the departing Spirit by the tree trunk near the middle. The Lady's fearful vision of sexuality as bestial in the first design makes Milton's doctrine of chastity seem like a true friend. But as it invades her mental space all joy is driven out, as in the case of that other victim of Puritan repression, Little Mary Bell (E 496). That this is indeed what the Lady's choice involves is also intimated by the twisted branches crossing over one another immediately above her head. Blake is evidently using the motif emblematically just as he uses trees and flowers in the *Songs*, since it reappears modulated in the Lady's repressive cruciform gesture in the fifth and sixth designs (Figs. 11, 13). Thus, without doing overt violence to Milton's text, Blake has managed to insinuate that this is the moment of her fall and the reason for her subsequent rigidity. And we, who can see the danger of which she is as yet unaware, perceive that Comus has only to raise his hat, as he will later raise his wand, for her to share the "Female Martyr's" fate in the seventh emblem of *The Gates of Paradise* (E 263).

The Boston version is again more economical iconographically but in one respect more daring. The fact that this is a moment of choice for the Lady is brought out more clearly. She is now more centrally located and her slightly more expansive gesture of uncertainty includes both Comus and the Spirit, who are equidistant from her, though as in the Huntington version she turns her face toward Comus and meets his earnest gaze. Incongruously, Comus still stoops and seems to plod along, but is now a youthful figure, while the Spirit departing with a gesture of dismay has lost his flower and some of his contempt for gravity, but his wings point heavenward and he has acquired a halo. Blake may have dispensed with the flower and twisted branch because he came to regard these clues as too obvious or needlessly reduplicative, or more probably they were made redundant by the amusing new solution that occurred to him as he worked the material through again. For the striking thing about Comus here is his resemblance to Milton himself as he appears dressed in somber Puritan garb in the *Il Penseroso* series (Figs. 62–66), which if Butlin's dating is accepted were produced at about the same time.[21] The similarity in this second design is fairly general, but the identification is endorsed by a much closer likeness between the aged Comus' face in the next design (Fig. 8) and that of Milton in old age as portrayed in the last *Il Penseroso* illustration (Fig. 66). Indeed, there is a distinct family resemblance between the physiognomies of the disguised Comus, the portrayals of Milton on plates 16 and 45 of Blake's epic (IB 242, 261), Milton in old age, and Blake's *Head of Milton* for Hayley's library (Fig. 1), discernible particularly in the moulding of the cheeks and eyebrows. The *Head* was based on engravings after William Faithorne's portrait (Fig. 2), which as Wittreich has pointed out had come to be regarded as the official public image of the poet, and Blake could therefore have expected any resemblance to it to be recognized.[22] The move should come as no surprise, since Blake's illustrations for the poems of Young and Gray had also entailed portrayals of those poets. This, then, it would appear is no longer a personification of Milton's Puritan virtue, but the young author of the masque in person seeking to indoctrinate the Lady. The substance of his counsel is suggested by the curious way in which he holds his hat as if to shield his genitals. In "Milton's Mysterious Dream" (Fig. 65), the penultimate *Il Penseroso* illustration, Blake shows Milton crossing his hands over his loins in a related gesture of repression, and it is not until *Milton* 16 (IB 232) that he is prepared to accept his own naked "Human Form" as "Divine" (*Mil* 32.13, E 131). The Lady's acquiescence in her virgin state is again perhaps echoed by the trees which enshrine her like the Madonnas of tradition within a gothic niche, though since their "Living Form" (E 270) is counterpointed against the Roman arches of Comus' palace (Fig. 10), they might also seem to hold out promise of her eventual redemption.

Several motifs already introduced are modulated in "The Brothers Seen by Comus Plucking Grapes" (Figs. 7–8), which appears to be a sequel revealing the effects of the Lady's decision on her male companions. She appears spellbound beneath the oak grove in the distance, though the hovering Spirit high above her keeps watch over her sleeping humanity. The Brothers, who in Milton are firm believers in the power of "Virgin purity" (427) and in "The unpolluted temple of the mind" (461), and are here very much under the eye of Comus, are obliged in consequence to pluck life's fruit without her. Under the rock of Milton's Puritanism, the vine of life in the Huntington version does not soar heavenward, like those in the *Songs of Innocence*, but threatens to become a snare. And now that he has the siblings in his power, Comus has grown young and vigorous and begins to show his rod. The Brothers, sexually and spiritually disarmed as Tayler (p. 245) notes, have the air of dreamy lotus-eaters. And if the barefoot one in green who leads in the three last designs is taken to be the elder (see n. 10 above), his position has been usurped in the psychic economy by his sandaled younger brother higher in the vine. Both are clearly as oblivious of their sister and their "native home" (76) as Comus' bestial victims, whose state they are approaching. In the symbolism of the *Marriage*, when the soul is thought of as something separated from the body and reason attempts to restrain desire, "it by degrees becomes passive till it is only the shadow of desire" (*MHH* 5, E 34). Or, as Tayler explains Blake's evident responsiveness to the Lady's description of her Brothers as "likest to Narcissus" (237), "Narcissus-like men are 'safe' in that their love is inward-turned . . ." (p. 245). These are "The self-enjoyings of self-denial" that replace the "moment of desire" in *Visions* (7.2, E 50). In Blake's later conceptual terms, man divided from his emanation becomes divided against himself. The homosexual overtones discerned by Dunbar (p. 19) in the Brothers' mutual admiration, but equally apparent in the admiring Comus, who in Milton tells the Lady how "as I past, I worshipt" (302), also fall into place as a logical consequence of the Lady's acceptance of

Milton's Puritan insistence upon premarital chastity. The plowman wears a hat like Thyrsis', and since Blake used plowing especially in the *Marriage* and *Milton* as a metaphor for creative work, this may again have been his way of associating the two figures and presenting the plowman as a vision of the poet "in fetters" (*MHH* 6, E 35), reduced to "the sordid drudgery of facsimile representations" (*DesC* 356, E 541) under Milton's iron law. In his *Canterbury Pilgrims* (B 878, 587) illustrations Blake would later portray Chaucer's plowman with a snub nose and hat not unlike his own, praising him in his *Descriptive Catalogue* note for his benevolence and industry (E 536).[23]

The main features of the Huntington version are retained in the Boston version, but there are important differences in detail. The Spirit hovering above the Lady now appears near the apex of the composition, but within a radiant mandorla like that associated with the Virgin Mary in traditional iconography.[24] Blake may therefore have used him here to signal that the star of Milton's doctrine is now in the ascendant, and transferred his role as watcher holding promise of redemption to the plowman, who has acquired a second ox. The Brothers now appear without swords beneath a much more formidable-looking rock, picking from a still fruitful but rather stunted vine. The one lower in the vine, who again will later lead, is now dressed in pink, his companion in green. In posture they mirror one another more exactly, and the simian rhythm of their limbs indicates more clearly that they are well on their way to joining Comus' bestial crew. They do, however, share, as Werner (p. 39) also notes, whereas in the earlier version each helps himself. But if the boys gathering grapes for the girl on the second plate of "The Ecchoing Green" (IB 48), or the youth handing down the "captive linnet" nest with its overtones of procreation to the maiden in the fifth illustration to Gray's "Ode on a Distant Prospect of Eton College," is regarded as a norm, again the gender of these secret sharers would appear to be at issue.[25] Erdman has suggested that this may also be the problem with the two female figures depicted beside "The Argument" of the *Marriage* (IB 99).[26] If the youthful Comus / Milton in the second design was the author of the masque preaching chastity to the Lady, Blake may have thought of the aged Comus / Milton, now no longer shielding himself with his hat, as the austere chronicler of "deeds / Above Heroic" (I.14–15) performed by a celibate Christ in *Paradise Regained*.

"The Brothers Meet the Attendant Spirit in the Wood" (Figs. 9–10) represents a turning point in these lost travelers' quest, and in both versions Blake invites us to contemplate it in relation to Comus' encounter with the Lady in the second design by repeating almost the same background tree configuration. In the Huntington version the Lady was torn by doubt, closeted alone with Comus inside the cranial cave of trees, unresponsive to the departing spirit with his flower of joy outside it. The reappearance of the cave motif here endorses the notion that the siblings may be regarded as aspects of a single psyche. But the ominous twisted branch has been eliminated, the Spirit of joy here dressed in golden yellow has returned, and the Brothers though still a little languid are no longer self-divided. They have resumed their phallic swords and gaze upon the flower haemony—the "Golden Key / That opes the Palace of Eternity" (13–14)—that the Spirit urges them to pluck. Thus Blake brilliantly exploits the traditional associations of the Spirit's pastoral guise as Thyrsis in the masque, to subvert his mentor's sage and serious doctrine by proclaiming that sex is innocent and profoundly Christian. Since this vision is the absolute negation of the Lady's view of sex as bestial, "dark veil'd Cotytto" (129) above the trees, whom Comus had invoked, and whose veil and leering serpents felicitously express the two faces or aspects of virginity, is excluded from the Brothers' mental space. And though she is in the traditional position of dominion like Comus above the Lady in the opening design, she is departing at a furious rate, perhaps, as Franson (pp. 165, 168) says, to join Comus at his Magic Banquet.

In the Boston series too this is a moment of incipient regeneration, but Blake conveys differently the idea that the Brothers are in spiritual transition, and broadens the implications of what their guide is saying. All three figures appear between incipient arboreal gothic arches which enclose them on both sides, so that the cave configuration in the Huntington design is still suggested. Thyrsis, now in light blue, adopts a similar attitude and the same position at the center of the composition as the Lady in the second design, intimating visually that his prophetic certainty is beginning to replace her doubts. The Brothers, placed symmetrically on either side of Thyrsis, are still clearly undecided since they move in opposite directions, the younger Brother in green still looks fearful, and the in Milton more hopeful elder Brother is not on Thyrsis' right side yet. Both, however, have resumed the "Godlike erect" (*Paradise Lost* IV.289) position of fully human beings, and where in the third design they were emasculated they are now armed for love and "Mental Fight" (*Mil* 13, E 95) alike. Putting the matter in this way is consonant with Blake's use of multivalent symbols, and with what seems to have been a desire to extend the significance of the haemony in Thyrsis' hand, which looks less flower-like than in the Huntington version and more like a five-pointed star. One reason for Blake's eliminating Thyrsis' snipping gesture may have been because he realized its susceptibility to vulgar misinterpretation. And Welch illuminates the question further by proposing that "the blossom represents honest temporal love . . . and an eternal 'center'—a minute particular, which if perceived imaginatively becomes infinite" (p. 518). In line with Franson's observation (pp. 170f.) that the Boston series seems to place less emphasis on the sensual than the Huntington designs, this is no longer solely an exhortation to pluck the flower of sweet delight, but also an epiphanic moment. And the Brothers listening to Thyrsis as poet and Spirit of prophecy, his nimbus-like hat and crook affirming the truly Christian nature of his message, are beginning to perceive the enormity of the errors Milton as the false prophetic tongue of Puritanism had voiced in the wider sense implied by Milton's presence in the second and third designs and explored more analytically in *Milton*. The night rider who departs in consequence may well, as Franson (pp. 167f.) thinks, be Hecate, whose triple nature comprehends Diana. But on *Job* 14 (B 710), the first version of which series in Butlin's dating antedates the Boston sequence, it is Diana herself who appears driving her serpent or dragon team opposite Apollo.[27] And again in *L'Allegro and Il Penseroso* 7 (Fig. 61) it is Cynthia who "checks her Dragon yoke" (59) above Melancholy. Given the importance in the present dramatic context of suggesting that the dualistic specter of virginity is now departing, it seems therefore more appropriate to take this as Diana and the (less obviously) leering serpents again as the other face of chastity.

The most conspicuous thing about both versions of "The Magic Banquet with the Lady Spell-Bound" (Figs. 11–12), at the nadir of the siblings' fall, is the complete *absence* of any signs of pleasure. Read sequentially from the Brothers' point of view, it may be regarded as a scene amplifying the moment of truth vouchsafed them by the Spirit of prophecy in the fourth design, a revelation of the consequences of disregarding Pleasure and of the Satanic face of Miltonic Virtue. Considered from the Lady's viewpoint, having elected to follow the Puritan path of Virtue—a little like Thel—as a refuge from her sexual fears, she is now as much under its spell as her Miltonic prototype. In the Huntington version she is shown sitting frozen with her arms crossed in the conventional gesture of modesty Blake was later to give to Mary in "Joseph and Mary, and the Room They Were Seen In" (B 920). But as has been generally recognized and as this analogy confirms, it is her chastity and no magic hocus-pocus that has her "nerves . . . all chain'd up in Alabaster / And [her] a statue" (600–1). The key to Milton's "Heaven doors" is the key to Blake's "Hell Gates" (*EG*, E 524). Repression, however logical to Urizen, leads inevitably to tyranny, of which Milton's domestic tyranny as Blake saw it and Comus' phallic dominion here are but two manifestations. As Malekin observes, "Milton's marital hierarchy" is essentially "rigid and external; it can only be imposed by emotional violence" (p. 162). No conceptual incoherence is entailed therefore in seeing Comus' wand both as a demonic phallic image and, in relation to his arm, as an allusion to Blake's hoary taskmaster's dividers, although in the earlier version the resemblance is less marked. Later, in "Christian Beaten Down by Apollyon" (Fig. 88) from the *Pilgrim's Progress* series, where Apollyon with his fiery phallus brings Christian to his knees, Blake was to make the connection between sexual repression and violence more explicit.[28]

The notion that Comus is withholding the cup of life and joy from the Lady is consistent with this line of thought. However, Milton describes him as "Much like his Father, but his Mother more" (57), and his red cloak and cup associate him also with the Great Whore of Revelation (17.2–18), whom Blake portrayed on *Night Thoughts* 345 and in a separate watercolor (B 584). And one might therefore here in the Huntington version at least prefer to think of it as Tayler (p. 244) does, as a type of Vala's "Poison Cup / Of Jealousy" (*J* 63.39–40, E 214) with which Comus seeks to reduce the Lady further to the abject status of his entourage and the yearning serpent-bound figures on her alabaster throne. The notion of jealousy, whether symbolized by the cup or the act of withholding it, is particularly suggestive in relation to Comus' followers, who have been transformed from beasts in the first design to five bird-like creatures for which Essick has suggested possible antiquarian sources.[29] This implies that Blake also thought of Comus' dimly lit, prison-like hall as a metaphoric cage, an image he had associated with possessive love and matrimony in his lyrics (see E 413, 460). Although a second cup, a pot, a jar, and a covered tureen are visible on the table, the conspicuous absence of food leaves little doubt that this is no liberating banquet of the senses, so that perhaps we should regard the five birds as the five lapsarian senses imprisoned in Milton's Puritan matrimonial cage.

The scene in the Boston version is even more evidently a vision of the House of Death. The hall has neither doors nor windows and the more schematic double Roman arches recall the tombstone and Mosaic tablet motifs on the title pages to *Thel* (IB 34) and *The Book of Urizen* (IB 183), which Milton as a Samson-like redeemer will eventually dispel in *Milton* 18 (IB 234; see *Night Thoughts* 537). The Lady, a lonely and embattled Puritan soul "clad in complete steel" (421), sits with her hands now resting on her knees like the seated colossus Blake engraved for Rees's *Cyclopaedia*—the epitome of Egyptian bondage.[30] Comus before her is more lithe and poised and has evidently grown young again at her expense, and his cloak, though less like the closed wings of an insect than in the earlier version, is now the color of "blue death" (*J* 33.10, E 179). He withholds the cup of life and joy and points to an alternative closed goblet; perhaps because it is sealed, serpentine demonic energy is emanating from it through the cloud in Comus' direction, hissing vengeance at the tyrant like its prototype in *Paradise Lost*. Since the wizened servant with the skull-like head who proffers it is distinguished from the others who are all part beast, and since Comus is a type of Satan, this figure may well be Death affecting a form "least like himself" as he appears in the *Night Thoughts* illustrations. The wider implications of the master-servant relationship between Comus and his crew, and his character as the spirit of negation of all liberty, are also cleverly brought out in this design. In counterpointing Comus' "stately Palace" (658 et seq.) against a "low / But loyal cottage" (319–20) in place of the "President's Castle" (957 et seq.) at the end, Blake may well have been prompted by the Lady's republican sentiments when she protests against what "lewdly-pamper'd Luxury / Now heaps upon some few with vast excess" (770–1). But he would probably also have agreed with Christopher Hill that "Milton, the leisure-class intellectual, living on money inherited from his father, had no appreciation of or sympathy for what it was like to be a wage-labourer."[31]

Moreover, throughout Blake's lifetime Milton's doctrines of discipline and obedience to reason as the voice of God, the very core of the Puritan ethic, had been used by those in power to chain the people to a military and industrial machine.[32] Here the gestures and expressions of those Comus has reduced to animals indicate that they too feel cheated by the dearth of food, a subject Blake had earlier broached visually in two of the full-plate designs to *Europe* (IB 164, 167). The elephant eyes Comus angrily and paws his empty plate, as does the rampant staring lion next to him.[33] The bird looks nonplussed at finding nothing in his cup and the dog is so hungry that he licks his neighbor's shoulder. All is not lost, however, for ears of wheat have replaced the figures in bondage on the Lady's throne in the earlier version, indicating that the Brothers' glimpse of a freer world has sown a seed in her. And though she appears in the same attitude as when last seen under the trees in the third design, she is no longer a backward-looking Lady and has turned to face her Brothers in the sixth, ready to move forward toward Eternity's sunrise.

If this splendid Magic Banquet scene is the visual high point of the series, "The Brothers Driving Out Comus" (Figs. 13–14) comes as the dramatic climax of the action, and represents the second stage in the siblings' spiritual regeneration. In the Huntington version the Brothers, now fully energized and acting together, assume center stage for the first time, as with swords raised they drive out Comus and his crew. Dunbar (p. 26) makes the pertinent analogy with the passage in the *Marriage* where the budding prophet, asked by the Angel how he had escaped from the Leviathan, replies: "All that we saw was owing to your metaphysics" (19, E 42). True to their master's protean spirit, Comus' crew have undergone further transformations, and Dunbar (p. 27) also remarks on their mask-like appearance as they dissolve amid the billowing smoke, a characteristic which corroborates the importance given earlier to Comus' two faces. For this is a symbolic scene of unmasking and casting out of Comus as the embodiment of Miltonic error, now naked and exposed. The importance of the cup is highlighted by the fact that Blake has focused on the very moment when the foremost Brother in green has seized it from Comus' outstretched hand, and now holds it aloft in a visually prominent position as his companion reaches for the wand. The Lady is not yet free of "cloudy Doubts & Reasoning Cares" (*GP* 4, E 261), as her still rigid attitude and her hands crossed over her breasts make clear. But the passional Brothers have now entered and so are driving Comus from her mental space, suggested by the cranial cave of smoke. And the ears of wheat on her throne make clear that the seeds of her regeneration have already been sown. That this is indeed also a symbolic moment of desire seems more certain as we follow the Lady's gaze up to the V formation of the trees, which replaces the twisted branches immediately above her in the second design and widens in the seventh. Dunbar (p. 28) suggests that the single star between them may be Venus, the morning star. The general line of movement of the Brothers divides the composition diagonally, so that

Comus and his crew's descent in the opening scene is now reversed.

Most of the variants in the Boston version seem directed toward reaffirming and clarifying rather than radically altering the symbolic import of the earlier version. The Lady is now centrally located, so that as man's lost soul or Emanation she is visibly the object of this mental contest. And though she is set back a little, in the context of the embracing figures on the *Marriage* title page (IB 98) or "The Reunion of the Soul & the Body" in Blake's illustrations to Blair's *Grave* (Fig. 97), the fact that she is about to be united with the Brothers as they rush forward is suggested visually in a way precluded by her position in the Huntington design. She is in the same passive rigid position as in the banquet scene, but the "black cloud" of Puritanism surrounding her is giving way before the advancing Brothers, who are not themselves caught up in it as they were in the earlier version, and who make no attempt significantly to seize authoritarian Comus' rod. Comus is now frontally presented in the manner of antique reliefs as he leaps off to the left, his attitude echoing that of Jehovah in Blake's *Laocoön* engraving (E 273). And though no longer naked, he is already engulfed in flames to indicate the burning up of error. His followers now look anything but threatening and their mask-like faces are all elderly and bearded, suggesting the demise of an outworn creed such as we witness in the fourth *Nativity Ode* designs (Figs. 49–50). That this is the moment when the cup of life and joy passes from Comus to the elder Brother is brought out much more clearly, and the cup itself is situated directly above the Lady. The diagonal movement which reverses the fall in the opening design is also accentuated, both by the line along which the smoke and spectrous heads give way, and by the angle of the Brothers' swords.

In "Sabrina Disenchanting the Lady" (Figs. 15–16), where the Lady is seated in the center of the composition with the male and female supporting cast arranged symmetrically on either side of her, the lost travelers' redemption is taken a step further. There is a consensus that Sabrina here is a benevolent deity, but where Milton saw her as a virgin protectress of distressed virginity, Tayler (p. 247) is surely right that Blake is pointing to the true significance of her effecting the Lady's bodily release, by surrounding her with nymphs bearing "winding shells" (873) as emblems of the body. For as Blake would have known, for instance from Porphyry's *Concerning the Cave of the Nymphs* translated by Thomas Taylor in 1789, nymphs were traditionally associated with the world of generation.[34] And the way Sabrina rises from the river's foam flanked by two young girls suggests that he thought of her as a procreative Venus Genetrix.[35] Blake may therefore have intended the five nymphs together as a regenerative vision of the five fallen senses in the Banquet scene, which are here to lead the lapsed soul back to psychic equilibrium through an increase in sensual enjoyment. Their healing function is denoted by the vessel containing "vial'd liquors" (847) that the figure on the right is about to open, which resembles that held by Jesus as the Good Samaritan in *Night Thoughts* 68.

But one might further contend that, again responding imaginatively to a hint from Milton and turning it to his own advantage, Blake has also presented this as a symbolic spousal scene. When Milton had the Spirit allude to the marriage of celestial Cupid and Psyche and their twin progeny Youth and Joy in his parting speech (1004 et seq.), he was making decorous reference to Lady Alice's destined and desired aristocratic fate in matrimony's golden cage. And given the number of echoes of the Psyche myth Irene H. Chayes has detected in Blake's work, we may be confident that he noted the allusion, particularly since in the Huntington version Sabrina wears her hair in a "Psyche-knot" adorned with pearls.[36] But Blake subverts both the emphasis Milton and Puritanism placed on "wedded Love" (*Paradise Lost*, IV.750) as a legal and hierarchic bond, and the implication that true Joy and Pleasure are only to be found in a celestial "allegorical abode" (*Eur* 5.7, E 62). For this is no prelude to domestic tyranny such as that suggested in the Banquet scene, but a liberating spousal scene which like the Song of Songs implies acceptance of the sensual, and it is freely entered into by the now innocent protagonists *after* the moment of desire. Sabrina is sprinkling drops of water from her "fountain pure" (912), the fountain of life, upon the Lady with her right hand, as she in turn opens her arms and turns to greet the Brothers. But Sabrina's expressive gesture also indicates that she is commending the passional Brothers to their lost Psyche, while her left hand is raised unequivocally in benediction. The Brothers themselves are now both united and at peace, and they bow in acknowledgment of the redemptive power of woman and the sacredness of their reunion. This Beulaic state is not to be their journey's end, but it must be entered into if the implications of Thyrsis' gesture are to be followed and they move forward to Eternity.

The Beulaic rainbow emanating significantly from the liberated Lady and arching over Sabrina in the Boston version confirms that this is indeed a spousal scene. Sabrina is a less queenly but more natural and more obviously maternal figure: her hair is no longer bound and her pearls have been eliminated, perhaps to avoid any possible confusion with the Whore (see B 584), and she is accompanied by two children but no attendant nymphs. She sprinkles laving water from an open shell upon the Lady's breast, and here too commends her to the Brothers. Tayler points out that in the "Epilogue" to *The Gates of Paradise* (IB 279) Blake indicates that the lost traveler's "Satanic dream arises in part from repressed sexual desire . . . by having Satan arise from the phallus of the sleeper (see the placement of Satan's right foot)" (p. 248 n.17). Here the Lady's more expansive welcoming gesture indicates that her "knees & elbows [were] only / glued together" (E 516) after all, and the position of her right hand shows how completely she has lost her fears. The leading Brother's attitude is one of receptivity, his sibling's one of reverence. It is also easier to see that Thyrsis with his nimbus-like hat is again exercising his prophetic prerogative, and reminding them and us that Beulah is not the final destination. For by eliminating Sabrina's adult attendants and presenting her in a more humble attitude as befits the body's vital but subordinate role, Blake has contrived to group the figures so as to again suggest a diagonal ascent, culminating in Thyrsis' pointing finger. Soon the Beulaic rainbow must give way before the Edenic rising sun behind.

With "The Lady Restored to Her Parents" (Figs. 17–18) both sets come to a quiet but essentially optimistic close. There is no dancing, singing, or overt sign of jubilation as in Milton, but it is nonetheless a family reunion and related to the Return of the Prodigal motif Blake used as an unambiguous image of redemption on *Night Thoughts* 269, in "Christ Offers to Redeem Man" (Figs. 23–24) from the *Paradise Lost* designs, on *Jerusalem* 99 (Fig. 85), and in "The Gate Is Opened by Goodwill" (B 1102) from the Bunyan series. And against the "marble built heaven" of Comus' hall, this "clay cottage" (*FR* 5.89, E 291) too has propitious and egalitarian connotations, as mooted earlier. On September 23, 1800, Blake wrote to Butts that "if I should ever build a Palace it would be only My Cottage Enlarged" (E 711), and a year later, still in Eden intermittently despite frustrations, he addressed another letter to him from "Felpham Cottage of Cottages the prettiest" (E 717). As Tayler (p. 248) intimates, the Parents in the Huntington version do look quite forbidding, and Dunbar (p. 33) proposes that the Lady, whose mobility has been restored completely, is here confronting her own former attitudes. Significantly in the context of Milton's patriarchal Puritan views, though, it is the father in black who is the more severe: he is the one who examines the Lady's left palm, whereas the mother, though dressed in purple which could have ecclesiastical overtones, draws her toward her sympathetically. Furthermore, the bluish shading on the Lady's palm, though not different in color from Blake's shading at other points in the sequence, is sufficiently heavy to suggest that it was not intended as an "Insignificant Blur or Mark" (*VLJ* 83, E 560). As with the snipping gesture in the fourth design, Blake was probably in a quandary here: he needed to make clear that like the maiden in "A Little Girl Lost" the Lady had overcome her fears in the wood, but was uneasy lest he be taken to mean that she had "dare[d] to soil her Virgin purity" (427) in Milton's sense. But if we with Blake read white where Milton and his age read black, and contemplate the siblings as a unit, we will perceive that the social disapproval the Lady is facing up to is balanced by a compensating vision vouchsafed to the Brothers, for they perceive that their pastoral counselor in the wood, who now readies himself for flight toward Eternity's sunrise like the Lark ascending in *L'Allegro* 2 (Fig. 56), was indeed a true messenger from heaven.

In the Boston version, where the roseate hues of the sunrise form an effective visual link with the rainbow in the previous design and the cottage has acquired a thatched roof like Blake's at Felpham, the siblings again as in the earlier version form a central group, but differently related—perhaps to suggest the notion that "Without Contraries is no progression" (*MHH* 3, E 34). The Brothers are still united but face in contrary directions, while the Lady advances to meet her parents. Their reunion is certainly not overtly jubilant like that on *Night Thoughts* 269, where the father dashes out to embrace the contrite prodigal on his knees before him. Anything too demonstrative would have been out of keeping with the restrained tone of the series, which matches the tone of the masque so perfectly and contributes to the initial sense of literal fidelity to Milton. But the inquisitorial overtones of the earlier version have been all but eliminated: the Lady gazes fearlessly at her darkly clad Father as she advances to embrace him, and instead of examining her palm he draws her toward him with anxious solicitude, and it is now the Mother dressed in purple who appears the less emancipated. The Brothers' attention is wholly absorbed by the departing Spirit of truth revealed. In Milton his final admonition to them and to us is a moralistic one: "Mortals that would follow me, / Love virtue, she alone is free" (1018–19). But if we have correctly followed the end of Blake's golden string through these designs, his Attendant Spirit is not holding out promise of virtue rewarded "in another Country" (632) where haemony is supposed to bloom. He is urging this humanized and reunited family and all who "by due steps aspire" (12) to "ope[s] the Palace of Eternity" (14), to cast out the errors of Milton and the Puritan tradition, to redeem the contraries by embracing pleasure, and to follow truth as it is revealed in the particulars of life by the Imagination, the spirit of true prophecy, moment by expanding moment.

Notes

1 See Erdman, ed., *The Complete Poetry and Prose of William Blake*, pp. 716–18, Letters 19 and 21.

2 Butlin, *The Paintings and Drawings of William Blake*, I.373f. Full particulars of all the Milton sequences and related extant preparatory sketches are provided in this *catalogue raisonné*.

3 See Erdman, pp. 806 and 809.

4 Tayler, "Say First! What Mov'd Blake? Blake's *Comus* Designs and *Milton*" in *Blake's Sublime Allegory*, ed. Stuart Curran and Joseph A. Wittreich, Jr. (Madison: Univ. of Wisconsin Press, 1973), p. 249.

5 Pamela Dunbar, *William Blake's Illustrations to the Poetry of Milton* (Oxford: Clarendon Press, 1980), pp. 9–34.

6 Behrendt, "The Mental Contest: Blake's *Comus* Designs," *Blake Studies*, 8 (1978), 87; 65–88.

7 Dennis M. Welch, "Blake's Critique of Election: *Milton* and the *Comus* Illustrations," *Philological Quarterly*, 64 (1985), 509f.

8 Warner, *Blake and the Language of Art*, p. 176.

9 Werner, *Blake's Vision of the Poetry of Milton*, p. 17.

10 This inconsistency is true of both sequences and was probably deliberate. In the Huntington set, for example, the Brother in blue wears the sandals in the third and fourth designs but in the sixth and seventh they have been transferred to the one in green. In the Boston set the Brother wearing pink has long hair in the third and seventh designs but short hair in the others. A fair surmise would be that Blake thought of color as the dominant factor, and varied the details to provoke us into thinking about the Brothers as parts of a divided whole.

11 Malekin, *Liberty and Love*, p. 81.

12 See Bernard de Montfaucon, *L'Antiquité Expliquée* (Paris, 1719–24), I.pls. 142 et seq., II.86–89 for depictions of Bacchus and a wide range of Bacchantes, Fauns, Satyrs, Priapi, Sileni, some of them suggestive in relation to Blake's Comus figure. Pierre D'Hancarville's *Collection of Etruscan, Greek and Roman Antiquities from the Cabinet of the Hon. W. Hamilton* (Paris, 1789), I.pl. 43 reproduces a scene in terra-cotta of a maiden with twin flutes following a Bacchic reveler stepping out like Comus in the first design, holding two torches and, interestingly in the context of Comus' two faces, wearing a comic mask, evidently an actor or entertainer at a Bacchic feast. Bacchic scenes were of course common on drinking vessels; see D'Hancarville, II.pl. 58; III.pls. 41, 90; IV.pls. 33, 83, 100, 105, 118—the last two suggestive in relation to Tayler's interpretation of Comus' wand. James Stuart and Nicholas Revett, *The Antiquities of Athens* (London, 1762–1816), Vol. I, Ch. IV, pl. xxi shows Bacchus and his Fauns routing the "Tyrrhanian Pyrates" from the frieze of the "Lanthorn of Demosthenes," engraved by James Besire, recalling Comus and the Brothers in the sixth design.

13 See David Bindman, *The Complete Graphic Works of William Blake* (London: Thames & Hudson, 1978), pl. 380; and John E. Grant, "Blake's Designs for *L'Allegro* and *Il Penseroso*, Part II: The Meaning of Mirth and Her Companions," *Blake Newsletter*, 19 (1971–72), 190–202.

14 J. Karl Franson, "The Serpent-Driving Females in Blake's *Comus* 4," *Blake: An Illustrated Quarterly*, 47 (1978–79), 171.

15 Robert N. Essick, "Blake's Newton," *Blake Studies*, 3 (1971), 149–62.

16 See Panofsky, *Hercules am Scheidewege* (Leipzig: Teubner, 1930), pp. 76f.; Edgar Wind, "Virtue Reconciled with Pleasure" in *Pagan Mysteries in the Renaissance* (New York: Norton, 1968), pp. 81–83; Paulson, *Book and Painting*, pp. 46, 52, 69, 82, 85, 89, 99–100, 106, 114, 126. The motif is also discussed in Rosemary Freeman, *English Emblem Books* (1948; New York: Octagon, 1966), pp. 9–18, and Jean H. Hagstrum, *The Sister Arts* (Chicago: Univ. of Chicago Press, 1958), pp. 190–95.

17 Shaftesbury, "A Notion of the Historical Draught or Tablature of the Judgment of Hercules" in *Characteristics of Men, Manners, Opinions, Times* (London, 1723–24), III.345–91.

18 Paulson, *Hogarth: His Life, Art and Times*, pp. 120–21.

19 See Panofsky, ills. 57, 60, 61, 65, 77, 78, 82, 83, 87, 88, 95.

20 See Wind, p. 83 and pl. 60; Panofsky, pp. 124–25 and ills. 96, 84.

21 Butlin, I.394.

22 Wittreich, *Angel of Apocalypse*, pp. 8, 12, 253–54.

23 In retrospect one wonders whether the portrayal of Milton in the Boston series replaces one of Hayley in the corresponding designs in

the earlier Felpham set, with Blake in the role of plowman, which an older, mellower Blake came to think better of. Comus' heavy eyebrows and domed forehead resemble Hayley's in, for instance, George Romney's portrait of him in "The Four Friends" in William Wells, *William Blake's Heads of the Poets* (Manchester, 1969), pl. C.

24 See George Ferguson, *Signs and Symbols in Christian Art* (1954; London: Oxford Univ. Press, 1961), p. 148; pl. 29.

25 See Tayler, *Blake's Illustrations to the Poems of Gray* (no. 5 in Blake's pagination of the "Ode").

26 It should, however, be emphasized that Blake is likely to have been more concerned with "Spiritual Causes" than with "Natural Effects" (see *Mil* 26.44, E 124), if in these cases he is indeed alluding to the taboo subject of homosexuality.

27 Butlin, I.409–10.

28 See Grant, "Visions in *Vala*: A Consideration of Some Pictures in the Manuscript," in Curran and Wittreich, p. 195.

29 Essick, *The Works of William Blake in the Huntington Collections: A Complete Catalogue* (San Marino: Huntington Library, 1985), p. 15.

30 See Essick and Donald Pearce, eds., *Blake in His Time* (Bloomington: Indiana Univ. Press, 1978), pl. 111.

31 Hill, *Milton and the English Revolution*, p. 265.

32 See R. H. Tawney, *Religion and the Rise of Capitalism* (1926; New York: Mentor, 1954), pp. 164f.; M. Weber, *The Protestant Ethic and the Spirit of Capitalism* (London: Allen and Unwin, 1930); and E. P. Thompson, *The Making of the English Working Class* (Chicago: Univ. of Chicago Press, 1968), pp. 1–52.

33 A point of incidental interest: the frontispiece to Edward Moor's *Hindu Pantheon* (London, 1810) engraved by Schiavonetti depicts the elephant god Ganesa dipping his trunk into a full bowl. See also B 908.

34 See Kathleen Raine and George Mills Harper, eds., *Thomas Taylor Platonist: Selected Writings* (London: Routledge, 1969), p. 304.

35 See J. Bell, *New Pantheon* (London, 1780), II.303–8.

36 Irene H. Chayes, "The Presence of Cupid and Psyche" in Erdman and Grant, eds., *Blake's Visionary Forms Dramatic* (Princeton: Princeton Univ. Press, 1970), pp. 234; 214–43.

"I am God Alone, there is No Other": The *Paradise Lost* Designs

Blake's two completed sets of illustrations to *Paradise Lost*—the smaller set (approx. 25 x 21 cm.) done for Thomas in 1807, is now in the Huntington Library; the larger one (approx. 50 x 39 cm.), for Butts, dated 1808, principally in the Boston Museum of Fine Arts—are the most impressive of his Milton sequences. They are less exuberant than the *Night Thoughts* and Gray designs from the previous decade, but they have a neoclassical simplicity, restraint, and compositional symmetry that seems appropriate to the measured stateliness of Milton's epic. And no doubt partly because of the subject of the Genesis myth that Milton amplifies, nowhere else in his pictorial canon is Blake's admiration for the human form more strikingly apparent. Both sets employ broad washes quite unlike the exquisite miniaturist coloring of the *L'Allegro and Il Penseroso* illustrations (Figs. 55–66), and both have suffered from prolonged exposure to light, though the Boston set, of which W. M. Rossetti wrote in 1863 that "the colour is throughout good, often splendid,"[1] has retained something of its original glory.

Iconographically the series reflect Blake's familiarity with the long tradition of commercial illustration of the poem, as has been shown by several scholars, and one or two analogues—for instance, the one, pointed out by Behrendt, between "Satan Watching the Endearments of Adam and Eve" (Figs. 25–26) and Rigaud's 1801 rendering of the same scene—are so close as to suggest that Blake may have consulted the work of other artists immediately before commencing.[2] Yet none of the commercial illustrations and few of the paintings on Miltonic themes by Blake's contemporaries approach his achievement as regards quality. The mood of these designs, too, is as remote from the rococo delicacy of a Burney or a Stothard as from the histrionic sublimity of a Fuseli or Barry, and as often as not we find Blake drawing on formulae developed by Raphael, Michelangelo, Dürer, Goltzius, and others in the mainstream of biblically inspired art. Indeed, the incidence of such allusions is rather higher than that to the tradition of Milton illustration, and in at least two cases it is these mainstream *topoi* that seem to provide the key to Blake's meaning. As much less time elapsed between the two completed sets than was the case with the *Comus* and *Nativity Ode* designs, variants are particularly enlightening. This is especially so where motifs have been further modified in the three designs to a third set (Figs. 79–81) that Blake began for John Linnell in 1822.[3]

Here too there is a consensus that Blake is at points critical of Milton's rationalism and his doctrine of atonement, and Behrendt (pp. 128f.) has argued that Jesus' prominence in the series represents a tribute to Milton's essentially Christocentric vision. Most scholars, moreover, have noticed that Blake seems to present Adam and Eve's fall as a "fall into Division" (*FZ* 4, E 301), and that as in Milton, Satan's degeneration proceeds by stages.[4] But beyond this, progress with the internal dynamics of the series has been impeded by the unspoken assumption that in this unique intertextual relationship Milton is the prophet, Blake the scribe—that the *Paradise Lost* designs are essentially magnificent pictorial footnotes. In consequence, commentary has here again encouraged the vertical movement of our imagination between poem and designs, while often missing iconographic continuities and contrasts which, when the designs are read horizontally, can reveal quite different emphases. Blake of course shared Shelley's respect for Milton's republicanism and had expressed his admiration for the infernal scenes of *Paradise Lost* as early as the *Marriage*. And to judge from the anecdote of Butts calling to find him and Catherine reading the poem naked in their garden (p. 2, above), he can scarcely have been less impressed with Milton's inspired vision of Eden as a state in which love is innocent and man in daily touch with the divine. Yet the comprehensiveness of his polemic against the errors "Miltons Religion" (*Mil* 22.39, E 117) shared with "All Bibles or sacred codes" (*MHH* 4, E 34) in the *Marriage* and *Milton* reminds us how clearly he also recognized the extent to which *Paradise Lost* had become an establishment text—an apology for an outworn creed which was still being used by kings and priests to enslave the vulgar. As late as 1822 Blake remarked on the poem to Crabb Robinson in terms that are more critical than laudatory:

> He reverted soon to his favourite expression 'my visions'. "I saw Milton in imagination and he told me to beware of being misled by his *Paradise Lost*. In particular he wished me to show the falsehood of his doctrine that the pleasures of sex arose from the Fall. The Fall could not produce any pleasure" ... the Fall produced

only generation and death and then he went off upon a rambling state[-ment?] of a union of sexes in man as in God—an androgynous state in which I could not follow him.[5]

The difficulty here is that Milton expressly states that Eve did not refuse her consort the "Rites / Mysterious of connubial Love" (IV.742–43). But if we take "pleasure" as the operative word, what Blake may have been implying is that he considered Milton's vision of unfallen sexuality a tepid and restrained affair compared to the passionately sensual scenes between Adam and Eve after the Fall. As Malekin justly observes, though "Adam and Eve copulate in their bower for mutual delight . . . in Book IV, lines 737–73, Milton stresses that it was then 'Founded in Reason, Loyal, Just and Pure,'" whereas "copulation after the Fall is sensual."[6] When we recall the central place of sensual enjoyment and spousal symbolism in Blake's system, there seems therefore every reason for suspecting that, as with the *Comus* designs, here too his critique of Milton may be more radical and imaginatively daring than the footnote hypothesis allows. Writing of painting in fifteenth-century Italy, Michael Baxandall observes that "a figure played its part in the stories by interacting with other figures, in the groupings and attitudes the painter used to suggest relationships and actions."[7] As Blake's poignant entreaty that we pay attention to the "Hands & Feet to the Lineaments of the Countenances" (*VLJ*, E 560) in his designs bears eloquent testimony, by the end of the eighteenth century this tradition and the shared values it assumed were dying. But when the interplay between figures, gestures, and motifs in the *Paradise Lost* designs is attended to as part of an intricately orchestrated narrative sequence, it becomes possible to see that they present not Milton's but Blake's own devil's party version of the Fall.

In broad outline, Blake's first three designs accurately reflect Milton's aims in the corresponding Books in the sense that they too serve to establish the spiritual poles of the ensuing psychodrama, Satan's facing outward in cruciform position in the first design being counterpointed against Jesus' facing inward in identical cruciform position in the third. And as mooted earlier, one of the problems in these opening designs is why Satan rousing his minions (Figs. 19–20) appears against a backdrop of clouds like Urizen on *America* 8 (Fig. 83) and elsewhere, whereas at the Gates of Hell (Figs. 21–22) he is more closely associated with the soaring flames behind him, suggesting affinities with the flaming Orc as he appears for instance on *America* 10 (Fig. 84), or with "Fire" in *The Gates of Paradise* (IB 271). The subsequent designs depicting Adam and Eve in Paradise dramatize the struggle between demonic and redemptive forces within the mind of man. And in the context of Blake's post-Enlightenment belief that "All deities reside in the human breast" (*MHH* 11, E 38), it is notable how frequently he uses overarching or encircling motifs (Figs. 25–26, 29–30, 37–38), which again like the cranial cave on the *Visions* frontispiece (IB 125), or the skull-like configuration of clouds and figures around the throne of God in some of his *Last Judgment* paintings (Fig. 89; B 868–70), point to the interior nature of events.[8] Adam and Eve's fall into division and Satan's gradual degeneration as he invades their mental space culminate in the Temptation scene (Figs. 35–36), where the couple are divided by the "Tree of Mystery" (FZ 93.24, E 365) and Eve in the toils of the serpent receives the fruit from its jaws. In the 1808 series both processes take place by more clearly demarcated stages through the replacement of "Satan Spying on Adam and Eve, and Raphael's Descent into Paradise" (Fig. 27) by "Adam and Eve Asleep" (Fig. 28), where Satan is depicted "Squat like a Toad, close at the ear of Eve" (IV.800), and she has already turned away from her fair consort. The puzzle in this new design is what to make of Ithuriel and Zephon's stellar or serrated halos, and of the way the former's pointing finger echoes that of Satan as it penetrates the Bower of Bliss (Figs. 25–26). This progression is counterpointed by three sequential designs (Figs. 29–34), corresponding to the admonitory middle sections of the epic, in which Raphael points the way to man's redemption. And in this context one of the fascinating features especially of the 1808 series is that Blake seems determined to absolve Eve from the responsibility for the Fall, which the rationalist in Milton had made her share with Adam, but which emotionally he and the twenty-seven "Churches" (*Mil* 37.15 et seq., E 139) of Christian tradition had no more forgiven her than he had forgiven Mary Powell, as his will was to reveal.[9] The last three designs are the most problematic in the series, raising questions about how much emphasis to place on the conciliatory tone of the Judgment scene, and whether the vision of the Crucifixion Michael grants to Adam should be construed *in bono* as is generally assumed or *in malo* as will be argued here. On this second issue it may be pertinent that in each of the three versions (Figs. 39–40, 81) Michael appears successively more spectrous.

Blake's two opening infernal scenes are among the designs more clearly indebted to the tradition of Milton illustration, and his frontal presentation of "Satan Arousing the Rebel Angels" (Figs.

19–20) most closely resembles those by Lawrence (P 104) and Westall (Fig. 90). At a literal level Satan presiding over this Ulro scene of "darkness visible" (I.63), his spear and shield resting against the rock behind him, is clearly bidding his despondent followers "Awake, arise or be for ever fall'n" (I.330). And the way his arms are extended in a cruciform gesture, which parodies that of Christ offering to redeem man, seems intended as a proleptic allusion to Book II, where he represents his vengeful mission to them as self-sacrifice. But it is also an imperious gesture which expresses his authority as "Thir dread commander . . . above the rest / In shape and gesture proudly eminent" (I.589–90). And how Blake may be manipulating Milton's allegorical figures to his own ends begins to emerge when Satan's commanding stance and gesture are thought of further as comprehending the archetypal act of self-assertion for which he was expelled from Heaven. Nowhere else in the series is Satan's violation of the hierarchy, which constitutes the mainspring of the entire action of *Paradise Lost*, referred to directly, since in his illustrations for Book VI (Figs. 31–32) Blake focuses on Christ's victory over the rebel angels. If, then, we take this provisionally as a moment analogous to that in the Bard's Song of *Milton* when Satan proclaims "I am God alone / There is no other!" (*Mil* 9.25–26, E 103), an explanation for the Urizenic clouds emerges. For as we have seen, what Los and Enitharmon's recognition that "Satan is Urizen" (*Mil* 10.1, E 104) implies in Blake's epic is that in his view, reason had assumed demonic proportions in Milton and Puritanism. By confirming them in their self-righteousness as the elect of God, and endorsing their mistrust of women and the passions, their rational faith had led to the devastation of Europe with wars. What therefore we may be witnessing here, felicitously placed at the opening of the series, is an archetypal act of usurpation on the part of reason.

The hypothesis will perhaps appear less fanciful when the design is contemplated in relation to *The Ancient of Days* (B 367–68), also used as the frontispiece to *Europe* (Fig. 82). There the Creator is depicted within his solar orb, kneeling with his "golden Compasses" to "circumscribe / The Universe" (VII.225–27; see Proverbs 8.27)—from Blake's point of view a highly Urizenic act. The similarity in the way Satan and the Creator are both hemmed in by billowing clouds is remarkable, and in the 1808 version, where Satan is proportionately larger, the effect is enhanced. This suggests that a deliberate cross-reference may be involved, hinting that Satan and Milton's rationalist Father are one and the same. A further reason for thinking so is that Christ in "The Rout of the Rebel Angels" (Figs. 31–32) is also inscribed within a circle, making it virtually certain that Blake had *The Ancient of Days* in mind when working on the *Paradise Lost* designs. Moreover, these two designs are not only formally but also thematically mirror images of one another. As Blake observed in *A Vision of the Last Judgment* about this time:

> Thinking as I do that the Creator of this World is a very Cruel Being & being a worshipper of Christ I cannot help saying the Son O how unlike the Father. First God Almighty comes with a Thump on the Head. Then Jesus Christ comes with a balm to heal it.
>
> (E 565)

In *Milton* Blake makes it clear that he regards Milton's vision of the Father as demonic by associating him fairly explicitly with Satan. In a magnificent satirical passage near the end—which as a gloss on "Satan Arousing the Rebel Angels" is potentially illuminating and furnishes a possible explanation for the reduction of his followers from sixteen to seven in the later series—Satan is revealed

> Coming in a cloud, with trumpets & flaming fire
> Saying I am God the judge of all, the living & the dead
> Fall therefore down & worship me. Submit thy supreme
> Dictate to my eternal Will & to my dictate bow
> I hold the Balance of Right & Just & mine the Sword
> Seven Angels bear my Name & in those Seven I appear
> But I alone am God & I alone in Heaven & Earth
> Of all that live dare utter this, others tremble & bow
> Till All Things become One Great Satan, in Holiness
> Oppos'd to Mercy, and the Divine Delusion Jesus be no more.
>
> (*Mil* 38.50 et seq., E 139)

Blake was to make this same identification on *Job* 11 (Fig. 91), and again later in the *Paradise Regained* series (Figs. 67–78), where in all but two of his appearances the Tempter is depicted with the long flowing beard of God the Father.

What we should consider therefore is that, while remaining scrupulously faithful to Milton on the literal level, Blake may in fact from the very outset of his series be challenging Milton's account of the Fall as the subversion of right reason by the passions and the will. Satan as "A mighty Fiend against the Divine Humanity mustring to war" (*Mil* 10.11, E 104) may here be Satan/Urizen/Jehovah who, as in *The Book of Urizen* and *Milton*, has usurped the throne of God in man—perhaps represented by the figure in the posture of the classical *Dying Gladiator* (H & P 116) behind Satan. If so, it would be tempting to identify the four figures in the fore-ground in the 1808 version with the four fallen Zoas or elements. To see this as a bid for power on reason's part would also explain why Satan's followers, who are not individualized in relation to Milton's catalogue of devils, are not only despondent but all male.

"Satan, Sin and Death: Satan Comes to the Gates of Hell" (Figs. 21–22), a design indebted to both Hogarth's (P 53) and Barry's (Fig. 92) and no doubt also to Gillray's renderings of the scene, is among the most dramatic in the series.[10] Burke had praised the episode for its sublimity and it evidently impressed Blake too.[11] It not only forms the basis for the conflict between Urizen and Fuzon in *The Book of Ahania*, where Urizen's "parted Soul" (2.32, E 84) Ahania is identified with Sin, it is also echoed in the eighth emblem in the *Gates of Paradise*, subtitled "My Son! My Son!" (E 263). A sense of continuity with the previous design is sustained by the reappear-ance of Satan, his arms again outstretched, but now flourishing his spear and shield like "Fire" in the fifth *Gates of Paradise* emblem (E 262). This analogy and Satan's close association with the wall of flames behind him might seem to undermine the Urizen hypoth-esis. But Blake's allegorical method is essentially kinetic, and when the scene is thought of as a sequel *causally* related to the previous one, this apparent iconographic inconsistency could be resolved as a coherent statement that when, as in Milton, reason usurps the throne of God in man, his energies become demonic and erupt in corporeal war.[12] The effects of such repression are also evident in the larger version, in the scaly loins of Satan.

This reading would also make sense of the relationship be-tween Satan and Death. The most immediately striking thing about these formidable antagonists is that they too are mirror images of one another. The effect is enhanced in the version belonging to the 1808 series, where the position of Satan's legs is reversed and the spectrous figure of Death—so much closer to Milton than the skel-etons of Milton illustration (P 4, 14, 40, 53, 92)—with his crown and "dreadful dart" (II.672) now faces inward. In both versions, more-over, the two figures are so nicely poised, with Sin in the center thrusting them apart, that the eye remains in doubt whether they are on the point of engaging in, or stepping back from, an initial encounter. The effect seems calculated to suggest that this is an allegory of psychic division. If what we are witnessing here is a vision of reason and energy interacting not as contraries but as negations, in which the figure of Death has assumed the role of disembodied abstract reason, it is a little worrying that in the larger version he appears without a beard. But as Butlin points out, since this latter design is undated and signed "W B inv," a form of signature Blake appears to have relinquished after about 1805, it may have originated as an independent illustration and been incorporated into the 1808 series subsequently.[13] And Blake could well have decided that it conveyed the idea of a divided personality more effectively, and avoided the reversal of the father/son relationship in Milton that his bearded Death entailed.

Sin, in some ways the most impressive figure of the three, seems symbolically as well as visually central to Blake's composition. In Milton, where Satan, Sin, and Death form a grotesque parody of the Trinity, the allegory which is based on James 1.15 is essentially moral and theological. In turning away from the God of Reason, Satan by incurring gives birth to Sin and spiritual Death, and the concupiscence inherent in his act of disobedience is expressed through their lustful and incestuous intercourse. But in Blake's more psychological view, man's preoccupation with sin is causally connected to the elevation of reason at the expense of his other living faculties or Zoas. When Urizen on his early appearance as "primeval Priest" seeks "for a joy without pain, / For a solid without fluctuation," he finds himself struggling "With terrible monsters Sin-bred" (*Ur* 2.1 et seq., E 71). And evidently Blake felt that Milton spoke more truly than he knew when he described the birth of Sin from Satan's head (II.745 et seq.), since he used it in *Milton* as the basis for the birth of Leutha in the more complex allegory of the Bard's Song. In the present context he may be taken as saying analogously that it is the *sense* of sin that divides body from soul, reason from energy, Orc from Urizen, and mankind from his fellows. Sin's voracious nether parts therefore would seem expressive of the perversion of love into lust that follows. Her serpentine appendages, which had given previous Milton illustrators so much trouble, are neatly coiled into two vortical configurations. Blake consistently used a variety of vortical forms in his iconography to signal expanding or contracting states of consciousness, and these are the first of three in the *Paradise Lost* designs.[14] Visually they enhance the sense of outward motion while also alerting us to the divisions within Satan. Sin's twin tails in the larger version end, like those of the fabulous beasts in Revelation 9.19, in serpent heads—added perhaps to identify her and her four yelping "Hell Hounds" (II.654) numerologically as an aggregate of the "Seven deadly Sins of the soul" (*Ur* 4.30, E 72). The portcullis of

Hell Gate, which compared to the "Bars of Death" being raised on *Night Thoughts* 126 looks utterly immobile despite its pendant chain, is grimly expressive of the spiritual bondage that acceptance of the tenets of Milton's oppressive religion entails. Sin's "fatal key" is from Blake's point of view the "Sad instrument of all our woe" (II.871–72) because it is the sense of sin that keeps man locked behind Hell Gate. Only Christ as the forgiver of sin, as he is seen descending with two similar keys on the first design to Blair's *Grave*, can liberate man from this state.

In "Christ Offers to Redeem Man" (Figs. 23–24), which, as Behrendt (p. 137) points out, unlike the first two designs has no real precedents in the tradition of Milton illustration, Blake again focuses on what is dramatically and doctrinally central to Book III. Like Milton at this point in the epic, he is concerned to establish the spiritual parameters within which the fall of Adam and Eve will subsequently unfold, but here too his differences with his Puritan mentor seem to be more fundamental than the footnote hypothesis allows. Particularly important is the way Christ in cruciform position forms a reverse mirror image of Satan in the first design. Blake could have portrayed Jesus facing outward, as he does Raphael descending to Paradise in the Huntington series (Fig. 27), and thus enhanced the sense of his imminent descent. But this contrast between an outward-facing Satan and an inward-facing Christ seems to go beyond mere acknowledgment of Milton's parodic skills, to invite our contemplation of the difference between external and internal notions of self-sacrifice. There is an equally telling contrast between the spectacle of discord between father and son in the second illustration and the harmony and love between Jesus and the Father here. And from a post-Enlightenment perspective, of course, Satan's readiness to sacrifice his son is precisely what is involved when Milton's Father declares that Adam

> with his whole posterity must die,
> Die hee or Justice must; unless for him
> Some other able, and as willing, pay
> The rigid satisfaction, death for death.
>
> (III.209–12)

Critics have been understandably perplexed by the discrepancy between Blake's known hostility to Milton's doctrine of atonement and the evident tenderness of this farewell, which seems so close in spirit to the reunion of Albion with his Emanation on *Jerusalem* 99 (Fig. 85) and to the Return of the Prodigal tradition it is based on.[15]

It may therefore be illuminating to consider the scene further as a modulation of the great iconographic *topos* referred to by Gertrud Schiller as the *Not Gottes* or *Pitié de Nostre Seigneur* tradition, in which the Father is portrayed supporting the broken body of Christ.[16] Dürer's woodcut of *The Trinity* (Fig. 93) is typical in its frontal presentation of Father and Son, shown ascending toward the Holy Spirit and surrounded by cherubim bearing most of the traditional *Arma Christi*, or emblems of the Passion. It would be hard to find a more cogent summary of the grislier aspects of the Christian faith. If in portraying the Father gently supporting the cruciform figure of the living Christ Blake is indeed invoking this tradition, it is surely to present, in the form of a visual pun, a more inward, life-affirming vision of at-one-ment than that subscribed to by Milton, Dürer, and the Churches. The resemblance of Jesus here to Blake's various portrayals of the risen Christ, likewise in cruciform position—on the *Night Thoughts* frontispiece dispersing clouds, and in watercolors of *The Resurrection* (Fig. 94) and *The Ascension* (B 574)—also argues against identifying him too closely with Milton's protagonist.

A God who hides his face could of course be sinister, but in the Huntington series he does later reveal his countenance above the descending Raphael (Fig. 27), and in the Boston version of the present design Christ himself is shown in half profile, perhaps to reassure us. Also pertinent is Behrendt's observation that the "Son's posture . . . places his heart against the Father's forehead" (p. 139). The force of this in context, though, surely is to suggest not the difference between them, but the *reconciliation* between the values of head and heart that in the Hell Gate illustration had been shown in dualistic opposition. If Satan in the first design is thought of therefore as perpetrating the archetypal act of self-assertion which separates man from God, Christ is here depicted in the exemplary act of self-surrender by which man again becomes at one with God—a reading which would account for what Dunbar describes as "the paradox of [Christ's] arrested motion."[17] As Blake was to express his humanist ideal in an inscription to his painting, the *Epitome of James Hervey's 'Meditations among the Tombs'* (B 967), a "God out of Christ is a Consuming Fire." This sense of unity rather than division is enhanced by the contrasting downward movement of the four wingless angels, which may be fruitfully compared to that of the lowest angel in the tenth *Paradise Regained* design (Fig. 76), who stoops to prevent Jesus' falling from the pinnacle. Evidently they are casting down their crowns less in "lowly reverant"

(III.349) affirmation of the hierarchy than as a gesture of renunciation of all such struggles for power and dominion as we have witnessed in the opening designs. In the 1808 version they have living "Crowns inwove with Amarant" (III.352), sharpening the contrast with Death's spiked crown. Numerologically this may therefore be taken as a fourfold vision of the highest happiness available to man.

The significance of the upper portion of the design as a redemptive emblem of peace, unity, love, and light is enhanced by the contrasting martial presence of Satan below, "Coasting the wall of Heav'n on this side Night" (III.71). He is presented laterally, flying from left to right in an attitude that may owe something to two of Stothard's portrayals of Satan (P 75–76). Continuity with the infernal scenes is maintained by his spear and shield, and in the 1807 version by his genital scales, but he has now also developed huge bat wings. Blake frequently associated these standard attributes of medieval devils with blinkered rationalism, for instance on *Jerusalem* 6 (IB 285), "To the Accuser" (*GP*, E 269), and in *Auguries of Innocence*, where "The Bat that flits at close of Eve / Has left the Brain that won't Believe" (E 494). In the 1807 version he gazes balefully and enviously up at the celestial group; in the 1808 version his expression is one of complete self-absorption. His spiritual isolation in both designs is graphically conveyed through his exclusion from Heaven by the cloud-barrier, and by his subordinate position beneath Christ's feet.

With "Satan Watching the Endearments of Adam and Eve" (Figs. 25–26, 79) Blake's narrative, like Milton's, shifts to the terrestrial world and to an exploration of the effect on man of these archetypal events in Heaven and Hell. Iconographically the shift is registered by the contrast between the more abstract settings of the opening scenes and the lush, verdant topography of Eden. In the five designs which precede the Fall in both sets (Figs. 25–34), two scenes showing Satan encroaching on our First Parents' pastoral world are followed by three which, again in broad conformity with Milton, make regenerative counterstatements.

Satan eavesdropping on Adam and Eve was first chosen as a subject for Book IV by Hayman (P 37), and it was his formulation that set the pattern for subsequent illustrators, including Brown (Fig. 95) and Rigaud (Behrendt, p. 147) whose versions Blake's resembles most closely. Here too Blake presents a scene emblematic of peace, harmony, and love, but one under threat from Satan, who provides the strongest visual link with the previous design. He is now as it were in the ascendant, appearing in the dominant position at the top of the design. And though no longer wielding his spear and shield, he is portrayed, much earlier than in Milton, in intimate association with the serpent coiled around him, cradling its head in such a way that they appear almost to kiss. This intimacy is not suggested in the separate watercolor on the same subject dated 1806 in the Fogg Art Museum (B 644). There, an older, lightly bearded Satan is seen hovering above, engulfed in flames, clutching his head in an attitude Blake associated with Despair in his sketch of "Various Personifications" (B 247) in the manner of Le Brun, while the serpent winds its way between the legs of Adam and Eve.[18] The final conception is undoubtedly more expressive and seems to emphasize that he is a self-divided being—if, that is, we again take his bat wings as emblematic of his rational portion and the crimson-tinted serpent, earlier associated with Sin, as the demonic form that energy assumes when repressed as sinful. In the 1822 version the Urizenic stars on his wings have spread over his whole body, making him appear more spectrous. In all three versions his index finger has already penetrated the fragile trellis of the "blissful Bower" (IV.690), within which Adam and Eve are seen "Imparadis't in one another's arms" (IV.506), thus violating what may be seen as a pastoral version of the perfect circle of the sun surrounding Christ in the seventh design (Figs. 31–32).[19] Adam and Eve are reclining on a bed of thornless roses, fringed beneath by lilies upon large vegetable leaves—a recurrent motif which reminds us that the action is taking place upon "this earth of vegetation" (*Mil* 14.41, E 109). They are intimate physically, but less passionately so than the embracing couple on the *Marriage* title page (IB 98), in "The Reunion of the Soul & the Body" (Fig. 97) from the *Grave* series, or the figures in the Lily of Havilah on *Jerusalem* 28 (IB 307). In all versions, moreover, they seem distracted by Satan's presence, and though Eve's body posture shows no self-consciousness, Adam raises his right leg defensively, obscuring his genitals from view. The way Adam and Eve's embrace is grotesquely parodied by Satan and the serpent suggests that they are an externalization of what is beginning to take place within the couple.

If we take this as the moment when Satan's archetypal fall into division begins to take hold in man, it would be logical to expect that Blake would have allegorized Adam and Eve too as body and soul, reason and energy. In the *Comus* series, as we have seen, it is the Lady who appears to be more closely associated with reason. And in two of the *Grave* designs (Figs. 96–97) the soul, like Psyche in Antiquity, is depicted as a woman—though here too Blake's flexible attitude to tradition is reflected in the fourth and fifth designs depicting the deaths of the "Strong Wicked Man" and the "Good Old Man," whose departing souls are in each case masculine. But in *Paradise Lost* Adam's greater rationality and Eve's more sensuous nature are central to Milton's patriarchal conception of the hierarchical relationship between them:

> For contemplation hee and valor form'd
> For softness Shee and sweet attractive Grace
> Hee for God only, Shee for God in him.
>
> (IV.497–99)

Blake's awareness of this is clearly attested by the iconography of *Night Thoughts* 119 (Fig. 98), where he responds to Young's "Sense and Reason show the Door, / Call for my Bier, and point me to the Dust" by depicting Reason and Sense before death's door as respectively the lapsarian Adam and Eve. It would thus have been quite natural for him to have reverted to this symbolism when he came to illustrate *Paradise Lost*. A further preliminary hint that Adam should be associated with reason and the soul, Eve with the body and the senses, is perhaps provided here by the fact that in both the 1808 and 1822 versions Adam holds a lily, Eve a rose, traditional emblems of purity and passion.

From this vantage it becomes possible with more confidence to interpret the dynamic interplay between the figures as a moment of incipient self-consciousness which begins to destroy the primal unity between man and woman, body and soul, reason and energy. Satan's pointing gesture is frequently one of accusation elsewhere in Blake, for instance on *Job* 10 and *Jerusalem* 93 (IB 372), and it establishes him further as Satan "The Accuser," whom Milton and the Churches "Worshipd by the Names Divine / Of Jesus and Jehovah" (*GP*, E 269).[20] The notion that he represents a process of self-accusation within Adam is supported by the fact that in all versions he and Adam look very much alike. Blake uses the same principle in the *Job* designs where Job resembles the Godhead he imagines. Under the influence of Milton's Puritan religion, we might say, therefore, that Adam has begun to reflect that "Womans love is Sin!" (*Eur* 5.5, E 62). Significantly, moreover, in relation to Milton's indictment of Eve, Blake presents this sense of sinfulness as a *mental* act by placing Adam's head in all versions under the more direct influence of Satan's accusing finger. In the Boston and 1822 versions he obtains an additional resonance by reversing Satan's position. The serpent now appears not only in the corresponding position but also on the same side as Eve, and Satan's finger, while still appearing to cast a spell over Adam's thoughts, is now also pointing accusingly at her. In the 1822 version she too has already been infected, for the rose she holds is no longer without thorns.

It is in this context that phallic interpretations of the serpent encircling Satan's loins fall into place. When man becomes self-conscious and selfish about sex, "Embraces" cease to be "Cominglings: from the Head even to the Feet," and are experienced as "a pompous High Priest entering by a Secret Place" (*J* 69.43–44, E 223). Satan's voyeurism, envy, and Narcissism too, which Blake's portrayal captures so successfully, are the effects of reason's hegemony and not, as Milton and his age believed, of its subversion. Adam's chaplet of roses suggests that he is not yet fully persuaded of the need for purity, but the setting sun and rising— and in the later versions waxing—moon behind him intimate that the long dark night of the soul lies just ahead.

In the Huntington series this design is followed by "Satan Spying on Adam and Eve, and Raphael's Descent into Paradise" (Fig. 27), in many respects a more beautiful design than "Adam and Eve Asleep" (Fig. 28), which replaces it in the Boston series. The subject was not without analogues in Milton illustration (P 11), but compositionally Blake's archangel descending the formalized steps within the V-shaped cloud-barrier seems more closely indebted to figures from spandrels in Renaissance churches, such as Raphael's *Mercury Descending from Heaven* in the Farnesina, engraved by Marcantonio (Fig. 99). In sequence the design presents a pause in the action in which Satan's advance is held temporarily in check. And the fact that it is initiated by a cruciform Father who though bearded is of open countenance and—very unconventionally and as an obvious contrast to the bat-winged Satan—has splendid eagle's wings should reassure critics who persist in associating him with the blind presiding figure in *The House of Death* (B 397–99). Raphael himself is a striking figure enveloped by his sixfold wings, his upturned gaze and gesture intimating dutiful devotion, his luxuriant hair cascading down his shoulders. His function as heavenly nuncio is conveyed visually by the way in which he comes between them and the Archfiend—the vignettes on either side of the cloud-barrier suggesting subordinate scenes in a formal triptych, the one life-affirming, the other life-denying. Satan facing outward appears bat-winged and serpent-bound again, but he has now invaded Eden. The trees to the left and right of him are dead and the darkness that accompanies him is spreading. His gesture may simply express dismay at Raphael's precipitous descent or, if he is frowning at Adam and Eve behind the cloud-barrier, perhaps also disapproval. If so, the voyeuristic pleasure he nonetheless derives may be read on the leering face of the now triumphant serpent above him. Adam and Eve shown facing inward and "talking hand in hand" (IV.689) still seem to be harmoniously united as they cross a sunlit glade toward vine-laden trees—a motif which, Essick observes, "suggests the traditional elm and vine *topos*, an emblem of ideal marriage."[21] One reason for Blake's not repeating the design in the Boston series may be that it shows Satan's successful invasion of Paradise, but registers no significant change in our Grand Parents since the previous design. But almost certainly he also came to see that its formal similarities to "Christ Offers to Redeem Man" made it a little too repetitive.

Both these problems are overcome in "Adam and Eve Asleep" (Fig. 28), a visually less prepossessing but iconographically much subtler alternative. It has no close precedents in Milton illustration, since artists tended to favor the more dramatic moment where Satan starts up "Discover'd and surpris'd" (IV.814) at the touch of Ithuriel's spear, but the toad does appear literally in a design by Lens (P 12) and in a sketch by Barry (P 122). Blake's disposition of his figures may owe something also to a delicate portrayal of "unawak'n'd Eve" (V.9) by Westall (Fig. 100). In relation to the previous design, it is now Ithuriel and Zephon who occupy the space above Adam and Eve, but unlike Satan there they are both *within* the overarching bower. They too, therefore, are likely to represent some aspect of what is occurring in the minds of the sleeping couple. The rift between Adam and Eve, moreover, has evidently developed further. Adam's right arm still encircles— though it barely touches—Eve as they lie outstretched on their lily-bordered bed of roses. But he has now crossed his legs in a repressive gesture that recalls the Lady's crossed arms in the first *Comus* series (Figs. 11, 13), and anticipates Milton's defensiveness in *L'Allegro and Il Penseroso* 11 (Fig. 65). Eve's whole body is still wonderfully expressive of unself-conscious innocence, but she is now in the subordinate position beneath Adam and has turned toward the toad. Both she and the toad are shown on vegetable leaves from which Adam appears to be excluded, and her "Tresses discompos'd" (V.10) encircle and seem to draw the toad into her orbit.

To gloss this simply as Eve's assertion of her "Female Will" (*J* 56.43, E 206), though no doubt acceptable to Milton, would be to ignore the possibility of a more dynamic interplay between all the figures. Eve's subordinate position as the body and the senses and her turning away from Adam as the rational soul may, in other words, be the result of Adam's attitudes, represented by Ithuriel and Zephon immediately above him. One reason for suspecting their innocence, as mentioned earlier, is the way Ithuriel's pointing gesture echoes that of Satan in the previous design. Another is that they are set apart from all the other angels by their stellar or serrated halos, recalling the "cogs tyrannic" (*J* 15.18, E 159) shown on *Jerusalem* 22 (IB 301), which could also associate them with the star-covered body of Satan as "Prince of the Starry Wheels" (*Mil* 343, E 97). One suggestive analogy occurs on *Night Thoughts* 121 (Fig. 101), where Christ is seen with hands and feet pierced by huge nails in the fiery furnace of Daniel 3.19, his crown of thorns offset by a large and jagged nimbus. And in the Banquet scene in the *Paradise Regained* designs (Fig. 72) Satan himself is seen against a huge serrated disk. A final—though more equivocal—reason for doubting that Ithuriel and Zephon are the redemptive guardians they may seem is that they are the only angels apart from Michael, the angel of Justice, in the penultimate design (Figs. 39–40, 81), to be armed like Satan and like Death with spears.

When Ithuriel and Zephon in the corresponding position to Satan and the serpent in the previous design are likewise seen as externalizations of what is now taking place within the dreaming Adam, complementing the toad-like Satan at the ear of Eve, it becomes possible to appreciate how subtly Blake has arranged all the particulars to explain exactly why things have degenerated further. Adam facing heavenward like the pious Puritan soul that he has now become is dreaming of militant transcendental angels, vigilant against sensual corruption. Ithuriel's finger of accusation pointing down at both Eve and the toad, and Zephon's gesture of revulsion, are alike expressive of reason's mistrust of the senses and Adam's growing persuasion that sexual pleasure must be sinful. Eve's subordinate position and her turning away from Adam are thus a *consequence* of his attitude, which closely corresponds to that of Albion when he rejects his emanation early in *Jerusalem*. Seen from Eve's perspective, the way she inclines toward the toad she is dreaming of suggests the incipient secretiveness, guilt, and self-disgust in matters sensual that Milton and Puritan tradition tended to engender. The palm fronds behind the couple form gothic arches, generally a propitious sign in Blake's iconography, but as they cross they obscure the overarching circle and seem to echo Adam's crossed legs. Accordingly, the modest bunch of grapes appears to function more as a reminder of what is in danger of being lost if, as the waxing moon intimates, their Beulaic sleep should become protracted into spiritual death.

This interpretation gains credence when Adam and Eve's attitudes and relative positions are contemplated in relation to those of the couple in the redemptive vision of *Milton* 42 (Fig. 102). There Milton and his Emanation Ololon, or possibly Albion and Jerusalem, are seen lying in attitudes of post-coital tenderness such as make life tolerable on England's "ancient Druid rocky shore" (*Mil* 6.25, E 102). Milton's posture is close to Adam's, but his hand rests fearlessly on his partner's thigh and in copy A, watermarked 1808, he is shown with a distinct erection. He is awake and gazes up at St. John's visionary eagle hovering overhead. Ololon is presented on the opposite side of her consort to Eve and she turns toward him, clasping him with her left arm in loving embrace.[22]

"Raphael Warns Adam and Eve" (Figs. 29–30) represents a regenerative countermovement, as the corresponding episode does in Milton, where Raphael appears in answer to the couple's morning prayers, immediately after Eve's account of her unsettling dream. Milton's symposial scene was popular with illustrators from the beginning, and in the 1808 version by Burney (Fig. 103) there is a precedent for Blake's central location of Eve. But his richly embroidered scene, framed by the delicate floral tracery of the Silvan Lodge, also has affinities with the intricate sixteenth-century engravings of Eden (see, for example, Fig. 104) that he admired. The Tree of Knowledge is given the prominence accorded it by Milton in Book IV, but the presence of the serpent coiled around it anticipates Book IX, and the Tree of Life, we should observe, is not included. More generally it is the spirit of Milton's Edenic panorama that Blake has tried to capture in his landscape, though some of the details do occur in Milton.

In the Huntington version the interaction between the three symposiasts is less complex than in the Boston version, and Raphael pointing heavenward and to the Tree is more the focus of attention. Adam and Eve appear united on their rose-upholstered seats, and Eve in "meek surrender, half embracing" leans on "our first Father" (IV.494–95). Adam's legs are ominously crossed, but his gesture, like Raphael's in his descent (Fig. 27), denotes submission and he seems to be listening to his guest. Raphael the "sociable Spirit"

(V.231) sits diagonally opposite them, on the same side of the rustic table heaped with "savoury fruits" (V.304). In Milton, Raphael is of course a moralist and rationalist, the essence of whose admonitory function is to warn Adam against the dangers of intemperance and uxoriousness:

> But if the sense of touch whereby mankind
> Is propagated seem such clear delight
> Beyond all other, think the same vouchsaf't
> To Cattle and each Beast; which would not be
> To them made common and divulg'd, if aught
> Therein enjoy'd were worthy to subdue
> The Soul of Man, or passion in him move.
> What higher in her society thou find'st
> Attractive, human, rational, love still;
> In loving thou dost well, in passion not,
> Wherein true Love consists not.
>
> (VIII.579–89)

From Blake's point of view such passages encapsulated precisely those Puritan fears from which he saw it as part of his prophetic mission to liberate mankind. In context, however, one would expect him to have retained Raphael's redemptive function on his own terms, and two particulars suggest that this is indeed the case. One is the way Blake has responded to the passage of great beauty in Milton describing Raphael's sixfold wings (V.277–85) by shaping them into an equally splendid vortical configuration, which points in the opposite direction to the flaming sword that spirals downward in the last design (Figs. 41–42). The other is that he has given Raphael a distinctly androgynous appearance.[23] Blake would hardly have missed the dualistic assumptions behind Raphael's account of how, when "Spirits embrace, / Total they mix, Union of Pure with Pure / Desiring" (VIII.626–28). But he appears to have recognized in it a visionary analogue to his own understanding of innocent sexuality as a matter of self-transcendent comminglings. And by presenting Raphael as an androgynous being, he would seem to be hinting that the archangel personifies the state of harmonious unity that, under Satan's influence, Adam and Eve have already begun to lose. Raphael's admonitory gesture may be taken as analogous to that of the prophetess in the *Arlington Court Picture* (B 969), who warns that if, like the sun-charioteer, man falls asleep imaginatively, he will find himself in the predicament of the man ensnared by the three Fates below.[24] He may, that is, be construed as saying that if Adam continues his quest for an abstract transcendental purity, he will find himself in the power of the serpent around the Tree of Mystery which, as the overarching trellis reminds us, "grows . . . in the Human Brain" (*SE*, E 27).

In the Boston version the interaction between the protagonists is more dynamic and more richly resonant. Adam now appears engaged in earnest colloquy with an even more resplendent Raphael, who has acquired an amaranthine crown. He no longer sits cross-legged but his gesture is expressive of uncertainty—as if he is only partly convinced by what Raphael is saying. Eve has moved from Adam's side to the center of the composition, immediately beneath the Tree of Knowledge, which has receded to accommodate her height and is more neatly encircled by a more obviously voyeuristic serpent. The trellised arch of the enclosing arbor is now fringed by lilies but no roses. Eve's relocation might appear to continue the theme of their gradual separation, already well established in this series in the toad design. But the conclusion that she is being negatively associated with the Tree to emphasize her greater frailty in Milton's sense, or that she is coming between Adam and the Divine Vision in an act of self-assertion, is not wholly in accord with the visual impression she makes. She seems the epitome of innocence as she stands there like an antique Venus, unself-consciously displaying her "Naked Human form divine" (*EG* 66, E 552), her head of golden ringlets inclined toward Adam in attentive expectation. The shell-like vessel in her left hand, which further associates her with the foam-born goddess and with Sabrina in the *Comus* series (Figs. 15–16), endorses the association of her with the body, while the huge bunch of grapes in her right hand perhaps initially suggests an allusion to her potential fruitfulness as "Mother of Mankind" (V.388).

Part of the explanation for Eve's medial position between the two disputants surely is that she is the subject of their discourse. And when she is thought of in relation to Sin in the corresponding position between Satan and Death in the Hell Gate scene (Figs. 21–22), it becomes more apparent that this is a vision of woman and the body as sinless. Moreover, since the Tree of Life, which is conspicuous in Blake's separate painting known as *The Fall of Man* (Fig. 105), is absent here, the force of the close association of Eve with the Tree of Knowledge is evidently one of contrast. To see in Eve, representing woman, the body and the senses, a humanized vision of the Tree of Life here would also provide a further explanation for her bunch of grapes. It would then follow that Adam too, like the Lady in the second *Comus* design (Figs. 5–6), is in the situation of Hercules at the Crossroads, as his almost identical gesture of indecision seems to intimate.[25] And Raphael is urging him to make a choice, his right thumb splayed so that he also gestures toward Eve, his left hand pointing heavenward at an angle which includes reference not only to three or more bunches of grapes but also to Christ's rout of the rebel angels in the next design (Figs. 31–32). Repression of woman and the senses and righteous Puritan devotion to the knowledge of good and evil are errors inspired by Satan/Urizen/Jehovah. Only by casting off such errors through Jesus as the Imagination, and accepting woman and the body in equal partnership as contraries, can man be restored to his original psychic harmony and unity of being.

Though in *Paradise Lost* Raphael's account of the War in Heaven is complemented by Adam's recollection of Eve's creation, the next two designs in Blake's pictorial narrative (Figs. 31–34, 80) should perhaps both be understood as amplifying the archangel's counsel, since in the second, Adam figures as dreamer rather than narrator. Like the opening infernal and celestial scenes, they appear to be complementary designs, "The Rout of the Rebel Angels" being clearly a vision of the rejection of error, followed therefore, one would expect, by "The Creation of Eve" as in some sense an "Image of truth new born" (*SE*, 31). The War in Heaven was popular with Milton illustrators, being selected for instance by Medina (P 7) and Cheron (P 20), and by Hayman (P 45), who anticipated Blake in focusing on Christ's intervention, while Barry (P 91) showed the rebels being driven out by Michael. But Blake's illustration is closer in spirit to the mainstream of Last Judgment paintings, and his own compositions on this subject (Fig. 89; B 868–74) date from the same period. Conceptually his vision of Jesus—and in *The Ancient of Days* the Creator—inscribed within the circle of the sun may also be indebted to such early emblematic designs as *The Garden of Eden* (Fig. 104) attributed to Cranach, where God appears above the perfect circle of the cosmos.

Leopold Damrosch, Jr., has with some justice observed that Christ appears to be the only absolute in Blake's system, and there is a consensus that here too, as in Milton's poem, at the midpoint in the series his action has exemplary redemptive implications.[26] But the hypothesis first advanced by Wittreich and endorsed by Behrendt, that Blake saw Milton's vision as essentially Christocentric and sought to celebrate this in these and the later *Paradise Regained* designs, should not be allowed to obscure the fact that Christ meant very different things to the two poets.[27] When the Son in Milton, having "into terror chang'd / His count'nance" (VI.824–25), intervenes to resolve the war in Heaven, he comes as the emissary of God's justice, wrath, and "Power Divine" (IV.780), and uses the words of Deuteronomy 32.35 to remind his "Saints" (VI.801) that "Vengeance is [God's], or whose he sole appoints" (VI.808). Milton's imagery is less sanguinary than that of Revelation 19, where Christ returns "clothed with a vesture dipped in blood" (19.13) and "in righteousness . . . doth judge and make war" (19.11), but his emphasis on justice is the same. To Blake this vision of the Redeemer was as false as Milton's legalistic doctrine of atonement. The essence of his disagreement with his precursor on the question of justice is contained in his repeated insistence in *Milton* and *Jerusalem* that one "Distinguish . . . States from Individuals in those States" (*Mil* 32.22, E 132). The idea is more fully articulated in *A Vision of the Last Judgment*, where he declares that

> whenever any Individual Rejects Error & Embraces Truth a Last Judgment passes upon that Individual . . . I do not consider either the Just or the Wicked to be in a Supreme State but to be every one of them States of the Sleep which the Soul may fall into in its Deadly Dreams of Good & Evil when it leaves Paradise following the Serpent . . . The Combats of Good & Evil is Eating of the Tree of Knowledge the Combats of Truth & Error is Eating of the Tree of Life.   (E 561–62)

By replacing the concept of sin by the principle of error, and by transferring judgment from the individual to the error he commits, Blake releases the individual from Puritan guilt with its debilitating effect upon his energies, increases the scope for mercy which the righteous tend to see as weakness, and absolves man from superstitious dependence on future rewards and punishments. Though expressed in religious terms, the principle is essentially secular and psychological and reminds us how much Blake was a product of the Enlightenment he criticized.

It is in this context surely that the significance of Christ's triumph depicted here should be understood—as a more humane alternative to Milton's portrait of Christ the Avenger. This is a vision of Milton's satanically repressive rationalist theology, which Adam has begun to listen to, being cast out by Jesus as the Imagination and the "bright Preacher of Life" (*J* 77.21, E 232). The true nature of Milton's hero is revealed on *Jerusalem* 35 (IB 314), where a bat-winged, bearded Satan wields a triple bow as he rides across the sky like the avenging Horsemen from the Book of Revelation.

The six tutelary angels surrounding Jesus, though prompted no doubt by Milton's description, based on Ezekiel 1.1–28, of Christ's chariot "convoy'd / By four Cherubic shapes" whose "wings were set with Eyes with Eyes the Wheels" (VI.750–55), form a configuration Blake consistently associated with the "Seven Eyes of God" (J 55.31, E 205; see B 497, 511, 538) or manifestations of the divine in human history. As an aggregate they appear to be more deliberately contrasted with Sin before Hell Gate in the 1808 version (Fig. 22), where she is surrounded by six demonic heads. Christ's bow has been rightly associated with the anti-dualistic "Bow of burning gold" and "Arrows of desire" that the prophet calls for in *Milton* (1, E 95), and with the fourfold bow wielded by the four Zoas restored to unity in Albion's bosom in the apocalyptic closing section of *Jerusalem*. The multiple arrowheads suggest that Jesus is acting with great energy and swiftness—recalling Blake's earlier and less effective illustration of Hyperion in the Gray designs (B 343). Their ethereal hafts, when contrasted with Satan's more substantial weaponry, seem to imply a distinction between mental and corporeal warfare. And by reducing them from seven to five in the 1808 version, Blake allows the six angels and Christ to exorcise the seven deadly sins, as it were, while also perhaps tilting numerologically at all Lockean five-sense philosophies unredeemed by the imagination. As in the opening designs, the rebel angels in both versions (though more certainly so in the Boston version) appear to be all male, and they are not identified as individuals evidently to make clear that they represent an aggregate of error.

"The Creation of Eve" (Figs. 33–34, 80), of which there are three versions, is formally one of the most beautiful designs in the series, but iconographically perhaps the most obscure. Though the subject was also chosen by Fuseli (P 100), Milton illustrators generally tended to avoid it, possibly because, given its centrality in biblically inspired art, it lacked novelty and put them too directly into competition with the great masters. In its simplicity Blake's design has affinities with early Florentines like Fra Angelico and Ghiberti (Fig. 86) whom Palmer remembered him admiring.[28] But it departs from tradition in at least two significant respects. First, Eve is shown, not emerging physically from the sleeping Adam's side, but hovering immediately above him. The effect, as comparison with Michelangelo's very physical portrayal on the Sistine ceiling reveals, is to enhance the sense that the spiritual event being portrayed takes place in Adam's dream.[29] Second, artists generally followed biblical authority in showing Eve being created by the

Father, who is usually depicted in the act of blessing her.[30] Milton has Adam plead with the "Almighty" (VIII.398) for a mate and his "Heav'nly Maker" (VIII.485) bring her to him, and Blake's separate watercolor of *The Creation of Eve* (B 512), where Adam with purplish "Hyacinthine Locks" (IV.301) is depicted being introduced to Eve by a full-bearded deity, indicates that he took these as allusions to the Father. But here, unconventionally, she is being drawn forth by Christ, with a gesture more commonly associated with the raising of Lazarus.

In sequence, coming as it does immediately after Christ's rejection of error, this should logically be a vision of truth aimed at restoring Adam's confidence in Eve. The difficulty is that to interpret this archetypal act of sexual division *in bono* would seem at odds with the negative implications both of Adam and Eve's gradual separation so far and of such events elsewhere in Blake's work. In "The Soul Hovering Over the Body Reluctantly Parting with Life" (Fig. 96) from the *Grave* series, where the soul is a young woman very like Eve, the dualistic implications are unequivocal. And on *Jerusalem* 31 (IB 310), where a stigmatized Christ hovers in flames over Adam as Eve erupts from his side in the traditional manner, the separation is portrayed as grotesque and painful. However, the implications there are ultimately propitious, as is clear from Blake's later account of how

> the Saviour in mercy takes
> Contractions Limit [Adam], and of the Limit he forms Woman:
> That Himself may in process of time be born Man to redeem.
>
> (*J* 42.32–34, E 189)

In "The Creation of Eve," however, there are no signs that the separation is a distressing experience for either party. How skillfully Blake has contrived to present a redemptive vision here, which again undermines the entire thrust of his Puritan precursor's disparagement of Eve, emerges more clearly when we reflect on it as a divinely inspired dream which replaces the dreams induced by Satan in the toad design (Fig. 28). In Milton, when Adam rapturously describes how Eve had first seemed to him "So lovely fair, / That what seem'd fair in all the World, seem'd now / Mean, or in her summ'd up" (VIII.471–73), he receives a stern rebuke from Raphael. But if we think of Eve as the content of Adam's dream, we can see that, by making her the wonderfully graceful naked beauty that she is, Blake would seem to be *endorsing* the passionate response in Adam that Milton's Raphael warns against, and signalling a change in Adam's attitude that replaces his preoccupation with purity and sin in the design showing Satan as a toad. He no longer crosses his legs and his whole body posture expresses open receptivity to this divine vision of his emanation Eve as sinless—to the "nakedness of woman [as] the work of God" (*MHH* 8, E 36). Indeed, the way Eve is suspended in midair invites comparison with the pendant Christ-child in the first design of the later *Nativity Ode* series (Fig. 44), in that it implies that her creation too is something of a miracle. That the moment is indeed auspicious is also supported by Eve's resemblance to two of the images of Jerusalem regenerating on *Jerusalem* 5 (IB 284). A contrast with the toad design is suggested by the now waning moon and by the marked absence of Urizenic stars.

Eve's resemblance to the hovering "Soul" in the *Grave* design, and Adam's closer association with the vegetable leaf, might suggest a reversal of the body/soul symbolism, analogous to Satan's transformation from Urizen to Orc in the opening designs. But considering the way Jesus draws Eve forth and the fact that this is a Beulaic scene "where Contrarieties are equally True" (*Mil* 30.1, E 129), it is perhaps more appropriate to think of Adam as a soul embodied and Eve as "Raised a Spiritual Body" (*SE*, E 30; see IB 59). As individuals they remain discrete, but through Jesus as the imagination toward whom Eve turns receptively, they have been raised to the consciousness that "Man has no Body distinct from his Soul" (*MHH* 4, E 34). To Blake this was the first essential step toward transcending the limitations of the natural world, perhaps represented by the oak groves in the background.

Christ in all versions also stands on a vegetable leaf, which in the Miltonic context is surely intended to indicate that he is "not a God afar off" but "a brother and friend" (*J* 4.18, E 146). Blake used variants of his gesture in two of his Bible illustrations, in *Christ Giving Sight to Bartimaeus* (B 490) and again in *Christ Raising the Son of the Widow of Nain* (B 561). These analogues tend to endorse the redemptive implications of this scene and to undermine the idea that Jesus might be imposing limits on Eve's separation. Werner (pp. 83–84) has perceptively observed furthermore that in the three versions Jesus becomes successively more like the Father, which is consistent with the unitary symbolism of the third design. One might add that as his hair becomes longer and his gown fuller, he also becomes, like Raphael, a more distinctly androgynous figure. As such, like Raphael he is an embodiment of the integral state toward which Adam and Eve are being encouraged to return.

"The Temptation and Fall of Eve" (Figs. 35–36), a design of great though quite un-Burkean sublimity and power, brings the series to a visual climax that complements the stately crescendo to which *Paradise Lost* rises in Book IX, as Milton turns his "Notes to Tragic" (IX.6). Several of Blake's contemporaries followed Milton literally in that they depicted Eve alone with the serpent, though Stothard (P 68) and Burney (P 85) also responded to the phallic suggestiveness of Milton's scene, showing it "erect / Admidst its circling Spires" (IX.501–2) before her. Blake brings together in the one design Satan's seduction of Eve (IX.494 et seq.), Adam's reactions as he drops "the Garland wreath'd" (IX.889–93) for her in horror, and Heaven's thunderous response to their disobedience (IX.1001–2). The way he places Adam and Eve on either side of a central tree, moreover, again reflects his tendency to turn for his models to mainstream compositions such as Dürer's engraving of *The Fall* (Fig. 106) in preference to the tradition of Milton illustration. In this case, however, he may also have been inspired by Grinling Gibbons's font in St. James's, Piccadilly (Fig. 107), where Blake had been baptized (BR 5), a work ingeniously designed to represent both the Tree of Knowledge and the Tree of Life. One of the constants in the iconography of the Fall reflected in both these works is that Adam and Eve are almost invariably depicted sharing the forbidden fruit.[31] And as J. B. Trapp has pointed out, with increasing frequency from the sixteenth century on the scene was given erotic overtones.[32] In both respects the pictorial tradition is in essential accord with Milton's portrayal of events in *Paradise Lost*: though Adam is not present when Eve eats of the forbidden fruit, he resolves to share her fate, and the immediate effects of the Fall are manifested in the scene of unbridled carnality (IX.1008–15) which Blake seems to have had in mind in the conversation recorded by Crabb Robinson. Both Milton and iconographic tradition are in harmony with standard Christian doctrine: by turning from obedience to God and the rule of right reason, Adam and Eve are guilty of idolatry and concupiscence.

In Blake's design, where, in line with his remarks to the diarist, all signs of pleasure are conspicuously absent, Adam and Eve face in opposite directions divided by the tree, and the erotic element has been transferred to Eve's relationship with the serpent. Adam is evidently as much under the dominion of Milton's accusing Godhead thundering in the heavens as Eve is in the power of the serpent, which she cradles exactly as did Satan above the Blissful Bower (Figs. 25–26, 79), receiving the fruit from its jaws again in such a way that they appear to kiss. As Satan has already been established as the Accuser, it is a fair inference that Blake was thinking of the angry heavens and the serpent here as complementary manifestations of the same demonic principle. A clear analogy occurs on *Job* 11 (Fig. 91), where the God of Righteousness, who affrights Job in his dreams by pointing to the torments of Hell that await those who disobey his commandments, is himself encircled by the serpent and reveals a cloven hoof, while jagged bolts of lightning like those surrounding Adam rend the skies. Thus while Blake follows Milton in showing Adam and Eve rejecting heavenly counsel and lapsing into selfishness and lust, as regards the *causes* of their fall he again reads black where Milton and his age read white. For despite the vision of Eve's innocence granted him by Jesus in the previous design, Adam has turned away from her toward the satanic Puritan God of Righteousness, convinced like Milton that they will be punished for following their impulses. The oppressiveness of the Christian Miltonic "law of ten command-ments" (*MHH* 23, E 43) and its inhibiting effect upon Adam are conveyed by the way the "Tree / Of interdicted Knowledge" (V.51–52)—the Tree of Mystery which springs from beneath Urizen's heel—totally dominates the picture and forms a massive and, in the 1808 version, thorn-infested obstacle to his communing with his Emanation.

Eve, like all Blake's Emanations, asserts her independent fe-male will again as a *reaction* to Adam's repudiation of her. In the 1808 version of the scene with Raphael in the Silvan Lodge (Fig. 30), she had inclined her head toward her spouse. Now she leans surreptitiously toward the serpent with the fruit, as though she was indeed "Crooked by nature" (X.855) like Adam's rib as he bitterly says later. These are in a sense the "self enjoyings" of Adam's "self denial" (*VDA* 7.9, C 50), and Eve is discovering that "stolen joys are sweet, & bread eaten in secret pleasant" (*Eur* iii.6, E 60). In *Night Thoughts* 296 Blake makes the demonic implications of such secretive behavior even more explicit, by presenting Young's personifi-cation of Pleasure as a serpent with human head and arms, coiled round the Tree of Mystery and urging an angel to be wise and taste. And by showing Adam and Eve looking guilty for having done so in the sequel, *Night Thoughts* 297, he suggests that such lapsarian views of Pleasure's demonic nature as Young and Milton express are the direct result of feeling guilty about it. The coldly erotic relationship between Eve and the serpent undoubtedly also pays tribute to Milton's vision of Satan's seduction of Eve as an archetypal rape. Blake had responded to this much earlier in *Satan Exulting over Eve* (B 384, 389), a color print dated 1795, in which an armed and bat-winged Satan hovers exultantly over the prostrate body of Eve in the toils of a huge phallic serpent, its head resting between her breasts. But the crucial difference between Blake's account and Milton's is that lust and violence are caused by Milton's rational dualistic hierarchy of values, not controlled by it. Abandoned by the pious soul, the body and the pleasures of the senses cease to be innocent and become obscene. In the 1807 version Adam holds up the broken rose garland of their innocent love, as if to emphasize that, like Milton's hero and like the "god-tormented" Theotormon after the Urizenic Bromion's rape of Oothoon in *Visions*, he now thinks of Eve as "Defac't, deflow'r'd, and unto Death devote" (IX.900). In the 1808 version the garland lies discarded at his feet.

In "The Judgment of Adam and Eve" (Figs. 37–38), which seems less concerned with the consequences of the Fall than with their resolution, Blake again appears to have turned to one of the mainstream iconographic *topoi* as a clue to his intentions. Milton illustrators who produced Judgment scenes include Cheron, Hayman (P 42), Barry (P 90), and Richter (see P, pp. 268–69), but their work has little bearing on Blake's rendering. In biblical tradition the Judgment is usually subordinated to the Fall, and often omitted in favor of the Expulsion. Blake's balanced composition, with Christ frontally presented in the center and the repentant Adam and Eve facing him on either side, is more closely related structurally to the great tradition of betrothal paintings. The formula goes back to Antiquity, and in Christian art from the Middle Ages on was most commonly used to depict the marriage of the Virgin.[33] Perugino, Raphael, and Dürer were among the distinguished Renaissance contributors to this subject, and Goltzius's *Marriage Founded Solely on Pure and Chaste Love, Which Is Blessed by Christ* (Fig. 108) and Duvet's elaborately ornate *The Marriage of Adam and Eve* (Fig. 109) are particularly suggestive variants in relation to Blake's illustration.[34] There is no question that he knew and was fond of this tradition, since he also used it as the model for the separate paintings of *The Creation of Eve* (B 512) and *The Angel of the Divine Presence Clothing Adam and Eve with Coats of Skins* (B 513), and for the marriage scene within the "more bright Sun of Imagination" in *L'Allegro and Il Penseroso* 6 (Fig. 60). The formula also lies behind his *Christ the Mediator* (B 497), another painting thematically pertinent to this design.

Commentary has tended to see Blake here as intent on bringing out Christ's dual role in Milton as "mild Judge and Intercessor both" (X.96). But assuming the marriage commonplace is more than merely a formal analogy, and in view of Blake's hostility to Milton's legalistic emphasis on justice, we are faced with the question of whether this is a judgment scene at all. It is true that in all Blake's *Last Judgment* compositions (Fig. 89), Christ does appear centrally enthroned as judge in the traditional manner. But in *A Vision of the Last Judgment* he makes clear that this is "the Saviour the True Vine of Eternity the Human Imagination," engaged in "throwing off the Temporal that the Eternal might be Established" (E 555). Moreover, the penitent Adam and Eve are always depicted as the first to be redeemed, whereas the righteous are cast out. Coming as it does immediately after the illustration of the Fall with Adam and Eve facing away from one another and divided by the Tree of Knowledge, the dominant impression made by this design is of reconciliation rather than of judgment. It is not strictly a spousal scene such as Duvet's, where Adam's and Eve's hands are united by the Father, since this would have created obvious incongruities with Milton's text. But Blake certainly had indirect Miltonic authority for the notion of reconciliation in the touching scene where Eve begs Adam for forgiveness (X.908 et seq.), which was thought to reflect Milton's own experience with the repentant Mary Powell, and which Blake might well have thought represented Milton's better self.[35] If, therefore, previous designs have revealed different aspects of the true Christ—as selfless Redeemer, victor over error, and bright preacher of life—here as in *Jerusalem* the emphasis seems to be on "The Spirit of Jesus" as "continual forgiveness of Sin" (*J* 3, E 145). That as such he is *himself* the Tree of Life is suggested visually by his presence in the same medial position as the Tree of Knowledge—the tree on which Milton and the Churches had first crucified then worshipped their false "Vegetated Christ" (*J* 90.34, E 250) in the name of justice and atonement. In both versions he shares the large vegetable leaf with the lapsarian Adam and Eve, again perhaps as a mark of solidarity—as a reminder that he is with us always here on earth if we have eyes to see. His conciliatory gesture intimates that it is through mutual forgiveness and the reintegration of soul and body, reason and energy, that man's resurrection to unity will be brought about.

In the 1807 version Adam and Eve both appear contrite and attentive in their leafy aprons. Adam inclines his head submissively, his hands clasped in prayer, his right heel threatening the serpent's head, while Eve covers her face in a gesture of repentance. But in the 1808 version Adam, again with clasped hands, looks directly across at Eve, as if imploring *her* forgiveness for his aberrant piety and rationalism. The revision nicely accentuates the importance of Adam's bringing Satan the Accuser's "Serpent Reasonings" (*GP* 7, E 268) to heel in this reconciliation of contraries, if man's life-denying preoccupation with the invading Sin and Death is to be kept at bay, and his psychic unity suggested by the overarching cloud-barrier to be continually restored. Jesus here thus appears to be remote from Milton's judge and his function closer to that he assumes in the misnamed *Fall of Man*, where, as Michael J. Tolley has pointed out, Adam and Eve are seen without their lapsarian aprons and Christ leads them through a predatory world as preserver of their innocence.[36] Indeed, in the 1808 version he seems to gaze intently at the spectator—as if challenging us to discriminate between justice and forgiveness.

The last two designs may perhaps be most satisfactorily integrated into this general line of argument if they are thought of as amplifying the consequences of pursuing justice rather than forgiveness. In "Michael Foretells the Crucifixion" (Figs. 39–40, 81), the more problematic of the two, Blake again breaks with Milton illustrators such as Cheron (P 22), Hayman (P 43), Richter, Westall, and Craig (see P, p. 269) who showed scenes from Milton's chronicle of fallen history, focusing instead on his doctrinally more central vision of Christ "nail'd to the Cross / By his own Nation" (XII.427). His presentation of the serpent pinned to the cross beneath Christ's feet, with Sin and Death slumped around it, is not wholly unprecedented, but it is altogether more powerful and expressive than most of the early crucifixion scenes in which the dead serpent appears beneath the cross.[37] The composition may also owe something to Michelangelo's *Lamentation of the Virgin Beneath the Cross* (Fig. 110), where the body of the deposed Christ lies under a hillock in an attitude similar to Eve's and beneath an equally plain cross. Michelangelo's seated Virgin also bears some resemblance to "Mary at Her Distaff" in the *Paradise Regained* series (Fig. 70).

What is at issue here is whether Blake is applauding Milton's vision of the crucifixion, as Behrendt (pp. 171–72) and with reservations Werner (pp. 95–97) have contended, or whether he is presenting it ironically as a demonic perversion of true self-sacrifice, which is life-sustaining. Blake believed Christ "ought not to have suffered himself to be crucified," as Crabb Robinson records (BR 540), and in three of his surviving *Last Judgment* scenes (B 871–72, 874) he shows the cross with the serpent nailed to it being cast out as a remnant of Druidism. In the Petworth *Last Judgment* (Fig. 89), however, the cross behind Christ is evidently to be spiritually discerned, and at points in both *Milton* (22.58, E 118) and *Jerusalem* the crucifixion is also used *in bono* as an emblem of true self-sacrifice:

> Jesus said, Wouldst thou love one who never died
> For thee or ever die for one who had not died for thee
> And if God dieth not for Man & giveth not himself
> Eternally for Man Man could not exist, for Man is Love:
> As God is Love: every kindness to another is a little Death
> In the Divine Image nor can Man exist but by Brotherhood.
>
> (*J* 96.23–28, E 256)

The absence of INRI from the head of the cross in the two later versions seems to reflect a desire on Blake's part to dissociate his vision of Christ from the historical Jesus, but this does not preclude the possibility of seeing him as the perennial victim under law. The fate of Satan, Sin, and Death might seem cause enough for jubilation, were it not for its overtones of self-defeating vengeance. But the fact that in all three versions Adam and Eve appear without their aprons could imply that by following Christ's example they will be restored to innocence.

Two considerations tend, however, to tilt the balance in favor of an ironic interpretation. One is that this is a vision presented by Michael, the angel of justice. Elsewhere in *He Cast Him into the Bottomless Pit* (B 585) Blake portrayed Michael propitiously, putting up a valiant though perhaps losing fight against the encircling Dragon. And in *Night Thoughts* 452, where he is shown wounding Satan in a scene taken from Milton's War in Heaven (VI.320–34), his conduct also seems unexceptionable. But here, as has been widely noticed, Blake presents him without Miltonic authority as the centurion who pierces Jesus' side. Furthermore, as mentioned earlier, in each successive version Michael becomes older and more Urizenic, assuming in the 1822 version a spectrous appearance reminiscent of Death before Hell Gate. These particulars at the very least suggest that Blake felt ambivalent about him, and could well indicate that he is indeed in league with all the other corporeal warriors armed with spears against Christ as the Divine Humanity. The second factor has to do with Blake's location of the sleeping Eve in a hollow below the cross. Chayes and Werner (p. 96) have both noticed that her attitude recalls that of Nature awakening beneath the stable in the first *Nativity Ode* design (Figs. 43–44), a resemblance which is consistent both with her Miltonic role as Mother of Mankind and her association with the body in the present series.[38] But Blake appears to have responded also to another parallel drawn by Milton himself when he has Michael remark to Adam:

> let Eve (for I have drencht her eyes)
> Here sleep below while thou to foresight Wak'st,
> As once thou slep'st, while Shee to life was form'd.
>
> (XI. 367–69)

For Eve lies at the bottom of the design in an attitude almost identical to that of Adam in "The Creation of Eve" (Figs. 33–34, 80). The visual parallel reinforces the notion that, whereas in Milton she is excluded from Michael's revelation, here the scene above her also represents what she is dreaming. Given her literal proximity to the earth and her resemblance to Nature and to Earth in the "Introduction" to *Experience* (IB 72), the logical inference is that this is a "female dream," analogous to Nature goddess Enitharmon's dream of the "eighteen hundred years" (*Eur* 9.5, E 63) of fallen history that follow the advent of Jesus in *Europe*.

Both factors tend to endorse what is surely the dominant impression made by the design as a whole, that this is a false image of self-sacrifice, a demonic travesty rather than the redemptive consummation of the living Christ's willing self-surrender in the third design—"allegorical and mental signification" turned to "corporeal command" (*DesC* 41, E 543). If so, it is closely related to *Jerusalem* 76 (IB 355), where Albion is likewise seen worshipping the dead Christ nailed to the Tree of Mystery and emitting a "dim religious light" (*Il Penseroso*, 160). In context it may be construed as depicting the consequences of disregarding Christ's conciliatory message in the previous design—of accepting Milton's redemptive vision of justice and atonement rather than Blake's more truly Christian vision of forgiveness. Adam has again moved away from Eve and gazes up at the "Dead Corpse from Sinai's heat" that the Churches "rear" upon their "Altars high" (*GP* 7–11, E 259). And under the auspices of the angel of justice he is worshipping the self-destructive work of Satan, albeit "by the Names Divine / Of Jesus & Jehovah" (*GP*, E 269). Eve, again subordinated and despised, participates in this first "lost Travellers Dream under the Hill" (*GP*, E 269), and she will awake to take up the power games of virgin harlotry that the patriarchal Churches in the fallen world will force on her in expiation, as Blake sees it, for Adam's original sin. The force of the absence of their lapsarian aprons would thus appear to

be the deeply ironic one that, from Blake's point of view, in following their natural desires and eating of the forbidden fruit in Milton's
sense, Adam and Eve were sinless.

If this reading of the design is accepted, then it is in complementary rather than antithetical relationship to "The Expulsion of
Adam and Eve from the Garden of Eden" (Figs. 41–42), which is
altogether more violent and angry in mood than Milton's rather
wistful parting scene, and brings the series to a satisfying dramatic
close. It belongs with the opening infernal scenes as among those
most influenced by Milton illustration, where Hayman (P 52),
Burney, and Craig (see P, p. 269) all anticipated Blake in presenting
Michael frontally between Adam and Eve, leading them out of
Eden by the hand. But even here Dunbar (p. 87) has drawn attention to an earlier mainstream analogy, *Lot's Escape* by Rubens,
which Blake engraved. Most of the Expulsion scenes in Milton
illustration are pastoral in setting, but Blake has effaced all trace of
pastoral innocence from his design. The three central figures are
shown entering a waste land of thorns and thistles, blasted as in the
Temptation scene by lightning bolts, and pursued by the four
Horsemen of the Apocalypse, who are not mentioned in Milton,
emissaries of a Satanic Father's just avenging ire. In the 1807 version they all look up or back as they descend the formalized flight
of steps, Michael sadly and regretfully, the again aproned Adam
and Eve with gestures of astonishment and fear at the "flaming
Brand" "Wav'd over" their former "happy seat" (XII.642–43). In the
1808 version, in which the steps are omitted, the couple look down,
more ominously preoccupied with the "sneaking Serpent" (*MHH*
2.17, E 33) which rears its head accusingly at Adam.

That Michael should have assumed Christ's medial position in
the Judgment scene is wholly appropriate, if we take this in sequence as a further manifestation of the consequences of replacing
mercy and forgiveness by justice, guilt, and punishment for sin.
The way he takes our First Parents by the hand might seem conciliatory, but it is less open and more coercive than Jesus' gesture.
Moreover, his visual association with the swirling flame immediately above him is a reminder that he is the Covering Cherub who
in Milton's theology keeps "guard at the tree of life" (*MHH* 14, E
39). His demonic allegiance with Satan/Urizen/Jehovah is also
cleverly suggested by the way the serpent insinuates itself between
his feet, its motion echoing that of the flaming sword. It is thus
precisely by accepting Miltonic justice and right reason as his guardian angel, and submitting to the "Wheel of Religion"—the "terrible

devouring sword" that "Jesus died because he strove / Against" (*J* 77, E 232)—that man undergoes the contraction of imaginative and sensual life, symbolized by the downward vortex, which for Blake constitutes the loss of Eden. So long as "Serpent Reasonings us entice / Of Good & Evil: Virtue and Vice" (*GP*, E 268), we will remain like Adam and Eve, outside the Gates of Paradise in the self-divided Ulro state of single vision and bondage to the fallen world toward which they are heading. Blake's doctrine of states implies that we can break these mental shackles at whatsoever time we please. But in keeping with his remarks to Crabb Robinson, there is little sign in this final design to what is perhaps his greatest Milton sequence of his agreeing with his Puritan precursor that there was anything fortunate about the Fall.

Notes

1   W. M. Rossetti, "Annotated Lists of Blake's Paintings, Drawings, and Engravings" in Gilchrist, *Life of William Blake*, 2nd ed. (London: Macmillan, 1880), II.219.

2   Behrendt, *The Moment of Explosion*, Fig. 46. According to Erdman, *Blake: Prophet Against Empire* (Princeton: Princeton Univ. Press, 1969), p. 291, Blake was personally acquainted with Rigaud.

3   See Butlin, *The Paintings and Drawings of William Blake*, I.388–89. There are also several preparatory sketches for the *Paradise Lost* series—see Butlin, II.723–27.

4   See Dunbar, *William Blake's Illustrations to the Poetry of Milton*, pp. 38, 41, 76; Behrendt, pp. 145, 149; and Werner, *Blake's Vision of the Poetry of Milton*, pp. 78, 86–88.

5   Morley, ed., *Henry Crabb Robinson on Books and Their Writers*, I.330.

6   Malekin, *Liberty and Love*, p. 160.

7   Michael Baxandall, *Painting and Experience in Fifteenth Century Italy* (Oxford: Oxford Univ. Press, 1972), p. 71.

8   See Mitchell, "Blake's Visions of the Last Judgment: Some Problems of Interpretation," *Blake Newsletter*, special supplement for MLA Blake Seminar, December 28, 1975, penultimate paragraph of unpaginated text.

9   See W. R. Parker, *Milton: A Biography* (Oxford: Clarendon, 1968), pp. 639, 647–49.

10 For Gillray's political use of the motif see Erdman, *Prophet*, pp. 221–23 and pl. VIIa.

11 Edmund Burke, *A Philosophical Enquiry into the Origin of Our Ideas of the Sublime and Beautiful*, ed. J. T. Boulton (London: Routledge, 1957), p. 59.

12 In the more distinct of the two separate temperas of *Satan Calling Up His Legions* (B 888–89), which is evidently a more complex allegory with roughly twice the number of figures as in the Huntington version of this scene, the two motifs are used together: Satan is again surrounded by heavy billowing clouds, but he is silhouetted against a column of fire. Another notable difference is that though the devils are again (so far as one can tell) predominantly male, both temperas depict a chained female with crescent moon endeavoring to rise on Satan's right, apparently at a literal level a portrait of "Astarte, Queen of Heav'n, with crescent Horns" (I.439).

13 Butlin, I.385; see further Butlin, "Cataloguing William Blake" in Essick and Donald Pearce, eds., *Blake in His Time* (Bloomington: Indiana Univ. Press, 1978), pp. 82f.

14 For discussions of the vortex in Blake's symbolism, see Hazard Adams, *William Blake: A Reading of the Shorter Poems* (Seattle: Univ. of Washington Press, 1963), pp. 29–34, and Donald Ault, *Visionary Physics: Blake's Response to Newton* (Chicago: Univ. of Chicago Press, 1974), pp. 141f.

15 Blunt, *The Art of William Blake*, pl. 49C. Samuel Palmer recalled how, reciting from this parable, Blake had been moved to tears—see Gilchrist, *Life of William Blake* (London: Dent, 1942), p. 302.

16 Gertrud Schiller, *Iconography of Christian Art*, trans. Janet Seligman (Greenwich: New York Graphic Society, 1971), II.219f. and Figs. 768–93.

17 Dunbar, p. 54.

18 For a discussion of the drawing manuals by Le Brun and others which Blake's sketch shows him to have been familiar with, see Warner, *Blake and the Language of Art*, pp. 35f.

19 The significance of the squared circle in Blake's iconography is discussed in Edward J. Rose, "'Mental Forms Creating': 'Fourfold Vision' and the Poet as Prophet in Blake's Designs and Verse," *Journal of Aesthetics and Art Criticism*, 23 (1964), 173–83.

20 See Damon, *Blake's Job* (Providence: Brown Univ. Press, 1966), p. 30 and pl. 10. Subsequent references to plate numbers in the engraved *Job* series are to this edition.

21 Essick, *The Works of William Blake in the Huntington Collections: A Complete Catalogue* (San Marino: Huntington Library, 1985), p.33.

22 Behrendt, p. 23, makes the interesting suggestion that we "see the eagle as an emblem also for Blake himself," who as prophet and

"presiding spirit . . . both *exhorts* [the couple] to increase their 'Mental Fight' and *chastizes* their lethargy."

23 For a discussion of hermaphrodism and androgyny in Blake, see Damon, *A Blake Dictionary* (Providence: Brown Univ. Press, 1965), pp. 181–82.

24 See Grant, "Discussing the Arlington Court Picture, Part II," *Blake Newsletter*, 13 (1970), 21.

25 See Panofsky, *Hercules am Scheidewege*, pp. 76f.

26 Leopold Damrosch, Jr., *Symbol and Truth in Blake's Myth* (Princeton: Princeton Univ. Press, 1980), pp. 19f, 280f.

27 Wittreich, *Angel of Apocalypse*, pp. 75f.

28 See Gilchrist, p. 302. For a discussion of Ghiberti's *Porta del Paradiso*, see Gombrich, *Norm and Form: Studies in the Art of the Renaissance* (London: Phaidon, 1966), pp. 1–10.

29 See Charles Seymour, Jr., *Michelangelo: The Sistine Chapel Ceiling* (New York: Norton, 1972), pl. 14.

30 See Roland M. Frye, *Milton's Imagery and the Visual Arts* (Princeton: Princeton Univ. Press, 1978), pp. 259–61 and pls. 163, 182, 214.

31 Frye, pp. 286–91 and pls. 152 et seq.

32 J. B. Trapp, "The Iconography of the Fall of Man" in C. A. Patrides, ed., *Approaches to Paradise Lost* (Toronto: Univ. of Toronto Press, 1968), pp. 251–52 and pls. 16–17.

33 See B. F. Cook, *The Townley Marbles* (London: British Museum, 1985), pl. 18; and James Hall, *Dictionary of Subjects and Symbols in Art* (London: John Murray, 1974), p. 200.

34 See Carlo Castellaneta, *L' Opera Completa del Perugino* (Milan: Rizzoli, 1969), p. 815 and pl. lvii; John Pope-Hennessy, *Raphael* (London: Phaidon, 1970), pp. 85–86 and Figs. 73–74; Roger Jones and Nicholas Penny, *Raphael* (New Haven: Yale Univ. Press, 1983), pp. 13–20 and pl. 24; and Panofsky, *The Life and Art of Albrecht Dürer* (1943; Princeton: Princeton Univ. Press, 1955), p. 103 and pl. 143.

35 See W. Hayley, *The Life of Milton*, ed. Wittreich (Gainesville: Scholars' Facsimiles, 1970), pp. 91–92.

36 In a paper delivered at the 1982 *Australian Universities' Language and Literature Association* Convention.

37 See Schiller, II.112–13 and Figs. 347 et seq.

38 Chayes, "Fallen Earth and Man in Nature: William Blake in Iconographic Tradition," *Studies in Iconography*, 10 (1984–86), 186f.

Apollo's "Naked Human Form Divine":
The *Nativity Ode* Designs

The ode *On the Morning of Christ's Nativity* is considered Milton's first major tribute to his Saviour in his new-found vocation as poet-prophet of Albion, a lyric prelude to *Paradise Lost* and *Paradise Regained*. And it has long been admired for what Blake would have regarded as its visionary qualities—its swift, expansive movement from the Nativity scene itself dwelt on by Catholic poets to the effects of the Incarnation: the descent of Peace, light, and celestial harmony, the redemption of Nature, the demise of the pagan oracles, and the binding of the "old Dragon" (168)—in a vision which both embraces and transcends the whole of human history from Creation to Apocalypse. Blake's two sets each of six illustrations to Milton's hymn, the larger (approx. 25 x 19 cm.) in the Whitworth Art Gallery, the other (approx. 16 x 12 cm.) in the Huntington Library, are the shortest and superficially least prepossessing of his watercolor sequences illuminating Milton's major poems. But there has been a growing recognition that his answering vision in another medium and a new philosophical key more than match the imaginative range and sophistication of his prophetic precursor's achievement.

Here again, however, determining the precise extent to which it is a dissenting vision, and the celebrative impulse behind the illustrations qualified by criticism, is not a straightforward matter. Behrendt has argued that in this series too Blake's principal concern is to illuminate the Christocentric nature of Milton's vision, to celebrate his rejection of classical culture, and to "liberate the poem from . . . misguided criticism."[1] And neither Leslie Tannenbaum's discussion of Blake's Christocentric typology, which clarifies how Blake could deny that art is progressive yet find fault with his precursors, nor Morton D. Paley's explorations of Blake's evolving attitude to the classics have diminished the plausibility of this point of view.[2] Nevertheless, the celebrative hypothesis does tend to assume that what is radical in one revolutionary era is necessarily so in the next, and it underestimates the extent to which Blake was intellectual heir to the Enlightenment. It is true that by 1809, the date of the Whitworth *Nativity Ode* designs, Christ had assumed a crucial role in Blake's thought. But it is hazardous to assume that the mere fact of his presence at the center of the *Nativity Ode* would have been enough to secure Blake's unqualified approval, for as is also apparent in the *Paradise Lost* designs, Christ is not a static symbol in Blake, a "Ratio" (*MHH* 5, E 35), as he felt he tended to be in Milton. And though related, his various manifestations as "secret child" (*Eur* 3.2, E 61), as rebellious prophet, as the seventh "Eye of God" (*Mil* 13.17, E 107) or historical advance in man's conception of the divine, as the forgiver of sins, and as the imagination, must be kept distinct since they function differently in different contexts. In *Europe*, which as Tolley has demonstrated is richly counterpointed against Milton's hymn, Blake presented the rebirth of energy at the Nativity as merely a prelude to Apocalypse, followed not as in Milton by a catalogue of its miraculous effects, but by a nightmare vision of "Urizen unloos'd from chains" (*Eur* 3.11, E 61), the "night of Nature" and the "Eighteen hundred years" (*Eur* 9.3–5, E 63) of Enitharmon's sleep which preceded the American and French Revolutions.[3] In this context, it may be significant that Moloch worship seems to be in full swing in the design traditionally titled "The Flight of Moloch" (Figs. 51–52). And though the way the series closes by returning to the opening scene with the stable in the foreground (Figs. 43–44, 53–54) does indeed suggest that "the 'time' elapsed is visionary," as Behrendt (p. 68) astutely observes, it could also signal an abortive Apocalypse, a return to the *status quo* in a perennial round of revolt and repression.

1809 was also the year in which Blake, roused perhaps by the beginning of the Peninsular War, wrote some of his most scathing attacks on the classics. Since he felt that "Shakspeare & Milton were both curbd by . . . the silly Greek & Latin slaves of the Sword" (*Mil* 1, E 95), he is likely to have been aware of the conventional nature of the youthful Milton's dismissal of the pagan gods. And he was probably also conscious that even in *Paradise Regained* Milton's reasons for rejecting classical wisdom were essentially theological, and thus closer to Dante's than to his own. But it nonetheless seems likely that he would have wished to illuminate the importance of so central a truth, however conventionally perceived. Another disconcerting particular in the series, however, suggests that he chose not to do so in any obvious way. In the Huntington version of "The Overthrow of Apollo and the Pagan Gods" (Fig. 50), the pedestaled statue of Apollo with its serpent-entwined stele is shown, in Hagstrum's words, "amid the ultimate apocalyptic destruction . . .

dumb, frozen, and helpless," his departing spirit plunging to the waves below.[4] In the Whitworth version by contrast (Fig. 49), Apollo though still on a pedestal has no supporting stele and looks very much alive; indeed, he is presented in the act of vanquishing a quite formidable-looking Python. How is this to be understood in relation to his departing spirit, which still suggests the notion of his overthrow? Such apparent incongruities seem to hint that here too Blake's pictorial commentary may be more dramatically counterpointed against Milton's hymn than has been recognized.

A preliminary word, though, is necessary about the order of composition of the two sets and the arrangement of the individual designs within each set. The Whitworth designs, done in pen and brown wash for Thomas in 1809, are as large as the Huntington set of *Paradise Lost* designs that Blake had painted for him two years earlier. And partly because they are more articulate iconographically—in the context of Blake's vituperations against chiaroscuro in his *Descriptive Catalogue* (E 547) the same year, they seem defiantly linear—they have usually been assumed to be the later set. But Butlin has proposed that the smaller, undated Huntington set painted originally for Butts, which is highly finished in pale, misty, luminous tones, should on stylistic grounds be grouped with the *L'Allegro and Il Penseroso* and *Paradise Regained* designs, both watermarked 1816, which are on the same intimate scale. He contends that "the strongest argument for placing the Butts series first is that the first design, 'The Descent of Peace,' follows the more imaginative idea of the tempera *Nativity* of c.1799–1800 (B 502)," which shows Christ miraculously suspended in mid-air. But "Blake could equally well have reverted to the earlier composition after showing the Nativity in a more conventional way in the Thomas version of 1809."[5] Blake does mention the *Nativity Ode* in a letter to Butts dated July 6, 1803 (E 729–30), in connection with the prospect of illustrating Cowper's Milton, but only the *Latin and Italian Poems* was to eventuate and the letter may indicate no more than that Blake contemplated such a series at the time. Butlin's hypothesis, moreover, helps explain why iconographically both sequences seem equally felicitous but in quite different ways and, unlike the two completed sets to *Paradise Lost* done within a year of each other, do not obviously suggest a process of revision and refinement in one direction or another. If the Huntington set was indeed executed around 1815–16, several years after the Whitworth set, then the sometimes radical differences between them could simply reflect two closely related but quite independent responses to the *Nativity*

Ode at different times. The survival of preliminary sketches for individual designs in both sequences (B 728, 730–31) is consistent with this notion and may indicate that Blake did not have access to Thomas's set when he came to do the second set for Butts. Some though never all the particulars in four of the six designs are reversed in the two versions. In the opening design (Figs. 43–44) Peace descends and Nature lies pillowed to the left of the stable in the Whitworth series but in the Huntington to the right; in the second (Figs. 45–46) the central shepherds are shown in the same attitude but they gaze heavenward in opposite directions; in the third (Figs. 47–48) the starry extension of the Dragon's tail has likewise been reversed; while in "The Flight of Moloch" (Figs. 51–52) only the presiding specter's position remains unchanged. These variants, for some of which possible explanations will be proposed, are quite compatible with the notion that Blake worked the second set up from memory, but they do not illuminate which came first. This discussion will not resolve the problem—though, despite what seems to be the greater iconographic daring of the Whitworth series, Butlin's hypothesis is certainly persuasive—but it may help us gauge the probabilities with more confidence.

If, as the recurrent image of the stable implies, the designs are to be read serially, their internal ordering is obviously important. Of the various proposed arrangements Behrendt's is undoubtedly the most purposeful.[6] Influenced by Arthur E. Barker's account of the tripartite structure of the hymn, Behrendt (pp. 67–69) argues that if "The Old Dragon" (Figs. 47–48) is placed in fifth instead of third position, the stable recedes and reappears by regular stages, revealing more clearly the "intellectual and artistic symmetry" (p. 68) of Blake's visual commentary.[7] And this arrangement has the further advantage of locating the binding of the Dragon in the same approximate position as in Revelation (20.2). But against this we must consider that the *L'Allegro and Il Penseroso* and *Paradise Regained* designs numbered by Blake follow the order of events in the poems.[8] This is also the case, as we have seen, with the unnumbered but trimmed *Paradise Lost* series, which, broadly speaking, have one design for each of the poem's twelve books, and with the *Comus* illustrations, although there Blake is especially apt to conflate more than one image or episode within a single design. Blake probably developed this methodical habit when illustrating Young's *Night Thoughts* and Gray's poems in the 1790s, where he was obliged to follow the order of the text by its presence offset within his exuberant designs. It is true that he experimented with the arrangement of the *Songs* and the full-plate illustrations to the *Book of Urizen* in various copies, but there his own text provided adequate internal control over the meaning of the work. In the absence of unequivocal evidence to the contrary, therefore, it seems prudent to assume that the *Nativity Ode* designs also follow the order dictated by the text.

Blake's strategy in the opening design, "The Descent of Peace" (Figs. 43–44), is characteristic of his method in the sequence generally. He focuses on the first three verses of Milton's hymn and draws in images from other points in the poem, while also discreetly introducing his own iconographic controls. No direct allusion to Milton's proem is made, but some of its functions are taken over by Blake's personification of Peace, a figure resembling his later heavenly messenger, the ascending Lark in *L'Allegro and Il Penseroso* 2 (Fig. 56). As Christ's "ready Harbinger" (49) she descends through the three concentric circles of the "turning sphere" (48), which forms a magnificent vortex like that expanding behind Milton as he descends from Eternity in Blake's epic (*Mil* 15.21 et seq., E 109). Her splayed palm and encompassing gesture—which Behrendt (p. 86) sees as a redemptive version of Urizen's dividers on the *Europe* frontispiece (Fig. 82)—indicate that like Milton in the proem she is introducing, indeed revealing, the Divine Vision opened to the spectator and to nature beneath her. The visual continuity established by her vortex with the "Globe of circular light" (110) in the next design (Figs. 45–46) implies that like the angel of the Lord in Luke 2.9–14, she also acts as herald to the angelic choir. Her function as spiritual nuncio is emphasized in the Whitworth version by the resemblance of her wand to the caduceus of Hermes.

The Nativity itself takes place within a stylized gothic stable oddly reminiscent of the tombs in Westminster Abbey that Blake sketched for Gough's *Sepulchral Monuments* (see B 4, 9, 18, 23, 26), and not unlike the winged ark with its little window on *Jerusalem* 44 (Fig. 111) and the Ark of the Covenant in his engraving of Raphael's *Joshua Passing Over Jordan*.[9] Prompted perhaps by Milton's description of Peace's "Turtle wing" (50) and olive crown (47), and his later allusion to the rainbow (143) and Osiris's "worship Ark" (220), Blake has recalled the stable's function in the Gospel story as a refuge from tyranny, by presenting it as a Beulaic ark in which the Divine Vision is kept afloat in time of trouble.[10] Hence perhaps the two oxen in lieu of the traditional ox and ass in both versions, and the addition of a window in the Huntington design. The Nativity scene in the Whitworth version is more conspicuously Beulaic, in that Joseph and Mary are shown tending a passive Christ-child, "meanly wrapt" (31) in swaddling clothes, his head surrounded by a modest aureole—an inauspicious figure altogether reminiscent of the "secret child" in *Europe*. Commenting on the opening plates of that poem, Tolley writes that "the birth of Christ represented the crucial challenge to Urizen's compasses; by circling Him tight round with swaddling bands, by the very milk of His mother's breast, Urizen and Enitharmon, forces of mortality, attempted to control the Infinite" (p. 119). In this context the Whitworth design seems less than jubilant, as though in 1809 Blake was convinced of the symbolic importance of Christ's birth, yet reluctant to endorse Milton's view of it as an event of unique historical and eschatological significance, and more than ever aware that in the ensuing 1800 years, Jesus had become Jehovah (cf. *MHH* 5, E 35).

The Huntington version, by contrast, with its naked, energetic Christ-child radiating light as he leaps from the swooning Mary's lap, seems redolent with hope. The image is apparently unprecedented in the iconography of the Nativity, though a source has been proposed in a Roman bas-relief of the *Birth of Dionysus*, and within Blake's canon such exuberant modulations of *Glad Day* (B 331–32) recur repeatedly.[11] But since Blake follows his tempera *Nativity* (B 502) in including Zacharias, Elizabeth, and the young John the Baptist opposite Joseph and Mary (though in reverse), his portrayal may also have been inspired by Elizabeth's vivid account in Luke 1.44 of how "the babe leaped in my womb for joy" at Mary's news that she was with child by the Holy Ghost. Evidently Blake wished to illuminate the spiritual rather than the historical significance of Christ's advent here, and he has emphasized this by presenting it as an epiphany, a Divine Vision the spectator is invited to share with the subordinate figures. Christ's cruciform gesture also establishes a much firmer line of continuity with the Cherubim raising their arms exultantly in the next design (Fig. 46), and with the sacrificial child in "The Flight of Moloch" (Fig. 52).

In both versions Blake also seems more optimistic about the pending redemption of Nature than Milton, who leaves her ultimate fate at the Last Judgment an open question, and whose emphasis on her "foul deformities" (44) would have given Blake little cause to revise his view that Milton never entirely freed himself from nature goddess Enitharmon's doctrine that "Womans love is Sin!" (*Eur* 5.5, E 62). And in both versions an intimate relationship is suggested pictorially between her and Peace. She lies in the lower foreground pillowed against a stone, her hair divided about it in token perhaps of her original fall into division, and she "hid[es] her guilty front with innocent Snow" (39). And as Chayes observes, Blake also seems to have associated her with Eve, placing her appropriately in subordinate position beneath Mary as the Second Eve, since her recumbent position resembles that of Eve in the eleventh *Paradise Lost* illustration (Figs. 39–40), and her snowy covering recalls Eve's fleecy garment in *The Angel of the Divine Presence Clothing Adam and Eve with Coats of Skins* (B 513).[12] In the Whitworth version she even crosses her legs in a gesture Blake consistently modulated to express repressed desire, as we have seen. But other signs are more auspicious, for unlike Eve she is awake and looks up responsive to the Divine Vision, listening even perhaps to the first strains of the angelic choir, and against the surrounding blizzard is evidently humanizing. In the context of the embracing figures in the recently completed series of *Last Judgment* paintings (Fig. 89; B 868, 870–74), she seems in the Whitworth version to be about to ascend and join with Peace on the side of the redeemed. Their position is reversed in the Huntington version, where Nature's legs are no longer crossed and her snowy covering is less pronounced, possibly to suggest that, unlike Eve and Milton's Nature, she is innocently unconcerned about her "naked shame" (40). But there, too, the pictorial relationship between them implies that Peace will descend to Nature, Nature be restored to Peace, that a "happier union" between "Heav'n and Earth" (108) is imminent.

In "The Annunciation to the Shepherds" (Figs. 45–46), Blake again responds creatively to several images in the central verses of the *Nativity Ode* (vii–xv), while concentrating appropriately on the climactic moment of the epiphany to the shepherds:

> At last surrounds their sight
> A Globe of circular light,
>> That with long beams the shame-fac't night array'd,
> The helmed Cherubim
> And sworded Seraphim
>> Are seen in glittering ranks with wings display'd,
> Harping in loud and solemn choir,
> With unexpressive notes to Heav'n's new-born Heir.
>
> (109–16)

Reverting to a motif he had originally adapted from Bryant in the *Night Thoughts* series, Blake depicts the Cherubim advancing above the distant stable, which has been extended laterally, their interlocking arms upraised in a gesture perfectly expressive of harmonious jubilation.[13] Within their globe of light they recall the passage in *A Vision of the Last Judgment*, where Blake distinguishes between the natural and visionary suns: "What it will be Questiond When the Sun rises do you not see a round Disk of fire somewhat like a Guinea O no no I see an Innumerable company of the Heavenly host crying Holy Holy Holy is the Lord God Almighty" (E 565–66). And in relation to the borders of the designs, the angelic choir forms a squared circle, a motif which in *Milton* 47 (IB 263), *Ezekiel's Wheels* (B 542), "The Rout of the Rebel Angels" (Figs. 31–32) in the *Paradise Lost* series, and elsewhere Blake associated with fourfold vision, as Edward J. Rose has shown.[14] Very similar figures appear again in a fourfold context in *Job* 14 (Fig. 112), where if we follow S. Foster Damon the "morning stars" are used to symbolize the imaginative realm.[15]

What this seems to imply is that Blake has effected a bold reversal of Milton's priorities in the first two designs. Whether or not Milton intended the angelic choir as the aesthetic center of his poem, there can be no question that doctrinally its importance is hierarchically subordinate to that of the infant Christ whose praises it sings. But in Blake we appear to move from a Beulaic vision in which Christ as the spirit of truth and love is born and cherished in the stable, to a fourfold Edenic vision of the choir as an emblem of harmony among men who in the aggregate form the Divine Body of Jesus. The effect is of an expanding "Vision of Light," analogous to that Blake described in a poem to Butts (E 712–13), which was to form the nucleus for the extended moment of *Milton* and to reappear greatly condensed in plate 34 of *Jerusalem* (E 180). In the Whitworth series, the notion that this heavenly light, which now illuminates the shepherds and floods out into the world, originated in the stable is suggested by the fact that Mary and Joseph are now alone. The way the Cherubim in the Huntington set echo Christ's cruciform gesture implies, less cryptically, that the Divine Body itself has as it were increased and multiplied. In the context of *Europe* this "humanized sphere," as Dunbar rightly calls it, supersedes the stellar globe of "Newtons Pantocrator" (*Mil* 4.11, E 98), and represents a millennial state in which the redemption of Nature begun in the previous design has been fulfilled.[16] Milton's "helmed Cherubim / And sworded Seraphim" also provided convenient emblems of the vigorous imaginative intellectual activity in the pursuit of truth and the rejection of error that Blake termed "Mental Fight" (*Mil* 1.13, E 95). In the flatter Whitworth globe, the rather regimented leading angels are more effectively delineated in that their upraised arms do not obscure their neighbors' faces. And the circumambient figures equipped with lute and harps to make their "stringed noise" (97) number a round apocalyptic eight. In the Huntington version Blake may have wanted to inhibit any confusion of these mental warriors with the avenging angels of Milton's "dreadful Judge" (164), for there the leading angels are all youthful, naked, and (save their helmets) unarmed, and advance with a lither, less military step, and the central figure in cruciform position stands out more prominently against the receding ranks, giving the globe a more three-dimensional appearance.

The humble recipients of this sudden revelation of man's and nature's potential are the shepherds. In both versions (though in reverse) the central figure is shown in a less dramatic modulation of the position adopted by other inspired figures in Blake's canon, such as William and Robert in *Milton* (IB 248, 253) or Job in *Job Confessing His Presumption to God Who Answers from the Whirlwind* (B 538). Surrounded by their watchdogs and sleeping flocks, his companions all either participate in or are awakening to the Divine Vision. In the Whitworth version all the shepherds appear to be male, but in the Huntington design Blake has made them more explicitly representative of the family of man. He has also increased their number from six to eight, a hint perhaps that they represent the millennial state in which Moses' prayer cited in the Preface to *Milton*, "would to God that all the Lords People were Prophets" (E 95), will be fulfilled for all mankind, rather than merely for the elect that Milton had in mind when he quoted it in *Areopagitica*.[17] In the Huntington version pyramid-like tents have been included, emblems perhaps of the state of bondage from which the shepherds have been delivered.

In the demonic sequel to this Divine Vision in the next two designs, "The Old Dragon" (Figs. 47–48) and "The Overthrow of Apollo and the Pagan Gods" (Figs. 49–50), both Blake's appreciation of the apocalyptic dimension to the *Nativity Ode* and his determination to illuminate it on his own terms emerge more clearly. The immediate subject of the first of these is Milton's account of how with the advent of Christ

> Th'old Dragon under ground,
> In straiter limits bound,
>> Not half so far casts his usurped sway,
> And wroth to see his Kingdom fail,
> Swinges the scaly Horror of his folded tail.
>
> (168–72)

And Dunbar (p. 100) suggests a further identification of Blake's terrifying beast with "Typhon huge ending in snaky twine" (226). Several particulars indicate that this design bears an intimate relationship both visually and thematically to "The Annunciation to the Shepherds." The most immediately apparent link is, of course, the stable, which again appears with lateral transepts, but surrounded now by slumbering flocks. The entrance is guarded by two Cherubim, the two perhaps from the Ark of the Covenant, who, Blake tells us in *A Vision of the Last Judgment* (E 562), appear above Christ as reminders that he has opened the temple and rent the veil, here standing aside to reveal the infant Christ. Further, by placing the stable above the Dragon, in the position of the Throne of God in his *Last Judgment* paintings, Blake endorses the significance of the Nativity at least insofar as it was regarded by Milton and Christian tradition as a symbolic victory of peace over war, truth over error, and, especially in the Huntington version where the three kings kneel before the entrance, spiritual over temporal dominion.

But continuity is also established by the starry extension of the Dragon's tail above the stable. This is an obvious allusion to Revelation 12.4, where the Dragon's "tail drew a third part of the stars of heaven" down, immediately before the War in Heaven, but in the context it also serves a very precise iconographic function: the line of descent it indicates, considered in conjunction with the way the Dragon and his crew gaze generally heavenward and not just at the stable, seems to imply that they have been routed in an encounter with the Cherubim in the previous design. Indeed, this dark Ulro world of discord is a demonic parody of the Edenic harmony within the globe of light—a contrast which is reinforced visually by the way both scenes are foregrounded, but in opposite segments of the two designs. In the Whitworth version the Dragon's vigorously "swingeing" tail shows that they have plummeted on the side of the damned in Blake's *Last Judgment* paintings (Fig. 89). This endorses the earlier suggestion that Nature is preparing to rise on the side of the redeemed in the opening design. The line of their descent has been reversed in the Huntington version, and their underworld is less like the Dragon's cave in the *Last Judgment* pictures. But Blake has intimated that they are victims of a mental war in Heaven with the Cherubim by making the figure pointing directly upward on the right do so with both hands, and by placing the stable much farther back.

Here too, then, Blake's emphases are subtly different from Milton's, and may be accounted for in terms of his post-Enlightenment attitude to the events in Milton's ode. Though Blake also went through a period of optimism about the prospect of an imminent millennium, unlike Cromwell's Latin Secretary and many of his contemporaries 150 years earlier, he never believed it would come about through a miracle of divine intervention of the kind envisaged in the hymn. And by alluding again to the War in Heaven in this design he seems to be insisting that if "God becomes as we are, that we may be as he is" (*NNR*, E 3), it is through emulation of Christ as mental warrior and "bright Preacher of Life" (*J* 77.21, E 232) that mankind will be redeemed, rather than through worship at the shrine of the Nativity. The Dragon's six heads in the Whitworth version indicate that Blake was specifically thinking here of Jesus as the seventh "Eye of God," further evidence of the close relationship between this set and *Europe* with its explicit historical time-scheme. And the way he is bound by his own tail suggests that these manacles are "mind-forg'd" (E 27), self-imposed. In the Huntington design the Dragon has his traditional seven heads, implying that the millennium is at hand, and Blake has sharpened the contrast with the unarmed Cherubim by giving him both sword and scepter. The looseness of the greenish tethers round his ankles is perhaps a sobering reminder that the banishment of corporeal war can be achieved only by ceaseless imaginative effort. The reversals here and in the opening design do, however, make the connection with Blake's *Last Judgment* pictures rather less intimate than in the Whitworth series.

The subordinate devils in the two designs are sufficiently different to support the hypothesis that the Huntington set was done without access to the Whitworth, but in both cases individual figures are hard to identify with confidence. Seated appropriately at the Dragon's right hand in the Whitworth version is the Great Whore, a voluptuous figure in several of Blake's other paintings and illustrations (B 541, 584, 868; *Night Thoughts* 345), but here shown "desolate and naked" as in Revelation 17.16, exposed, like Spenser's Duessa, as the hag she really is. The fiend diagonally opposite her could be Satan bidding them "Awake, arise, or be for ever fallen" (*Paradise Lost* I.331), since he somewhat resembles Blake's portrayals of him in the *Paradise Lost* series, and in *A Vision of the Last Judgment* (E 556–58) he and the Dragon are kept distinct. If the Cherubim in their globe of light represent fourfold man, the four principal male devils could be the four fallen Zoas or Elements, and the subordinate figures, with the Whore as Vanity, the "Seven deadly Sins of the soul" (*Ur* 4.30, E 72). In the Huntington version the flames are localized around Satan, there is a scaly amphibious creature in the lower foreground, and an earthbound female like the worm-encircled mother beyond Death's Door in *The Gates of Paradise* (E 267) has replaced the Whore, but one would expect all the Elements to be male as in the sixty-ninth Dante illustration.[18]

In "The Overthrow of Apollo and the Pagan Gods" (Figs. 49– 50), the differences between the two versions appear to be more fundamental than at any other point in the series. In both sets Blake has incorporated several particulars from Milton's account of the flight of the pagan deities, while focusing on stanza nineteen of the ode:

> The Oracles are dumb,
> No voice or hideous hum
>   Runs through the arched roof in words deceiving.
> Apollo from his shrine
> Can no more divine,
>   With hollow shriek the steep of Delphos leaving.
> No nightly trance, or breathed spell,
> Inspires the pale-ey'd Priest from the prophetic cell.
>
>   (173–80)

The central figure, as has often been remarked, is based on that neoclassical touchstone of sublimity and grace, the *Apollo Belvedere* (Fig. 113), and Blake may well have been familiar with the tradition which "held that Augustus had had it taken from the site of Apollo's oracle at Delphi."[19] The Whitworth Apollo, however, is essentially a free, imaginative modulation of the classical prototype, quite different from the statue in the Huntington design, where Blake adheres to the prototype more closely. By adding masculine strength to the slightly feminine grace of the original, and showing Apollo strangling an obviously puissant Python rather than shooting one present only emblematically, he has also created an altogether more dynamic deity, with attributes that recall not only Apollo but also Hercules and Christ, as Behrendt too (p. 85) has registered.

If this design is simply a celebrative tribute to Milton's vision of paganism eclipsed by Christianity represented by the Star of Bethlehem, why did Blake present an Apollo not only majestic but triumphant? The obvious explanation—that he wished to show Apollo forsaken by his indwelling spirit at the very height of his powers—seems at first attractive. And the hypothesis could be supported by analogy with the "Death of the Strong Wicked Man," the fourth illustration in his series to Blair's *Grave*, published the previous year. But this would not resolve why Blake, who had depicted the strong wicked man *in rigor mortis* so expressively, and was to present Apollo as a very convincing statue in the Huntington design, should have chosen not to do so here. Indeed, Blake seems to have deliberately enhanced the sense of Apollo's vitality and vigor by counterpointing him against the rigid idol petrifying on the hill behind him. Furthermore, Blake can scarcely have been unconscious of the parallel with Hercules that his portrayal would suggest, as a surviving pencil sketch in which he depicts "The Infant Hercules Throttling the Serpents" (B 304) tends to confirm. If so, he must also have been aware that, as Hercules was a traditional type of Christ, the parallel in the context of Apollo's demise would be ambiguous. Werner's proposal that he may have thought of both deities as types of Christ now superseded by his advent fits intellectually, but does not resolve the visual ambivalence of the Whitworth rendering.[20]

One must therefore consider the more problematic hypothesis that, with the same imaginative daring as he was to display when illustrating *L'Allegro and Il Penseroso* and *Paradise Regained*, Blake has exploited these parallels to distinguish his own vision of man's redemption from Milton's by transforming Apollo into a redeemer. When this design is contemplated in relation to the iconographic continuities already established, it becomes possible to see it as the appropriately placed climax to a visionary progression again analogous to that in Blake's ecstatic poem to Butts, where he describes how

> My Eyes more & more
> Like a Sea without shore
> Continued Expanding
> The Heavens commanding,
> Till the Jewels of Light
> Heavenly Men beaming bright
> Appeared as One Man.
>
> (E 683)

We have moved, it would appear, from the birth of Christ in the first design to a vision of the Divine Body as a "Multitude of Nations" (*VLJ* 76, E 557) in the globe of light, and now, as if stepping back to view the general contours of Blake's lost *Last Judgment* painting, we perceive Apollo as a macrocosmic image of renovated fourfold Man.[21] Inspired perhaps by Milton's own allusion to Christ as "mighty Pan" (89) or to how "the chill Marble seems to sweat" (195), Blake has shown Apollo come dramatically to life, a symbolic event comparable to Albion's awakening and "Resurrection to Unity" (*FZ* 4.4, E 301) in the prophecies. Like the redeemed Milton at the close of Blake's brief epic, and like Christ on the pinnacle in "The Third Temptation" (Fig. 76) from the *Paradise Regained* series, this Herculean Apollo has "cast his Spectre into the Lake" (*J* 37, E 184; cf. *Mil* 39.10–11, E 140). He has achieved a decisive victory over Python, a classical counterpart of "that old serpent, which is the Devil, and Satan" who in the previous design lay bound, but only for "a thousand years" (Revelation 20.2). The crucial difference between this Last Judgment and those envisioned by Dürer or Michelangelo or Milton, however, is that Apollo's is an act of self-purgation. This accomplished, Apollo stands like the risen Albion in *Glad Day* (B 331), another fourfold vision based on classical statuary, unself-consciously displaying his "Naked Human form divine" (*EG* 66, E 522), as earlier Nature had begun to do.[22] The serpent's victory over Adam and Eve, who had sought to hide their naked shame, is thus reversed.

The priests as "Guardian[s] of the secret codes" (*Eur* 12.15, E 64) are none too pleased, but the vestals are learning their "own humanity . . . to adore" (*EG* 72, E 520). A distracted Pythia is seen behind them, her hair on end like Pride's in *Night Thoughts* 302, in straiter limits bound within her cavern. Blake would probably have recognized this deliverer of notoriously ambiguous oracles as a pagan counterpart to "Mystery Babylon the Great" (Revelation 17.5) in the previous design, and as the appropriate consort for Python that her name implies. Above a classical colonnade ominously like the trilithons in Stukeley's reconstructions of Abury and Stonehenge, other pagan deities representing all the superstitions that have enslaved mankind are seen departing.[23] A horned "Isis . . . and the Dog Anubis" (212) and a winged solar disk with double-headed serpent adapted from Bryant can be specifically discerned above the bolts of lightning.[24] The shipwreck, like that in Dürer's woodcut illustrating the opening of the Seventh Seal (Revelation 8.9), and the tiny figure retreating before the rising tide, seem to imply that the old order is on the point of being cleansed by flood, as in "The Old Dragon" it was purged by fire.[25] The Star of Bethlehem, which significantly did not appear above the stable earlier and is omitted from the Huntington version of this scene, may thus signal that it is with Apollo's exemplary triumph that man's salvation lies, rather than with the birth of the secret child, as Milton and his age believed. Its function in the last design (Fig. 53), where it appears as the flickering "Handmaid Lamp" (242) of "Heav'n's youngest-teemed Star" (244), is to lighten our way during the intervals when the Divine Vision is asleep.

This reading of the Whitworth version has in the interests of clarity been presented without pausing to consider objections, and to show that a redemptive interpretation of Apollo does seem to fit organically into the internal iconographic structure of the sequence. What makes it problematic, of course, is that the series was executed during precisely the period when Blake was perfecting epic poems which rejected classical models for "the Sublime of the Bible" (*Mil* 1, E 95), and working toward the philosophical conclusion that "The Classics, it is the Classics! & not Goths nor Monks, that Desolate Europe with Wars" (E 270). On the subject of classical sculpture specifically, he wrote in the *Descriptive Catalogue* to his abortive one-man exhibition of 1809 that of "the Greek statues . . . perhaps the Torso is the only original work remaining; all the rest are evidently copies, though fine ones, from greater works of the Asiatic Patriarchs . . . Those wonderful originals seen in my visions . . ." (E 531). But Blake's attitude to classical philosophy and art was a complex one, as all investigations have concluded. Peter F. Fisher pointed out that "the positive influence of the classical tradition was assimilated without comment, and Blake obviously agreed with the Platonic theory of ideas which were essentially his own imaginative 'Forms'—the 'Existent Images' of eternity."[26] Moreover, his assimilation of the great works of classical sculpture from casts in Pars's drawing school, engravings, and neoclassical imitations was so complete that as Joseph Burke has observed, "an eidetic image . . . appeared to Blake, not merely as a kind of living sculpture, but in a shape suggested by antiquity."[27] And the many instances of indebtedness to classical models which Paley (pp. 171f.) has been able to trace in Blake's later works indicate that his reservations about the rationalist abstractions of classical philosophy and the warrior code that "Turnd Love into a Boy" (E 479) did not lead him to abandon the habits of a lifetime.

The specific objection that as a solar deity and symbol of reason Apollo is unlikely to have appealed to Blake as a redeemer is a real one, despite Milton's allusion to Christ as a "greater Sun" (83). And later he was to present Apollo *in malo* in *L'Allegro and Il Penseroso* 3 (Fig. 57), naked but sceptered and wearing a spiked crown within his solar orb, and dominating a diminutive Milton's vision in the background. Virgil's fourth Messianic *Eclogue*, in which the return of the golden age is associated with a renewal of Apollo's reign, provided an important precedent, but one Blake could well have reacted to negatively.[28] As an illustrator, however, Blake was always a great opportunist, and within the constraints of literal fidelity to Milton he had to improvise with what he encountered in the hymn. Moreover, the difficulty begins to recede when one recalls Apollo's humanist credentials as physician, lyrist, Python-slayer, and leader of the Muses, albeit the "Daughters of Memory" (*Mil* 1, E 95). Blake also alludes to him positively in his note to the now lost painting of those "naked civilized men," *The Ancient Britons*:

> It has been said to the Artist, take the Apollo for the model of your beautiful Man and the Hercules for your strong Man, and the Dancing Fawn for your Ugly Man. Now he comes to his trial. He knows that what he does is not inferior to the grandest Antiques. Superior they cannot be, for human power cannot go beyond either what he does, or what they have done, it is the gift of God, it is inspiration and vision.   (E 544)

> The Strong man represents the human sublime. The Beautiful man represents the human pathetic, which was in the wars of Eden divided into male and female. The Ugly man represents the human reason. They were originally one man, who was fourfold; he was self-divided, and his real humanity slain on the stems of generation, and the form of the fourth was like the Son of God.
> (E 543)

This is by no means the only occasion in the *Descriptive Catalogue* on which Blake reveals that he shared the general enthusiasm for classical art that events such as the arrival of the Elgin marbles and the opening of the Townley galleries were currently generating.[29] But Blake's explanation of his painting is of special relevance to the Whitworth design in that it presents Apollo and Hercules in close association as two facets of fallen man. It is only a step imaginatively to reverse this symbolism and present a Herculean Apollo as a fourfold image of the eternally "Divine-Humanity" (*J* 38.19–20, E 185). Blake's association of these famous statues with his own archetypes also illuminates why in the redemptive last plate of *Jerusalem* (IB 379) he should have modelled the central figure on the *Farnese Hercules* (H & P 118), but endowed him with something of the Belvedere's grace. How Blake could use both models in redemptive contexts and yet fulminate against the classics without inconsistency is best understood, however, by thinking of them not as Apollo and Hercules but as representing those "wonderful originals" seen in his visions. Moreover, the Greek and Roman delight in the human body, which Winckelmann too was aware Christianity had neglected, is clearly another facet of classical culture which Blake silently assimilated.[30] From this point of view, what more appropriate corrective to the transcendental dualism of Milton's religion could there be than to place Apollo's Naked Human Form Divine at the visionary climax of the sequence?

The Huntington Apollo resembles the Belvedere statue much more closely, and this may well be a consequence of Blake's having studied it afresh in 1815 or 1816 when he was making sketches from casts in the Royal Academy for illustrations to Flaxman's essay on sculpture in Rees's *Cyclopaedia*.[31] If so, this would corroborate Butlin's dating. Paley (p. 172) is surely right to interpret Apollo here as a negative emblem more in line with Milton's hymn. His vacant eye and statuesque appearance leave little doubt that this is Apollo turned to stone, and that as with the strong wicked man his specter swooping up out of him and startling the tiny figure above the water signals his demise. One may assume that here he is specifically Apollo as rationalist sun-god, a fallen version of the triumphant figure in *L'Allegro and Il Penseroso* 3, his locks bound up, his arrow spent, his dwindling fires consuming the last remnant of a sacrificial ox, his vestals cowering in terror.[32] He has been eclipsed by the "more bright Sun of Imagination" (E 655) represented by the angelic choir, as pagan wisdom and pagan oracles were superseded not by the Nativity but by the voice of inspiration in the Gospels. For "What Jesus came to Remove was the Heathen or Platonic Philosophy which blinds the eye of Imagination The Real Man" (E 654).

Since this conception seems less inspired iconographically and makes for less of a crescendo, if Apollo is indeed a redemptive figure in the Whitworth series, why did Blake abandon his original idea? For one thing, the Huntington solution is in some respects intrinsically more satisfactory. It gives greater emphasis to the importance of rejecting pagan error, for instance, and creates a nicely balanced contrast between this design and "The Old Dragon," where the errors of Judeo-Christian culture are cast out. But it is entirely consistent with the mixture of praise and censure of antiquity we find in the *Descriptive Catalogue* that Blake should have used the Belvedere Apollo in the way proposed in 1809 and become more resolutely anticlassical by 1815. Blake was also an inveterate experimenter, and need have felt no more compunction about rejecting the Whitworth model in the fourth design than in the first. It is always tempting in such cases to speculate about the influence of individual purchasers, in this instance Thomas Butts. Could Blake not have relinquished his more radical interpretation in deference to the piety of his most loyal patron?

In both versions of the next design, traditionally entitled "The Flight of Moloch" (Figs. 51–52), Blake's epiphanic vision of a man-centered millennium in the globe of light and in the Whitworth Apollo is replaced by an archetypal scene of human sacrifice, which in the historical context of the Nativity was of course a gruesome reality. And the case can be made that it represents a brilliantly improvised contradiction of Milton's account of how

> sullen Moloch, fled,
> Hath left in shadows dread
> His burning Idol all of blackest hue;
> In vain with Cymbals' ring
> They call the grisly king,
> In dismal dance about the furnace blue.
> (205–10)

All the particulars indicate that the cult of Moloch here is very much alive. The scene corresponds to the moment in *Europe* immediately after the Nativity when Urizen is "unloos'd from chains" and his sons "Seize all the spirits of life and bind / Their warbling joys" (*Eur* 3.11–4.4, E 60). Both scenes are related to St. John's prophecy that after the binding of the Dragon and immediately before Jerusalem's descent, "Satan shall be loosed out of his prison" (20.7) for a time. As both his close resemblance to Blake's Accuser in the Epilogue to *The Gates of Paradise* (IB 279) and his scarlet hue suggest, the powerful bald and bat-winged figure above Moloch would appear to be not his expiring spirit but Satan himself, his arms extended in a gesture Blake consistently associated with dominion. He may be envisaged as departing to his own place, leaving Moloch not exactly "rejoic[ing] thro the Land" (*J* 68.38, E 222), but evidently reinstated for a further eighteen hundred years, his furnaces blazing, his priests and vestals dancing around him in frantic jubilation.

Hagstrum (p. 123) sees his most prominent victim as "a fiery Orc who leaps out of the furnace," but in both versions he is being abandoned to the flames by his reluctant parents. Blake's iconic frontal presentation perhaps leaves this a little ambiguous, but it is certainly expressive of the child's resistance. Since Moloch and

Nebuchadnezzar would have been typologically related in Blake's mind, and the child is shown in cruciform position, there is almost certainly an allusion here to Daniel 3.25, which Blake cited in the passage from the *Descriptive Catalogue* quoted above. But this promise that man will eventually be delivered from the fiery furnace appears to be subordinated to the negative implications of the crucifixion image, amounting to an inversion of Milton's pious reflection that "The babe lies yet in smiling Infancy, / That on the bitter cross / Must redeem our loss" (151–53); what Blake's pictorial commentary seems to be asserting is that, taken literally, this cornerstone of Milton's faith was itself a remnant of Druidism. The point is made more explicitly in the Huntington series, where the cruciform Infant in "The Descent of Peace" (Fig. 44) and the sacrificial victim here form positive and negative mirror images of one another. Analogously, in *Night Thoughts* 121 (Fig. 101), which draws on the iconography of the Passion and the Harrowing of Hell, Blake had foregrounded the suffering adult Christ crowned with thorns and pierced by huge nails, while invoking the redemptive promise of the Daniel episode by showing him striding through billowing flames.[33]

Several other redemptive motifs encountered earlier are recapitulated in demonic form in both versions of the design, indicating that from the first Blake conceived this as a turning point, a massive negation of the millennial vision that had gone before. That "mighty Angel" Peace (*Mil* 36.12, E 135) has been displaced by Satan as harbinger of discord, who like God appearing to Moses reveals only his "back parts" (Exodus 33.23). The choric globe of angels where the sexes were commingled (cf. *J* 69.43, E 221) has become a segregated band of priests and virgins, "drunk with unsatisfied love" (*J* 68.62, E 222) and locked in a dance of death. Plying their trumpets and cymbals, they recall Milton's description in *Paradise Lost* of

> Moloch, horrid King besmear'd with blood
> Of human sacrifice, and parents' tears,
> Though for the noise of Drums and Timbrels loud
> Their children's cries unheard, that pass'd through fire
> To his grim Idol.[34]
>
> (I.392–96)

Youthful, dynamic Apollo in the Whitworth series has been replaced by a hoary, slothful Moloch, whose name "betokeneth a king."[35] He is the perennial tyrant to whom Christ as Orc or Love or

Truth or Imagination or the Eternal Divine Humanity is perennially sacrificed, an aggregate of such historically pertinent figures as Herod and Nero. In the Huntington version he bears some resemblance to Blake's satirical portrait of George the Third wearing a papal crown on *Europe* 11 (IB 169).

The furnace of Moloch's throne on its Druidic circular dais has multiple openings as described in Banier,[36] formed in both versions by gothic arches, used *in malo* apparently to parody the peace and spirituality of the simpler gothic stable. Again prompted perhaps by Milton's mention of Osiris's "worshipt Ark" (220), in the Whitworth version Blake has presented Moloch's throne as a demonic ark, a pompously ecclesiastical perversion of the Nativity stable on which the crowned and sceptered Moloch sits like a monstrous Covering Cherub. This effect is relinquished in the Huntington design, in which Moloch's position is reversed and he now holds a spiked poignard with which to dispatch his victims. But the gothic openings to the furnace are topped by battlements, together perhaps alluding to the twin powers of Church and Caesar, to whose interests humanity is sacrificed. In the Whitworth design the Druidic nature of all such ceremonies is also perhaps emphasized by the surrounding mountains. Stukeley, Mallet, Davies, and others comment on the fact that stone circles occur on high ground in open places, and that both in earliest antiquity and among northern tribes, such sacred edifices were not roofed over for fear of presuming to confine the deity.[37] But perhaps the most poignant contrast in both sequences is between the innocent Divine Family in the opening designs and the distracted parents sacrificing their offspring for king and country in the foreground here. A similar scene occurs in "A Little Boy Lost" from the *Songs of Experience*, where the priest took the child "in trembling zeal"

> And burn'd him in a holy place,
> Where many had been burn'd before:
> The weeping parents wept in vain.
> Are such things done on Albion's shore.
>
> (E 29)

In the first design, the converging figures of Nature and Peace had anticipated a time when "Heaven, Earth & Hell, henceforth shall live in harmony" (J 3.10, E 144). Here the way the parents fall apart reinforces the sexual message of the segregated dancers—like them, their relative position has been reversed in the Huntington version—and brings home that all has again been plunged into division.

In purely artistic terms, the way Blake's final design, "The Night of Peace" (Figs. 53–54), in both sequences balances his first seems to pay gracious tribute to the symmetry of Milton's hymn, without, however, reproducing the abruptness with which Milton bids us adieu. And unlike the previous designs it confines itself to the details of Milton's final stanza:

> But see! the Virgin blest,
> Hath laid her Babe to rest.
>> Time is our tedious Song should here have ending;
> Heav'n's youngest-teamed Star
> Hath fixt her polisht Car,
>> Her sleeping Lord with Handmaid Lamp attending:
> And all about the Courtly Stable,
> Bright-harness'd Angels sit in order serviceable.
>
> (237–44)

But doctrinally Milton's lines are merely neutral, whereas in the iconographic context Blake has established it is clear that we are here presented with a scene of armed neutrality or, more aptly, guarded optimism. As mooted earlier, the modulated repetition of the opening scene also serves to emphasize that, with the reinstatement of Moloch and the divine right of kings, the cycle of revolt and repression Blake explored in the Lambeth prophecies has come full turn.

But all is not lost. One of the remarkable things about Blake, despite the poignant *Notebook* entry for "Tuesday Jan. 20, 1807, between Two & Seven in the Evening—Despair" (E 672), and his fear of perhaps being too passive, is the extraordinary buoyancy of his temperament, the tenacity of his faith in the dignity and potential of man. And here the Holy Family should be taken as principally an emblem of man's sleeping humanity, preserved in the arkite stable against his resurrection. In the Whitworth version Joseph remains awake: perhaps like the prophetic eagle *cum* Michelangelesque thinker *cum* watchman on *Jerusalem* 78 (IB 357), his function now is to keep the "Divine Vision in time of trouble" (*J* 44.15, E 191). The guardian angels surrounding the stable, whom Behrendt (p. 90) rightly associates with the Cherubim in their globe of light, correspond to the Angels of the Divine Presence who watch over Milton's slumbering humanity in *Milton*. In the Huntington version they are again more youthful and have been increased from four to eight, and the thatched transepts of the Whitworth stable have been eliminated, creating a more precise mirror image of the stable in the first design. Promise that Satan has been loosed but for a season, that harmony will return and man once again ascend the "Fiery Chariot of his Contemplative Thought" (*VLJ*, E 560), is held out by the harping angels and "Heav'n's youngest-teamed star." Blake indicates that the star has come to rest above the stable by depicting the two horses reposing rather charmingly upon a bed of cloud. The Whitworth version seems a shade more pessimistic, though, for both they and their mistress with her "Handmaid Lamp" are seen against a sky filled with Urizenic stars, and they look round as if expecting deliverance from elsewhere. Judging from the glum expressions of the guardian angels and the mass of fodder Dunbar (p. 112) notices, they all anticipate that before the dawn a long dark night still lies ahead. In the Huntington version the stars have been eliminated, as have the cattle, and the two guardians in the foreground and two of the three figures in the sky all gaze upon the Christ-child reverentially. This seems entirely consonant with the greater importance Blake appears to have attached to him in the sequence as a whole. Where in the Whitworth series he seems to have had the Nativity in mind principally as a historical event, in the Huntington version he has concentrated on the symbolic significance of Christ's advent. In both series he has traced its wider implications from a post-Enlightenment perspective, acknowledging the high seriousness of Milton's theme, but exposing the negative implications of some of his most central orthodoxies, and simultaneously presenting his own, more truly humanist answering vision with marvellous imaginative ingenuity.

Notes

1   Behrendt, "Blake's Illustrations to Milton's *Nativity Ode*," *Philological Quarterly*, 55 (1976), 91; subsequent page references to this article are internalized. See further the same author's *The Moment of Explosion*, pp. 38–41. Alexander N. Hutchison in "Blake's Illustrations to Milton's *On the Morning of Christ's Nativity*," *British Columbia Library Quarterly*, 36 (1972–73), 9–10, also holds the view that "Blake does not take liberties with the text of the *Hymn* . . . he subordinates his desire for revision to the delight he took in exploiting the imaginative possibilities of Milton's verbal imagery."

2   Leslie Tannenbaum, *Biblical Tradition in Blake's Early Prophecies* (Princeton: Princeton Univ. Press, 1982), pp. 86–123; Morton D. Paley,

"'Wonderful Originals'—Blake and Ancient Sculpture" in Essick and Pearce, eds., *Blake in His Time*, pp. 170–97; see also his "The Truchsessian Gallery Revisited," *Studies in Romanticism*, 16 (1977), 155–78.

3   Tolley, "*Europe*: 'to those ychain'd in sleep,'" in Erdman and Grant, eds., *Blake's Visionary Forms Dramatic*, pp. 115–45.

4   Hagstrum, *William Blake: Poet and Painter*, p. 27.

5   The fact that both sets are signed "W. Blake," a form Butlin has discovered Blake tended to adopt around 1806 in preference to his monogram, also argues against an early date for the Huntington set; see Butlin, "Cataloguing William Blake," in Essick and Pearce, pp. 82f.

6   If one includes Rossetti's probably random ordering in his "Descriptive Catalogue" of Blake's work in Gilchrist's *Life and Works of William Blake*, 2nd ed. (London: Macmillan, 1980), II.222, five different arrangements and a formidable array of different titles for the *Nativity Ode* designs have been proposed. Details are given in Behrendt's article, pp. 68 and 93 n.11.

7   Arthur E. Barker, "The Pattern of Milton's *Nativity Ode*," *University of Toronto Quarterly*, 10 (1941), 167–69.

8   See Adrian Van Sinderen, *Blake, the Mystic Genius* (Syracuse: Syracuse Univ. Press, 1949), where Blake's notes accompanying the *L'Allegro and Il Penseroso* designs which he numbered 1–12 are reproduced; and David Bindman, *Catalogue of the Blake Collection in the Fitzwilliam Museum Cambridge* (Cambridge: Heffer, 1970), pls. 25–34, where Blake's numbering of the *Paradise Regained* designs is visible.

9   See Easson and Essick, eds., *William Blake: Book Illustrator*, Vol. 2, XVI.pls. 1, 9; XX.pl.5.

10 See Nicholas O. Warner, "Blake's Moon-Ark Symbolism," *Blake: An Illustrated Quarterly*, 54 (1980), 44–59; Jacob Bryant, *A New System, or, An Analysis of Ancient Mythology* (London, 1775), II.59f., 198f.; Paul Henri Mallet, *Northern Antiquities*, trans. Thomas Percy (1770; rpt. London, 1847), p. 98; Edward Davies, *Celtic Researches* (London, 1804), pp. 24f., 157, 309, 316; and *The Mythology and Rites of the British Druids* (London, 1809), pp. 90f., 154f., 293. In the *Descriptive Catalogue* Blake writes that "the British Antiquities are now in the Artist's hands" (E 533), and the arkite symbolism Warner has found in his epics makes clear that he was familiar with the kind of parallels these syncretist mythographers were drawing between Noah and other heroes such as Osiris, Perseus, Dionysus, and Deucalion, who were exposed in arks but returned to renew civilization. Further pictorial support for an arkite stable here can be adduced from the fact that Noah in the *Epitome of James Hervey's Meditations Among the Tombs* (B 967) and Moses leaping from a rather different ark in *The Finding of Moses* (B 533) appear in postures similar to that of the Christ-child in the Hun-

tington design. *A propos* the stable's resemblance to the tombs Blake sketched in the Abbey, it is interesting to find Bryant writing that "as the confinement during the deluge was esteemed an interval of death, the Ark from thence was represented as a bier or coffin" (II.328). Conceivably Blake was also familiar with the traditional association of the Ark of the Covenant with "Mary, in whom the divine Son was hidden," noted by Gertrud Schiller in *Iconography of Christian Art* (Greenwich: New York Graphic Society, 1971), I.109.

11 See C. H. Collins Baker, *Catalogue of William Blake's Drawings and Paintings in the Huntington Library*, 2nd ed. (San Marino: Huntington Library, 1969), p. 26.

12 Chayes, "Fallen Earth and Man in Nature: William Blake in Iconographic Tradition," *Studies in Iconography*, 10 (1984–86), 186–91.

13 See Geoffrey Keynes, *Blake Studies*, rev. ed. (London: Oxford Univ. Press, 1971), p. 27.

14 Rose, "Mental Forms Creating: 'Fourfold Vision' and the Poet as Prophet in Blake's Designs and Verse," *Journal of Aesthetics and Art Criticism*, 23 (1964), 173–83.

15 Damon, *Blake's Job* (New York: Dutton, 1966), p. 38.

16 Dunbar, *William Blake's Illustrations to the Poetry of Milton*, p. 98.

17 See Hill, *Milton and the English Revolution*, pp. 159–61; and Michael Fixler, *Milton and the Kingdoms of God* (London: Faber, 1964), pp. 127, 134, 153.

18 See Albert S. Roe, *Blake's Illustrations to the Divine Comedy* (Princeton: Princeton Univ. Press, 1953), p. 134 and pl. 69; and Milton Klonsky, *Blake's Dante* (New York: Harmony Books, 1980), p. 153 and pl. 72.

19 Francis Haskell and Nicholas Penny, *Taste and the Antique* (New Haven: Yale Univ. Press, 1981), p. 148.

20 Werner, *Blake's Vision of the Poetry of Milton*, p. 26.

21 See Mitchell, "Blake's Visions of the Last Judgment," a booklet published by *Blake Newsletter* for the 1975 MLA Blake Seminar.

22 See Blunt, *The Art of William Blake*, p. 34 and pls. 6–7. There were also precedents for Blake's use of classical figures in millennial contexts during the French Revolution. Jacques-Louis David, for instance, was involved in a project to erect a "colossal Hercules representing the French people ... on the Pont Neuf"; and for the Festival of the Supreme Being in 1794 he built "an enormous plaster-and-cardboard mountain," on the summit of which was another Hercules holding a statuette of Liberty. See Simon Schama, *Citizens: A Chronicle of the French Revolution* (New York: Knopf, 1989), pp. 830–35 and pls. 208–209.

23　See William Stukeley, *Stonehenge, a Temple Restor'd to the British Druids* (London, 1740), pls. XII, XIII, XV, XVI. In *Abury, a Temple of the British Druids* (London, 1743), p. 67, Stukeley writes that Phut, whom he equates with Apollo, "planted the country about the mountain Parnassus, where he built . . . a great serpentine temple, like ours at Abury, at the bottom of that mountain, by the city of Delphos. This I gather from the Greek reports of the serpent Python of an immense bulk, bred of the slime left on the earth, by the general deluge, which Apollo here overcame. . . ."

24　Bryant, I.pl.VIII. See Raine, *Blake and Tradition* (Princeton: Princeton Univ. Press, 1968), II.261.

25　See Panofsky, *The Life and Art of Albrecht Dürer*, pl. 80. The classical sources for the belief in the destruction of the world by fire and water are given in Richard Payne Knight, *An Inquiry into the Symbolic Language of Ancient Art and Mythology* (1818; rpt. London: Society of Dilettanti, 1835), p. 52.

26　Peter F. Fisher, "Blake's Attacks on the Classical Tradition," *Philological Quarterly*, 40 (1961), 13. This remains the most searching study of Blake's complex relationship to classical antiquity, but Blake's archetypes have less in common with Plato's than Fisher believed, and Tannenbaum, pp. 86–123, should be read as a corrective.

27　Joseph Burke, "The Eidetic and the Borrowed Image: An Interpretation of Blake's Theory and Practice of Art," in Essick, ed., *The Visionary Hand* (Los Angeles: Hennessey & Ingalls, 1973), p. 284.

28　Virgil, *The Eclogues*, ed. and trans. Guy Lee (Harmondsworth: Penguin, 1980), p. 57.

29　See Edward Miller, *That Noble Cabinet: A History of the British Museum* (London: André Deutsch, 1973), pp. 97–107; William St. Clair, *Lord Elgin and the Marbles* (London: Oxford Univ. Press, 1967), pp.166f.; B. F. Cook, *The Elgin Marbles* (London: British Museum, 1984), pp. 60–66; and his *The Townley Marbles* (London: British Museum, 1985), pp. 59–62.

30　Blake owned a copy of Johann Winckelmann, *Reflections on the Painting and Sculpture of the Greeks*, trans. Henry Fuseli (London, 1765).

31　Essick and Pearce, eds., *Blake in His Time*, pl. 110.

32　The mythographers would have provided Blake with ample evidence of the ubiquity of sun worship. See, for example, Bryant, I.13f.; Montfaucon, *Antiquity Explained*, trans. David Humphreys (London, 1721–22), I.72, IV.255; Antoine Banier, *The Mythology and Fables of the Ancients Explain'd from History* (London, 1740), II.378f., III.270, 308; Stukeley, *Abury*, pp. 9, 67; Mallet, pp. 87f., 110; Sir William Jones, *On the Gods of Greece, Italy and India*, in *Works* (London, 1799), I.268;

Edward Moor, *Hindu Pantheon* (London, 1810), pp. 6–21, 121–22, 192, 277f., and pls. 87–89; Davies, *Mythology*, pp. 30f., 291f.; and Knight, pp. 18, 22, 38f.

33 See Schiller, I.pls.529 et seq.

34 In his *Observations on the Antiquities of Cornwall* (Oxford, 1754), pp. 121–23, William Borlase gives an indignant circumstantial account of the different methods of human sacrifice among the Druids noted by classical historians, including what Blake termed the "Wicker Man of Scandinavia" (*J* 47.7, E 196). He explains that "the more dear and beloved was the person, the more acceptable they thought their offering would be accounted. Hence, not only beautiful captives and strangers, but children, and Princes were, upon great occasions, offer'd upon their Altars." His concluding remarks provide a fairly precise gloss on this aspect of Blake's Moloch design. "Whilst they were performing these horrid rites," he observes, "the drums and trumpets sounded without intermission, that the cries of the miserable victims might not be heard, or distinguish'd by their friends, it being accounted very ominous, if the lamentations of either children or parents were distinctly to be heard, whilst the victim was burning."

35 Banier, II.48; see Bryant, I.70.

36 Banier, II.48–51.

37 Stukeley, *Stonehenge*, pp. 23–24; Mallet, p. 107; Davies, *Mythology*, pp. 291f., 305; Borlase, pp. 107f., 116; Bryant, I.235f.; Abraham Rees, *Cyclopaedia* (London, 1819), XII, under "Druids."

"A Negation is not a Contrary":
The *L'Allegro and Il Penseroso* Designs

If the *Paradise Lost* series is the most sublime of Blake's Milton sequences, his set of twelve small (approx. 16 x 12 cm.) watercolor illustrations to *L'Allegro* and *Il Penseroso* is surely the most exquisite and immediately appealing. Commissioned originally by Butts and now in the Pierpont Morgan Library, they are undated, but are painted, on paper watermarked 1816, in bright iridescent tones that have lost none of their freshness with the passage of time. They are also the least classical, the most rococo of the Milton sequences, and the nicely balanced daylight and nocturnal scenes capture with consummate decorum the airy feel that Milton's swift cataloguing of the delights of Mirth and Melancholy gives to his twin poems. The correspondence is partly attributable to the fact that the aerial regions of the designs are as alive with Miltonic personifications, goblins, nature sprites, and fairies as are the landscapes. Yet the eye is not overwhelmed by this plethora of figures, perhaps because the recurrence of circular configurations—notably in "The Sun at His Eastern Gate" (Fig. 57), "The Youthful Poet's Dream" (Fig. 60), "The Spirit of Plato" (Fig. 63), and "Milton's Mysterious Dream" (Fig. 65)—has a restful and formally integrating effect.

There is also a good deal of impish humor in the series, reminiscent of the *Marriage* and some of the Gray designs. The breezy figures circling Mirth's head (Fig. 55) seem, for instance, to comment on the giddy thing she is, while the more factious spirits around Milton in "The Spirit of Plato" imply that the *Timaeus* is making even him a little dizzy. In "The Sun at His Eastern Gate" Blake depicts Milton as a diminutive figure in the landscape, all but eclipsed and perhaps blinded by his own Apollonian vision. This, moreover, is the only time that Milton appears for certain in the *L'Allegro* series, whereas he is depicted five times in the *Il Penseroso*—always dressed like Melancholy herself in "robe of darkest grain" (33). Thought of in the context of works which placed artists between opposed facets of their art, such as Reynolds's *Garrick Between Tragedy and Comedy* or Thomas Banks's *Shakespeare Between the Dramatic Muse and the Genius of Painting*, this suggests that he considered "divinest Melancholy's" (12) hold over Milton to have been excessive.[1] Dr. Johnson too had noticed this imbalance in the poems themselves, observing that "no mirth can, indeed, be found in his melancholy; but I am afraid that I always meet some melancholy in his mirth."[2] Blake's irreverent attitude to Milton here and in the roughly contemporaneous Boston *Comus* series contrasts sharply with the mid-century sentimentalism of Hayman's "The Poet by the Pool" (P 51), or the bardolatrous portrayals by Fuseli (Fig. 114) and Flaxman (P 69).[3]

Hermeneutically, the *L'Allegro and Il Penseroso* designs are as tantalizingly suggestive and elusive as they are beautiful, and the descriptive notes Blake transcribed on separate sheets beneath the relevant sections of the poems give little away. The various models advanced as underlying organizational principles are "Seldom without some Vision" (E 554), but none of them renders a complete account of the particulars. The diurnal cycle is of course suggested in the *L'Allegro* series, where dawn (Fig. 56) is followed sequentially by sunrise (Fig. 57) and "A Sunshine Holiday" (Fig. 58). But the intrusion of the nocturnal vision of "The Goblin" (Fig. 59) before the setting of the natural sun (Fig. 60), and the corresponding intrusion of "The Sun in His Wrath" (Fig. 64) in the nocturnal *Il Penseroso* series, indicate that this pattern is not rigidly adhered to. The mensural and seasonal cycles Rose proposes may well be numerologically represented, but Blake has made no attempt to depict the changing seasons in his pastoral settings.[4] Attempts to equate the contrasting segments of the series with Innocence and Experience, or, conversely, Experience and a putative higher Innocence, also seem to do violence to Blake's living form, and it bears remembering that the *Songs* themselves are not rigidly divided, and that we repeatedly encounter the voice of Innocence amid the oppression of Experience. Thus Anne K. Mellor's association of the *L'Allegro* designs with Innocence fails to account for the inane or frivolous character of most of Mirth's companions.[5] The view shared by Grant and Behrendt, that "divinest Melancholy" (12), given her traditional association with poetic genius, might be a more auspicious and innocent guide in the education of a prophet, is undermined by her status as a "Pensive Nun, devout and pure" (31) and by the austere company she keeps.[6] The extent to which both Mirth and Melancholy are ironically presented, as Karl Kiralis proposes, also of course has bearing on the vexed question of whether in "Milton in His Old Age" (Fig. 66) the poet finally transcends his doctrinal errors as in *Milton*, or remains entrapped by them.[7]

A hypothesis that has not been explored in discussions of these designs is that Blake may be criticizing Milton precisely for his *failure* to think of Mirth and Melancholy as dynamically interrelated contraries. If Blake intended to commend Milton for his ability to enter equally into the delights of his sanguine and melancholy poets, Behrendt's contention that "Milton's progress" in the series "results from his correct response to the dynamic tension between contrary states he experiences, . . . a movement Blake discerned clearly in Milton's poetic development" (p. 128) would seem quite plausible. But, in the context of Blake's doctrine of contraries, the striking thing about Milton's companion poems surely is that each speaker *negates* the rival tutelary's claims. L'Allegro commences his oration with "Hence, loathed Melancholy" (1), while Il Penseroso correspondingly dismisses the pleasures of Mirth with "Hence, vain deluding Joys" (1). When one considers this in the light of Blake's explicit statements about Milton as a true but self-divided poet, "of the Devils party without knowing it" (E 35) in the *Marriage*, and "Unhappy tho in heav'n" (E 96) in *Milton*, there would seem every reason to suspect that he would have regarded it as yet another symptom of the deep-seated dualism that had prevented Milton, for all his liberalism, from transcending the limitations of his age. What Blake may be prompting us to see, in other words, is that both Mirth and Melancholy are inadequate because they are one-sided muses—tutelaries respectively of Cavalier excess and Puritan repression.

This hypothesis suggests that the historical Milton is the focus of Blake's interest, and tends to endorse Werner's conclusion that the series leaves off where *Milton* takes up, with Milton unredeemed.[8] But it also helps to accommodate a number of awkward particulars insisted on by Grant (I.122), such as the negative overtones in "The Sun at His Eastern Gate" and "The Spirit of Plato," that have resisted easy synthesis. The fact that the designs propel the imagination beyond the immediate context of the poems to contemplate larger aspects of Milton's life and times might seem to argue against linear analysis, yet Blake himself carefully numbered the series 1–12 on the separate sheets he annotated.[9] Moreover, as Rose (p. 61) points out, they can be read both sequentially and in pairs, and the correspondences between individual *L'Allegro* and individual *Il Penseroso* illustrations that his analysis reveals can be further shown to form two coherent, parallel narratives within each segment. To the extent that the inaugural designs sum up the strengths and weaknesses of Mirth and Melancholy, they too may be said to function a little like the prefaces to *Milton* and *Jerusalem*. At the same time, the rival goddesses are also of course the moving spirits behind each narrative, and their tutelary influence is suggested visually by the way their attitudes are echoed by the sanguine and melancholy poets at the conclusion of each series, so that each is in this sense circular in structure. As Mellor (p. 277) points out, the position of Mirth's arms (Fig. 55) is echoed by that of the supine poet in "The Youthful Poet's Dream" (Fig. 60); and there is a similar correspondence between Melancholy presented frontally with sable gown and heaven-bent gaze (Fig. 61) and Milton seated in his "mossy Cell" (169) with his arms raised rather higher in the last design (Fig. 66).

Within these parameters the narrative development resembles that in the *Nativity Ode* series in that it seems to be broadly apocalyptic. Both symbolic subnarratives begin with an epiphany, the implications of which are then worked out in the subsequent designs. In the *L'Allegro* series, Earth in the lower segment awakens to the sound of the Lark (Fig. 56), but the new day that breaks over Milton in the next design (Fig. 57) appears to be an Age of Reason, dominated by Apollo as an imperious Sun King. The effects on England's public life are presented in "A Sunshine Holiday" (Fig. 58), a scene apparently of Natural Religion, since the revellers ignore the Christ-like admonisher who urges them to ascend the vortex and so transcend the natural sun. The effects on private life are suggested in the nightmare scene of sexual frustration depicted in "The Goblin" (Fig. 59). And the implications for the arts are revealed in the last design (Fig. 60), where what Blake describes as "The more bright Sun of Imagination" appearing to the "Youthful Poet" (E 684) in his dream remains dualistically divided. In the *Il Penseroso* series correspondingly, "Milton in his Character of a student at Cambridge" (E 684) is shown gazing up at the chaste moon-goddess Diana (Fig. 62), evidently a vision of the guiding principle of chastity that Milton adopted in matters of the heart. His idealistic and essentially Platonic view of love impels him in "The Spirit of Plato" (Fig. 63) to consult the sage more deeply. And this in turn leads to his evasion of the heat of the sun (Fig. 64), to apocalyptic dreams frustrated by his sexual fears (Fig. 65), and an old age of lonely isolation (Fig. 66).

In electing to portray Mirth surrounded by her companions, rather than leading the poet as in Hayman (P 36) or alone as in Westall (P 111), Blake was following a precedent established by Fuseli (P 93) and Romney (Fig. 115)—though he ignores Fuseli's overt eroticism and omits the musical instruments of the subordinate figures in Romney.[10] As so often in commercial illustration, moreover, he defines Mirth at least in part in relation to her more sober rival, depicting her as at once "Buxom, blithe, and debonair" (24), the epitome of grace and energy. The contrast between her long rose-garlanded hair, light clinging dress, and carefree mien, and veiled Melancholy's dark robe and sedate deportment, is particularly suggestive in relation to the Choice of Hercules tradition discussed earlier, since it implies that she plays Sense to Melancholy's Reason. This would be in line with Milton's characterization of her as the daughter of "lovely Venus" (14) and "Ivy-crowned Bacchus" (16), and (if we follow Warburton's gloss) the sibling of the "sister Graces" (15) "Meat and Drink."[11] It would also accord with her general resemblance, noted by Grant (II.197), to Sense escaping from under Reason's pall on *Night Thoughts* 81, and with the further resemblance of her gesture to that of Eve as Sense on *Night Thoughts* 119 (Fig. 98). The typological analogy Kiralis (p. 49) draws between Mirth and Melancholy and those other victims of a dualistic rational culture, the Wife of Bath and the Prioress in Blake's *Canterbury Pilgrims* pictures (B 587, 878), would seem therefore to the point.

Mirth is also defined by the company she keeps, and the inane or frivolous antics of the troupe she leads suggest that, like Comus on his opening appearance (Figs. 3–4), she too is something of a Mistress of Misrule. Blake insists that the "Personifications" the sanguine poet invokes "are all brought together in this design" (E 682):

> Haste thee Nymph, & bring with thee
> Jest & Youthful Jollity,
> Quips & Cranks & Wanton Wiles,
> Nods & Becks & wreathed smiles,
> Sport that wrinkled Care derides
> And Laughter holding both his Sides.
> Come & trip it as you go
> On the light phantastic toe
> And in thy right hand lead with thee,
> The Mountain Nymph Sweet Liberty.

And on the basis of the second state of the only engraving Blake completed for the series, where Sport, Care, and Laughter are labelled, most of them have been convincingly identified.[12] Grant (II.192) moreover draws attention to reservations about Mirth that Blake expresses in a letter to Trusler: "Fun I love but too much Fun is of all things the most loathsome. Mirth is better than Fun and Happiness is better than Mirth—I feel that a Man may be happy in This World" (E 702). From this perspective the gesturing of the high-stepping Jest and Youthful Jollity flanking Mirth may seem empty rather than innocent, a point which comparison with the clowns in Blake's picture of "Vanity Fair" (Fig. 116) in the *Pilgrim's Progress* series tends to confirm. Too much fun may also be entailed in the case of Sport deriding Care above Mirth's right arm and "Laughter holding both his Sides," emblems perhaps of the coarse and cruel faces of Mirth. The animal attributes of the grotesque Quips and Cranks and Wanton Wiles on her left are perhaps intended as visual puns, commenting on their batty, asinine, or kittenish behavior.[13] Sweet Liberty being led by Mirth might seem beyond reproach, especially since in both states of the engraving an apocalyptic bow is added to her quiver. Yet the point of the visual connection between her and the bubble-blowing trumpeter, made by Mirth's extended arms, could be that liberty guided by sense or energy divorced from reason and imagination are mere libertinism— a vacuous apocalypse.

When one considers Mirth's halo of Wreathed Smiles, however, and the fact that her less attractive attributes are confined to her companions, it is hard not to suspect that Blake had a soft spot for her, as he had for Eve and for the Virgin Mary as belonging to a class of "innocently gay and thoughtless" (E 559) beings, like the damsel tripping toward her grave in *Night Thoughts* 253. As Grant (II.193) points out, in the second state of the engraving he relocated her left hand, so that she appears to sponsor a diminutive child (in the same attitude as the Lark in the next design) being launched by the mother toward the father. The group is evidently a collective emblem of the sustaining power of happiness at the higher reaches of mirth, and bears comparison with the Nativity scene within the flower of "Infant Joy" from the *Songs of Innocence* (IB 66). From this vantage Blake's inscription would appear to be two-edged: "Solomon says Vanity of Vanities all is Vanity and what can be Foolisher than this" (E 686) can be read both as an indictment of Mirth and her companions, and as a reminder of the importance to human happiness of redeeming Mirth from vanity. Significantly, however, they are all heading away from "eternity's sun rise" (E 470).

In the next two designs, "Night Startled by the Lark" (Fig. 56) and "The Sun at His Eastern Gate" (Fig. 57), Blake transforms the sanguine poet's observation of the natural dawn into an expanding visionary moment analogous to that in the first two *Nativity Ode* illustrations (Figs. 43–46). There are no apocalyptic overtones in the lines describing the lark that Blake transcribed:

> To hear the Lark begin his flight,
> And singing startle the dull Night,
> From his Watch Tower in the Skies,
> Till the dappled Dawn does rise.

But in his note Blake declares that "The Lark is an Angel on the Wing. Dull Night starts from his Watch Tower on a Cloud. The Dawn with her dappled Horses arises above the Earth. The Earth beneath awakes at the Larks Voice" (E 682). The last sentence in particular, which draws attention to a personified figure not present in Milton, intimates that all is to be spiritually discerned. The relationship between Earth and the Lark is conceptually analogous to that between Nature and Peace in the first *Nativity Ode* design. Here, too, the Lark is a joyful messenger, and his kinship with the innocent side of Mirth is perhaps implied in his youthful appearance and by the way his features and the angle of his head appear to mirror hers. His powerful golden wings and expansive gesture as he mounts are marvellously expressive of energy released, making him seem a younger version of the risen Albion in *Glad Day* (B 331). His body posture also quite closely resembles that of the spectrous Goblin (Fig. 59), which raises the possibility that the two may be related as positive and negative mirror images of one another. His hair rises to a peak to suggest his beak, his mouth is open, and he may confidently be assumed to be singing a new song. These propitious signs are to some degree endorsed by Blake's use of the lark in a justly celebrated passage in *Milton* to herald the reunion of Ololon and Milton:

> The Lark is Los's Messenger thro the Twenty-seven Churches
> That the Seven Eyes of God who walk even to Satans Seat
> Thro all the Twenty-seven Heavens may not slumber nor sleep
> But the Larks Nest is at the Gate of Los, at the eastern
> Gate of wide Golgonooza & the Lark is Los's Messenger
> When on the highest lift of his light pinions he arrives
> At that bright Gate, another Lark meets him & back to back
> They touch their pinions tip tip: and each descend
> To their respective Earths & there all night consult with Angels
> Of Providence & with the Eyes of God all night in slumbers
> Inspired: & at the dawn of day send out another Lark
> Into another Heaven to carry news upon his wings

> Thus are the Messengers dispatcht till they reach the Earth again
> In the East Gate of Golgonooza, & the Twenty-eighth bright
> Lark met the Female Ololon descending into my Garden
> Thus it appears to Mortal eyes & those of the Ulro Heavens
> But not thus to Immortals, the Lark is a mighty Angel.
>
> (*Mil* 35.63–36.12, E 136)

The context in the design is, of course, quite different, since the Lark appears at the beginning of the series and is the herald of Apollo. Yet here too he is a mighty Angel, formidable enough to startle a very "ancient Night" (*Paradise Lost* II.970), ensconced within a crenellated tower reminiscent of Blake's sketch of Windsor Castle in the fourth illustration to Gray's "Ode on a Distant Prospect of Eton College."[14] Warton had noted that in *Of Reformation* Milton refers to God himself "in his high watch-tower in the Heavens," and the Urizenic appearance of Night against the stars suggests that Blake intended him as an emblem of the traditional feudal order.[15] Immediately beneath him Aurora appears trailing rosy clouds of glory from her outstretched arms, and gazes up at the ascending Lark as her dappled horses streak across the yellow-tinged horizon. Propitiously, too, she has drawn her veil, the contours of which, as Grant (I.122) points out, suggest a bow.[16] In so doing she anticipates the time when the male and female figures separated by the cloud-barrier will be united, and "Heaven, Earth and Hell, henceforth shall live in harmony" (*J* 3, E 145). The degree of commerce between heaven and earth appears to function as an index of meaning in several subsequent designs.

In the sequel, "The Sun at His Eastern Gate" (Fig. 57), which corresponds to the epiphany of the angelic choir in the *Nativity Ode* series, Blake depicts the fulfillment of the Lark's prophetic song, the birth of a new age. The lines from Milton that he transcribed present a pastoral panorama, in which equal attention is given to the various aspects of the scene that the sanguine poet surveys:

> Sometime walking not unseen
> By hedgerow Elms on Hillocks green
> Right against the Eastern Gate
> When the Great Sun begins his state
> Robed in Flames & amber Light
> The Clouds in thousand Liveries dight
> While the Plowman near at hand
> Whistles o'er the Furrow'd Land
> And the Milkmaid singeth blithe
> And the Mower whets his Scythe

> And every Shepherd tells his Tale
> Under the Hawthorn in the Dale.

Blake's note adds that "The Great Sun is represented clothed in Flames Surrounded by the Clouds in their Liveries, in their various Offices at the Eastern Gate. Beneath in Small Figures Milton walking by Elms on Hillocks green. The Plowman, the Milkmaid, the Mower whetting his Scythe, & the Shepherd & his Lass under a Hawthorn in the Dale" (E 683). Thus, by emphasizing the personified Great Sun, surrounded by an aureole of curling flame within a huge orb of amber light, and subordinating the liveried clouds and pastoral spectators, Blake again gives an apocalyptic interpretation to Milton's essentially naturalistic scene. And by drawing attention to Milton's presence in the landscape, he leaves the way open to the inference that this is a moment of illumination for Milton, the implications of which are defined by the particulars.

Commentators have repeatedly asserted that this is an auspicious moment, yet there are good grounds for suspecting that Blake in fact intended to suggest a false dawn, an ominous apocalypse. It is true that as the deity who regulates the activities of the clouds with their rain jars and the harvest spirits yielding up the earth's fruits, the Great Sun might seem above reproach. His frank display of his naked form, to which Dunbar (p. 129) draws attention, would also seem commendable, particularly if Apollo in the Whitworth *Nativity Ode* series (Fig. 49) is indeed a redemptive figure, as suggested earlier. His imperious bearing, however, his scepter, and the fact, noted by Grant (I.122), that he wears the spiked gothic crown that Blake consistently used as an emblem of tyranny, are less reassuring. Comparison with the equally radiant nimbus of Goltzius's *The Sun God*, proposed by Hagstrum as a possible source for Blake's figure, suggests that merely as an added emblem of the Great Sun's rays this crown would have been superfluous.[17] Rose (p. 63) notes the analogy with Los stepping from his fiery orb on *Milton* 47 (IB 263), a design illustrating the moment in the poem when Blake describes how

> Los behind me stood; a terrible flaming Sun: just close
> Behind my back; I turned round in terror, and behold
> Los stood in that fierce glowing fire; & he also stoop'd down
> And bound my sandals on in Udan-Adan; trembling I stood
> Exceedingly with fear & terror, standing in the Vale
> Of Lambeth: but he kissed me and wishd me health.
> And I became One Man with him arising in my strength:

Twas too late now to recede. Los had enterd into my soul:
His terrors now posses'd me whole! I arose in fury & strength.

(*Mil* 22.6–14, E 116)

The parallel does not seem close enough, however, to warrant Werner's claim (p. 144) that the Great Sun here is Los, despite Blake's association of both figures with the lark. It is true that the squared circle common to both these epiphanic pictures is often emblematic of fourfold imaginative vision, but Blake uses the motif both *in bono* and *in malo*, as we have seen in the mirror image designs of "The Rout of the Rebel Angels" from the *Paradise Lost* series (Figs. 31–32) and the frontispiece to *Europe* (Fig. 82). Moreover, can one imagine the Great Sun, as Blake has characterized him, stooping to bind another's sandals?

A more instructive parallel surely is with the awesome figure of Satan in a very similar attitude in the Tate Gallery watercolor catalogued by Butlin as *Satan in His Original Glory: 'Thou wast perfect till iniquity was found in thee'* (Fig. 117). The subtitle, from Ezekiel 28.15, used on its own by Rossetti in his catalogue, is clearly the more relevant, and in fact the reference on the original mount from which it is taken is to "Ezekiel ch. 28th v. 13th &c" (B I.469), that is, to the sequence of verses dealing with the corruption of the Prince of Tyre.[18] Satan's majestic bearing, his imperial scepter, orb, and train, his expansive sixfold wings, and his exalted position above the "starry floor" (E 18) all suggest that this is a vision of him as Ezekiel's archetypal Covering Cherub (28.16), declaring "I am God alone / There is no other!" (*Mil* 9.25–26, E 103; see Ezekiel 28.2). The notion that he and the equally imperious Great Sun are kindred spiritual and political oppressors would certainly accommodate the latter's crown and scepter. It would also suggest that Blake's distinction between the spiritual and guinea suns as formulated in *A Vision of the Last Judgment* (E 566), though routinely cited in discussions of this design, may not have the direct relevance it has to the second *Nativity Ode* illustration.

Blake's quite different formulation of the same distinction as reported by Crabb Robinson seems much more pertinent:

> By way of example of the difference between [the natural and spiritual worlds] he said, "*You* never saw the spiritual Sun. I have. I saw him on Primrose Hill. He said 'Do you take me for the Greek Apollo?' 'No!' I said. '*That* (pointing to the Sky) That is the Greek Apollo—He is Satan!' "   (BR 541)

Since Blake has manifestly depicted the Great Sun as a splendid neoclassical "Greek Apollo," the logical inference would seem to be that he and Los as he appears stepping from the sun on *Milton* 47 are not complementary but antithetical inspirational figures. Blake, that is, would again appear to be tilting at the demonic hold of the rationalist classical tradition over Milton, and over the cultural life of his age and the age of Enlightenment that followed. Apollo's relationship to Mirth would thus appear to be a dual one. As spirits of the natural world they are in league, and the confident bearing with which both advance suggests the—from Blake's point of view naive—optimism of all rationalist philosophies of the five senses divorced from the imagination. As personifications of Sense and Reason they exemplify the dualistic tendencies inherent in this tradition. The patriarchal oppression that results is perhaps detectable in the fact that Apollo's ministering clouds, harvest sprites, and trumpeters appear to be predominantly dependent women and children.

That Milton is the principal recipient of this vision is less explicit than in, say, *Ezekiel's Wheels* (B 542), in the interests no doubt of maintaining literal fidelity to the poem. But the contrast in scale between him and Apollo is equally striking and emphatic, and as in the case of the little visionary between the giant's legs on *Jerusalem* 62 (IB 34), the intention is also clearly partly humorous. There is humor too in the way the Great Sun sweeps the head-clutching storm cloud aside with his left hand, and in the fact that in a sense he is blowing his own trumpet, since five little heralds within his orb (three of them with flaming halos) are trumpeting his praise. The two angels watching from the wings as he prepares to ascend from the hilltop up the formalized steps of the sky have apparently just blown their fanfare. Two butterfly spirits in the hawthorn trees are struggling to rise, but for the moment they are trapped.

If, then, the Great Sun's advent represents from Blake's point of view an abortive apocalypse, a manifestation of Lucifer as the spirit of rational enlightenment, one might expect the remaining *L'Allegro* designs to amplify some of the effects of his triumph on England's green and pleasant land. "A Sunshine Holiday" (Fig. 58), which exemplifies Blake's remarkable ability to introduce a rich variety of figures without losing either lightness or visual coherence, is based principally on the following lines:

> Sometimes with secure delight
> The upland Hamlets will invite

> When the merry Bells ring round
> And the jocund Rebecks Sound
> To many a Youth & many a Maid
> Dancing in the chequerd Shade
> And Young & Old come forth to play
> On a Sunshine Holiday.

Blake in his note adds that "In this Design is Introduced

> Mountains on whose barren breast
> The Labring Clouds do often rest

Mountains Clouds Rivers Trees appear Humanized on the Sunshine Holiday. The Church Steeple with its merry bells. The Clouds arise from the bosoms of Mountains While Two Angels sound their Trumpets in the Heavens to announce the Sunshine Holiday" (E 683). If one excepts the principal giant figure wearing a crenellated crown, who appears to be in some distress, the whole mood of this verdant scene with its amber sun and roseate sky is so delightfully summery, and its foreground activities so reminiscent of happy scenes like those which illuminate the "Nurses Song" (IB 65) or "The Ecchoing Green" (IB 47) in the *Songs*, that it seems uncharitable to suspect the innocence of these sunshine revellers, the more so since Blake's term "humanized" encourages association of the scene with the climactic passage at the end of *Jerusalem*, where Nature is redeemed and

> All Human Forms identified even Tree Metal Earth & Stone, all
> Human Forms identified, living going forth & returning
> > wearied
> Into the Planetary lives of Years Months Days & Hours reposing
> And then Awaking into his Bosom in the Life of Immortality.
> > (J 99.1–4, E 258)

What should give us pause before assuming Blake's unqualified approval of the scene, however, is that the Christ-like admonisher pointing heavenward in the oak tree on the right sets up a dialectic between the dancing celebrants in the glade and the trumpeters and spirits bearing urns and baskets up the vortex past the natural sun. He somewhat resembles the bearded figure in red casting a spell upon the waters of materialism in the *Arlington Court Picture* (B 969), but his function, like Raphael's in the *Paradise Lost* series (Figs. 29–30), seems closer to that of the veiled prophetess pointing up at the sleeping sun-charioteer and down at the shell-helmeted figure in the toils of the three Fates.[19] What may be inferred from his gesture is that he is reminding these holiday makers of the existence of a spiritual realm, but also perhaps that regular communion between the natural and the spiritual realms is important if barren nature is to be perceived and recreated in man's image as humanized and fruitful.

From this vantage the striking thing about the dancers is that they seem completely self-absorbed and oblivious to the admonisher, while their perception of the humanized landscape beyond is impeded by the heavy line of oaks behind them. As devotees of Mirth it would appear that they partake not only of her energy but of her heedlessness as well. That they are organized around a maypole, a traditional symbol of fertility as Mellor (p. 257) notes, might seem grounds for optimism. But as the gothic tower above the tree line pointing heavenward reminds us, such pagan rituals were also a form of Natural Religion going back to Druid times, as Blake, whose antiquarian interests were extensive, and who may have known John Brand the pioneer folklorist personally, would certainly have been well aware.[20] The figures in the domestic group under the oak tree have their backs to the admonisher and to the regenerative butterfly-spirit, trumpeter, and tiny flyer ascending on the right. This suggests that the aged couple on crutches may be contemplating the span-long infant in its mother's arms as an emblem of generation rather than regeneration, a surmise which might explain why the family appears to lack a father. It should also be noticed that in contrast to the situation in "London" from the *Songs of Experience* (IB 88), where a bearded elder on crutches is led by a young boy, here the dependent children cling to the old man—though Blake has characteristically made his minutest particular the most telling, showing the younger one trying to redirect his companion's attention to the prophet in the tree. One is put in mind of Frederick Tatham's report that as a child Blake was himself once chastised by his mother for declaring that he had seen "the Prophet Ezekiel under a Tree in the Fields" (BR 519).

The giant couple who dominate the landscape and are included in the prophet's gesture may be assumed to be humanized mountains, and constitute the meeting ground, as it were, between heaven and earth. The female Mountain supports one "upland Hamlet" in her lap, giving her a general resemblance to such figures as the personified Mount Athos in Fischer von Erlach's *Plan of Civil and Historical Architecture* (Fig. 118), as Paley notes, while her bearded consort, who resembles ancient Night in "Night Startled by the Lark" (Fig. 56), holds another in his hand.[21] Both gaze directly out from the picture, as if challenging the spectator's powers of spiritual discernment. The hermeneutic riddle posed by the principal Mountain, past whom the cloud-spirits are laboring upward, is that her pained expression and barren breast, to which she draws attention with her left hand, seem to be contradicted by the hamlet she sustains and the water cascading like long tresses down her side, from which the foremost river deity is drinking, both of which imply that she is a bounteous figure. Her crenellated crown suggests that Blake associated her with Cybele—referred to by Milton as "tow'red Cybele, / Mother of a hundred gods" in *Arcades* (21–22)—and with Earth as portrayed, for instance, in Hertel's 1758–60 edition of Cesare Ripa's *Iconologia* (Fig. 119). There the crown and waterfall motifs occur together, along with the garland, which Blake transposes to the male Mountain's brow, and other emblems of Earth's fruitfulness. Ripa, who makes the connection between Earth and Cybele, glosses her crown as symbolizing the inhabited parts of the earth, her bare breast as the source of all fruitfulness, and the waterfall and trees as representing the regions covered by water and forests.[22]

One way to construe Blake's modulation of Ripa's images that would make sense of this visual paradox is to see the fruitfulness of the otherwise barren Mountain as contingent on the fructifying commerce of the laboring cloud-spirits with the heavens. Though none of them is actually depicted resting on her breast, wisps of cloud mark the line of their ascent across her chest, and these are both visually and logically the more obvious source of the cataract, emblematic of rain, that flows down into the rivers. At the same time, her gesture, reinforced by her distressed expression, suggests that Blake has retained the Miltonic allusion to her barren breast as a reminder of the consequences of following the thoughtless revellers' example. So long as man is prepared to look up and mount the vortex past the guinea sun, fallen Nature will reveal her human face, "And the desert wild / Become a garden mild" (E 20). But among these revellers the triumph of Apollo as the Satanic god of reason, optimism, and Enlightenment seems to have brought in its wake the triumph of Natural Religion—a comprehensive term in Blake's usage referring to a number of traditions, including Deism, experimental science, associationist psychology, and empirical philosophy and history. Consequently, Nature's human status and her bounty are at risk, as the female Mountain's challenging gaze and gesture invite us to perceive. There is even perhaps the suggestion in the curious way she and her consort are juxtaposed, he looking back from behind her with one hand around her right shoulder as if to redirect her, that she has already begun to "Turn away" and is reluctant to "Arise" (E 18) in response to the two trumpeters. That this is the case with the unreflecting devotees of Mirth might also be inferred from the admonisher's melancholy expression. His own plight, trapped and almost invisible in the Druid oak, would appear to exemplify the fate of the spirit of prophecy under the double yoke of Reason and Natural Religion. His resemblance to Christ, therefore, far from being fortuitous, would seem completely logical.

If "A Sunshine Holiday" presents the effects of Apollo's reign on the public, conscious life of England, one would expect "The Goblin" (Fig. 59), which breaks the diurnal pattern maintained so far, to be a complementary vision of his effects upon man's inner life—of the powerful unconscious forces his tyranny releases. Certainly the Goblin himself is a nightmare figure, much closer to Blake's *Pestilence* (B 518), "Apollyon" (Fig. 88), or *The Ghost of a Flea* (B 966) than to Fuseli's Puckish slumbering *Lubber Fiend* (P 126), which is more in keeping with the convivial tone of Milton's poem:

> Then to the Spicy Nut brown Ale
> With Stories told of many a Treat
> How Fairy Mab the junkets eat
> She was pinchd & pulld she said
> And he by Friars Lantern led
> Tells how the drudging Goblin sweat
> To earn his Cream Bowl duly set
> When in one Night e'er glimpse of Morn
> His shadowy Flail had threshd the Corn
> That ten day labourers could not end
> Then crop-full out of doors he flings
> E'er the first Cock his Matin rings.

The disturbing effect of Blake's figure is only partially allayed by his descriptive note, which also provides a gloss on the activities of the figures in the foreground: "The Goblin crop full flings out of doors from his Laborious task dropping his Flail & Cream bowl, [and] yawning & stretching vanishes into the Sky, in which is seen Queen Mab Eating the Junkets. The Sports of the Fairies are seen thro the Cottage where 'She' lays in Bed 'pinchd & pulld' by Fairies as they dance on the Bed the Ceiling & the Floor & a Ghost pulls the Bed Clothes at her Feet. 'He' is seen following the Friars Lantern towards the Convent" (E 683).

The way in which the Goblin dominates the pictorial space seems to imply that he is the dominant spirit, whatever we make of his pending departure. It is also consistent with the notion that, despite the contrast between his contorted form and Apollo's classical beauty, they may be complementary figures, analogous to Urizen and Orc on *America* 8 (Fig. 83) and 10 (Fig. 84). If Apollo is an objective correlative of the diminutive Milton's faith in reason, then the Goblin is likely to be in the first place a projection of the psychological drama being enacted by the figures in the foreground. And a causal connection between the two designs would make Dunbar's suggestion that the two human protagonists are "in the throes of serious sexual discord" (p. 137) the more persuasive. "She" is humorously shown through the cottage lattice being pinched by the impish spirits of unsatisfied desire (significantly, if one thinks of the regenerative subterranean activities on the *Marriage* title page [IB 98], one is emerging from the ground), and haunted by a specter like the ghostly sentry in the fifth design for Gray's "A Long Story," his attempt to pull off the bedclothes being expressive of her virgin fears. "He," depicted wearing the hat but without the stick of Blake's mental traveler on *Night Thoughts* 419 or *Gates* 14 (E 266), has turned his back on her and follows the Friar, perhaps in search of alternative gratification, to the single-towered convent. However, as the term was applied historically to religious institutions for either sex, he may be in pursuit of higher things. Warton's note explains that *"Friar's lantern, is the Jack and lantern,* which led people in the night into marshes and waters," and Blake might have literalized Milton's metaphor to make the ironic point that such celibate ideals amount to a "Will-o-the-wisp" or "ignis fatuus," rather than a truly Christian calling.[23] That the couple are reenacting the story of the Fall as Blake depicts it in his *Paradise Lost* series could also be inferred from the presiding presence of Queen Mab. In Shakespeare's account of her in *Romeo and Juliet,* she is "the fairies' midwife" who "gallops night by night / Through lovers' brains" and makes them "dream of love" (II.iv.54 et seq.). Blake has transformed her into a chaste moon-goddess enjoying the junkets served up to her in solitude: evidently, like Eve in the Temptation scene (Figs. 35–36), she too has discovered that "stolen joys are sweet, and bread eaten in secret pleasant" (E 60).

In context, therefore, the Goblin becomes a richly suggestive figure. His manneristically distorted figure as he flings out of the barn, and his features, which as Dunbar notes "are contorted into a yawn that 'reads' more like a howl of rage" (p. 138), are most directly expressive of the emotional pain being experienced by these misguided mortals. Warner also draws attention to his "dance-like posture reminiscent of the dancing faun" that George Cumberland sketched in his personal notebook as exemplifying "enthusiastic action," which as she points out "is a concept directly related to Blake's ideas of energy."[24] But though this makes the way the Goblin echoes the attitude and explosive upward movement of the energetic Lark seem more pertinent, it is harder to see him, as Warner does (p. 169), as playing a positive role in Milton's ongoing education. For one thing, the opposition between the Lark's ascent and the Goblin's flight is implicit in the poem, and is echoed in the lines "When larks gin sing / Away we fling" quoted by Warton from "the old Song of Puck or *Robin Goodfellow*" as one of Milton's probable sources.[25] But more important, the Goblin is surely one of Blake's most memorable demonic images of energy run amuck when oppressed by reason. And we can accommodate the fact that he is vanishing by thinking of him in relation to Milton's earlier vision of Apollo, and the effect of his sage and serious doctrine on the couple here, as rapidly becoming the merest "shadow of desire" (*MHH* 5, E 34). From this vantage the iconographic logic of associating the starry sky absorbing him and the clouds across his loins with Urizen becomes apparent. A reading of his discarded flail and bowl as phallic and vaginal emblems would also fit into this pattern. Since the "drudging Goblin" in Milton and the folk tradition he draws on is essentially a bondslave, it seems likely that Blake too would have thought of him as a symbolic victim of political oppression. There seems little doubt about his capacity for violence, particularly when one compares him with Blake's portrait of the Savage Man in *The Characters in Spenser's 'Faerie Queen'* (B 879), who is equipped with both flail and spear.

Most commentary has followed Grant (III.xi–xiv) in reading the beautiful closing design in the *L'Allegro* series, "The Youthful Poet's Dream" (Fig. 60), as an auspicious vision significantly qualified by irony. And this indeed is what the spiritual events outlined so far would lead us to expect. The design focuses primarily on the lines summarizing L'Allegro's pleasure in the theatrical delights of city life, to which Blake appended one of the few notes which give any clue to his allegorical intent:

> There let Hymen oft appear
> In Saffron Robe with Taper clear
> With Mask & Antique Pageantry

Such sights as Youthful Poets dream
On Summers Eve by haunted Stream
Then lo the well trod Stage anon
If Johnsons learned Sock be on
Or Sweetest Shakespeare Fancys Child
Warble his native wood notes wild.

"The Youthful Poet sleeping on the bank by the Haunted Stream by Sun Set sees in his Dream the more bright Sun of Imagination, under the auspices of Shakespeare & Johnson, in which is Hymen at a Marriage & the Antique Pageantry attending it" (E 684). Blake's note makes explicit the distinction between natural and spiritual suns, but does not specifically identify the youthful poet with Milton himself. It is possible that his omission was deliberate and intended to increase the suggestiveness of the design, for the way the poet's reclining attitude, which echoes that of the *Barberini Fawn* (H & P 105), reiterates that of Mirth herself, but on a horizontal plane, intimates that he is under her dominion. And his pink lace-collared suit, long hair, broad-brimmed hat, and air of gay abandon give him a cavalier appearance which could be intended to suggest a generalized portrait of the artist as fun-loving court poet, *contrasting* with Milton dressed in Puritan black in the *Il Penseroso* series. Jonson, shown on the left, was not only the author of courtly entertainments such as his *Masque of Hymen*, but also the leading spirit among a tribe of poets devoted to the delights of Mirth; and the Royalist allegiances of Shakespeare are as indubitable as his proclivity for laughter. By leaving the poet's identity unspecified, Blake perhaps also wished us to see in him an allusion to Milton's Orpheus, deep in "golden slumber" (146) and dreaming of marriage to his "half-regain'd Eurydice" (150). On the other hand, he may simply have assumed that the youthful poet would be identified with Milton as the young author of *L'Allegro* and *A Mask Presented at Ludlow Castle*—or even perhaps as the "Lady of Christ College," as he was known, according to his earliest biographer, John Aubrey, on account of his "exceeding fair" complexion.[26] Crabb Robinson records that when asked

> which of the three or four portraits [of Milton] in Hollis's Memoirs is the most like—[Blake] answered 'They are all like. At different Ages. I have seen him as a youth And as an old man with a long flowing beard. He came lately as an old man.   (BR 543–44)

And to see the dreaming poet as another such manifestation of the bard would also include, more satisfactorily, the idea of poetic succession so central to *Milton*. There is a precedent for this aspect of the design in the twelfth illustration to Gray's "The Bard," where Spenser is seen instructing a "fairy Fiction" in "Truth severe," and Milton and Shakespeare are about to descend a flight of steps behind him.[27]

If, then, we read this design in direct apposition not only to "Mirth" but also to "The Sun at His Eastern Gate," which the reiteration of the squared circle motif and Blake's note both clearly invite, and see it as a further manifestation of the consequences of the youthful Milton's epiphanic vision of Apollo for his imaginative life, several particulars fall into place. For one thing, it provides an explanation for the passivity of the poet noted by Grant (III.xi), which accommodates the reading of the Goblin as the "shadow of desire" and is entirely consonant with the negative side of Blake's famous dictum that

> The reason Milton wrote in fetters when he wrote of Angles & God, and at liberty when of Devils & Hell, is because he was a true Poet and of the Devils party without knowing it.
>
> (*MHH* 6, E 35)

It also illuminates why the "more bright Sun" of Milton's imagination is dualistically divided into a celestial and an infernal region, much as is the *Marriage* title page (IB 98). A haloed Hymen in his "Saffron Robe" is seen in medial position in the upper segment— like Christ between Adam and Eve in the tenth design for *Paradise Lost* (Figs. 37–38)—officiating at what is perhaps the dreamed-of marriage of Milton himself, rather than as in the poem of the "Soft Lydian Airs" (136), to "Immortal Verse" (137), since they would seem to be accounted for by the musicians in the lower segment. If so, the fact that it is the bride rather than Hymen who holds the "Taper clear," and that all the wedding guests are distinctly angelic, may well be a humorous reminder of the predominantly restrained and pious character of much of his immortal verse. The reasons for this are suggested in the lower segment, representing the energizing infernal source of art, where all three principals are haloed. The presiding figure is (a little incongruously) holding an unblown trumpet and, according to Grant (III.xii), a censer—emblems perhaps of the conflicting ecclesiastical and apocalyptic impulses within Milton. If so, this might explain why the two flanking Lydian Airs are out of step and have not succeeded in "Untwisting all the chains that tie / The hidden soul of harmony" (143–44). The notion that Blake may also be including references to the Orpheus story is supported here by the flames engulfing the aspiring spirits, restrained like Eurydice confined in Hell. For such harmony to be achieved and the poet as Orpheus to be fully restored to his half-regained Eurydice, we may infer, these energizing spirits must ascend the stairway and unite with the angelic figures in the upper segment. In Milton's case this was impeded by the hold Apollo had over his imaginative life. Werner's proposal (p. 153) that Blake may have had in mind the microcosmic globe that Jonson used in his *Hymenaei* seems therefore highly pertinent, since with its antimasquers representing "untemp'red Humors" and "wild Affections," dominated by "Reason" astride the globe, it epitomized the same dualistic tradition.

Another way of understanding Shakespeare and Jonson's sponsorship of the imaginative sun might be to see them as representatives of Nature and Art, but conceived of as negations rather than as contraries, divided by the globe and vying for control over Milton's imaginative life. Learned Jonson, whose emblematic book and quill are matched by Milton's, seems intent on the masque-like proceedings, while Shakespeare with his panpipes gazes intently at the spectator and motions toward the enclosing Druid oaks with a gesture (also reiterated by Milton) which seems to take in the ensuing design. Both Jonson and Shakespeare, however, were "curbd by the general malady and infection from the silly Greek and Latin slaves of the Sword" (*Mil* 1, E 95), and from this point of view they may be taken as representatives of the entire rationalist tradition stretching back through the Middle Ages to Antiquity. It is perhaps therefore in protest against the effects of this tradition on Milton's imaginative life that the small fugitive beneath his feet is raising the alarm. Three nymphs, whom Grant proposes may be Milton's three "Daughters of Inspiration, his threefold artistic emanation" (III.xiii), are being carried Eurydice-like back down the river Lethe, the river of spiritual forgetfulness, toward the infernal realm where Melancholy was "Of Cerberus and blackest midnight born" (2). The ideal unity that Milton has only partially envisaged is represented by an emblematic Orpheus and Eurydice in passionate embrace on this side of the river.

"Melancholy" (Fig. 61) is integrated into the sequential narrative by the way Shakespeare seems to announce her, and the three nymphs appear more than a little alarmed at the prospect of her tutelage. But her advent also constitutes a new departure, and like "Mirth," this design too stands a little to one side of the ensuing designs, establishing the Goddess's character in contrast to her rival and in terms of the company she keeps, and introducing some of the iconographic motifs that will later reappear. Chromatically it is a beautifully variegated nocturne, the dominant blues, grays, and greens being lightened by the white robes of the subordinate figures and offset by touches of warm color in the flaming chariot and the flowers. Hayman (P 51), Burney (P 83), and Westall are among the artists who contributed portrayals of Melancholy, but Blake's leading lady again perhaps most closely resembles Romney's solitary figure (Fig. 120), though the presence of her companions makes her seem less conventionally romantic. Here again Blake's transcription provides a key to the identity of the specific figures:

> Come pensive Nun devout & pure
> Sober stedfast & demure
> All in Robe of darkest grain
> Flowing with majestic train
> Come but keep thy wonted state
> With even step & musing gait
> And looks commercing with the Skies
>
> And join with thee calm Peace & Quiet
> Spare Fast who oft with Gods doth diet
> And hears the Muses in a ring
> Ay round about Joves altar sing
> And add to these retired Leasure
> Who in trim Gardens takes his pleasure
> But first & Chiefest with thee bring
> Him who yon soars on golden Wing
> Guiding the Fiery wheeled Throne
> The Cherub Contemplation
>
> Less Philomel will deign a song
> In her sweetest saddest plight
> Smoothing the rugged Brow of Night
> While Cynthia Checks her dragon yoke
> Gently o'er the accustomd Oak.

And again Blake's note stresses the inclusiveness of his composition: "These Personifications are all brought together in this design surrounding the Principal Figure Who is Melancholy herself" (E 689).

During the eighteenth century the possibility was raised that Milton might have been indebted to Dürer's *Melancholia I* for his conception, and since Blake was fond of this print and kept it above his work table, he is likely to have made the same connection.[28] The way Melancholy's attitude of heavenly contemplation is reiterated by Milton seated in his peaceful hermitage in the last design, for instance, seems to acknowledge the traditional association of Melancholy with genius.[29] Yet many of the devices surrounding Dürer's Saturnine geometrician—her twin compasses, her scales, the hourglass and bell, and the bat bearing her inscription—tend in Blake's own iconography to be used *in malo*, as emblems of the anti-humanist and life-denying implications of the rationalist transcendentalism of the Churches.[30] The putative connection with Dürer's figure would also be compatible with the hypothesis that Blake associated Melancholy with Reason and Virtue in contrast to Mirth as Sense and Pleasure, and thought of her too therefore as a less than ideal mentor for an aspiring prophet.

Certainly the first impression she and her companions make pictorially, when set against her frolicsome rival, is not merely of quietude but of complete passivity. Blake is of course being faithful to his text in depicting her veiled and dressed in black, but the fact that he later shows Milton similarly clad suggests that he thought of her more specifically as the "Sober stedfast & demure" muse of Puritanism, to whom Milton significantly devoted over twice the number of lines he did to Mirth. Her evident devotion to the Cherub Contemplation, whose fiery-wheeled throne Hurd rightly associated with "the fiery-wheeled car in Ezekiel, x.2.seq." and *Paradise Lost*, VI.750–53, might seem more auspicious.[31] But though Blake has given his Cherub splendid eagle's wings, he has depicted him kneeling on a dais surrounded by what appears to be a single fiery wheel that, unlike that in *Ezekiel's Wheels* (B 542), has no eyes. Moreover, his Cherub extends his arms—in a gesture reiterated by Milton in the closing design (Fig. 66)—as if in acknowledgment of the wonders of the night sky which—again like Milton—he is gazing out upon. All this might well imply that from Blake's point of view Milton's melancholy muse, like Dürer's, is all too prone to single vision, and that his Cherub Contemplation is also something of a Covering Cherub.

Melancholy also appears to be a sexually divisive goddess, as Grant (I.128) suggests, for not only does she come between fair Peace and Quiet on the left and Spare Fast and Retired Leasure opposite, but in keeping with her prudish nature her gesture even seems to hint that she would have it so. Moreover, in contrast to Jest and Youthful Jollity, who had taken a lively interest in each other, albeit behind Mirth's back, here the male figures are evidently indifferent to their female counterparts. Spare Fast is shown with his arms crossed abstemiously, and like a good classical scholar his attention is fixed on the Daughters of Memory around Jove's altar—whom Blake in a letter to Hayley described as "an iron-hearted tyrant" and "the enemy of conjugal love" (E 756). Youthful (and therefore presumably affluent) Retired Leasure, facing the other way, is even more self-absorbed, and though surrounded by lilies and roses seems, with his folded arms and vacant smile, the picture of idleness rather than of innocence. That both are confirmed celibates is also implied by their location under the influence of Cynthia, seen checking her dragons yoked to the rising moon, which will appear higher in the sky in the next design (Fig. 62).

Peace and her companion Quiet, on the other hand, are at least exchanging confidences, and given Blake's reservations about the patriarchal nature of Milton and Puritanism, it may not be accidental that the most hopeful signs in the picture come from the female side. Quiet, with her hair in a bun and her hands clasped as if in prayer, still inclines toward Melancholy, but she is listening to what her companion has to say. Peace, with free-flowing locks, is in the corresponding position to Sweet Liberty led by Mirth—on the side, that is, on which the redeemed ascend in Blake's *Last Judgment* pictures. Moreover, not only does she hold an emblematic shepherd's crook like Thyrsis in the *Comus* series, she also repeats the suggestive snipping gesture he makes in the fourth Huntington design (Fig. 9), and in contrast to her more staid friend she has a flaming halo. The message we may surmise she is imparting is that peace lies not with Melancholy's devotion to purity, but with acceptance of the moment of desire.

If so, then perhaps the contorted figure of Night above them, like that of the Goblin, should be understood as expressive of the nocturnal discord induced by unsatisfied desire. She is shown sitting cross-legged on a harp or lyre, but holding her copious locks back from her ear to listen to the tiny figure of Philomel, the nightingale. Like the Lark in the *L'Allegro* series, her function too is that of a messenger, sent to smooth the rugged brow of Night with her harmonious song, and since she is depicted as a naked ascending figure, perhaps she has been dispatched by Peace. The contrast between Night's cramped, tormented figure and Philomel's liberated grace suggests that Blake may also have been thinking of the traditional association of melancholy with madness, and the belief that madness could be cured by music.[32]

These preliminary pictorial reflections on Milton's vision of Melancholy and her companions are pursued more fully in the ensuing five designs, which make up the second subnarrative of the series. Unlike Mirth, whom we meet only once, Melancholy makes a second personal appearance, leading Milton in "The Sun in His Wrath" (Fig. 64), and generally her influence is more pervasively felt than that of her rival in the *L'Allegro* series. "The Wandering Moon" (Fig. 62) makes a rather solemnly romantic first impression, but once its visual puns have been appreciated it emerges as one of the wittier designs in the sequence. Compositionally, it bears some resemblance to an engraving in Basin's *Dictionnaire des Graveurs* (Fig. 121), picturing a moon goddess pushing aside the clouds.[33] In the lines Blake transcribed, Milton's Penseroso imagines taking a nocturnal walk

> To behold the wandring Moon
> Riding near her highest Noon
> Like one that has been led astray
> Thro the heavens wide pathless way
> And oft as if her head she bowd
> Stooping thro' a fleecy Cloud
> Oft on a plat of rising ground
> I hear the far off Curfew sound
> Over some wide waterd shore
> Swinging slow with sullen roar.

Blake's note explains that "Milton in his Character of a Student at Cambridge, Sees the Moon terrified as one led astray in the midst of her path thro heaven. The distant Steeple seen across a wide water indicates the Sound of the Curfew Bell" (E 684).

The most immediate effect of this mention of water is, perhaps, to establish a sense of continuity with the final *L'Allegro* design, where Milton was last seen dreaming at sunset by a stream already in shadow, which threatened to carry off his terrified threefold emanation. Now we see him awake, very differently dressed in academic mortarboard and gown, and on the near side of a much wider stretch of water, gazing up at the distracted figure of Diana in what is evidently for him an epiphanic moment. Moreover, the fact that it occurs in the corresponding position in this half of the series to Earth's vision of the Lark, which is followed by Milton's vision of Apollo, creates the expectation of a parallel developmental pattern here. If, therefore, Apollo in "The Sun at His Eastern Gate" represents the illuminating principle in Milton's conscious

life, we may reasonably surmise that this is intended as a complementary revelation of the guiding principle that a misguided Milton
adopted in matters of the heart. What the sage and serious poet
appears, that is, to be experiencing, as he gazes up at Diana as an
older girl lost in heaven's wide pathless way, is a vision of woman
as chaste. As the youthful Puritan's ideal of womanhood, she corresponds to the likewise errant Lady in *Comus*, and there is a distinct
resemblance between her and Blake's portrayals of the Lady, particularly in her moments of distress. The fact that, in contrast to
Cynthia in the previous design, this wandering Diana is the same
size as Milton also supports the notion that she is a further manifestation of Milton's Emanation. Blake was to use the same technique
in the ninth illustration to *Paradise Regained* (Fig. 75), where Christ
awakens from his troubled dreams to a mirror-image vision of
Morning. But since Diana is clearly in considerable distress, her
actual state seems closer to that of the unredeemed Ololon as "a
Virgin of twelve years" in *Milton* (36.17, E 137), before her virginity
separates from her and flees shrieking into the abyss.

That the Wandering Moon is indeed a goddess not only fair but
chaste is also brought home by the witty double pun that Blake has
engineered: she is being both chased and chastened by the stellar
scourges to the left and right of her—variants of the one wielded by
the kingly "scourge of Heav'n" in the seventh illustration to Gray's
"The Bard"—and perhaps also needled by the pointed shafts of
light she strides across within the cloud barrier. As a vision of one
under the scourge of reason and tormented by her chastity, she
may also therefore be seen as the female counterpart of the Goblin.
Part of the fun here arises from the fact that, in the sense that Diana
is a projection of Milton's inmost psyche, he is the one who is erring
and in torment. The way that the steeple to which Blake's note
draws attention points directly up at the virgin goddess may be
intended as a reminder that chastity was an ideal espoused by the
Churches—a point already broached in "The Goblin" through the
husband's departure for the convent. But Blake is also likely to
have recalled how deeply Milton's vision of pure love in *Comus* is
interfused with Christian Neoplatonism, and from this point of
view Milton's exalted vision here leads naturally to his immersion
in Plato in the next design. The tiny red flowers, emblems of passion, in the redemptive lower-left-hand corner serve as a corrective.

In "The Spirit of Plato" (Fig. 63), which continues in the same
humorously ironic vein, aspects of Plato's thought are highlighted
so as to reveal the classical origins of many of the errors that had

clouded Milton's vision. Though nominally a nocturnal scene, it is, like "The Sun at His Eastern Gate" and "The Youthful Poet's Dream," quite brightly colored, and its modulation of the visionary orbs in those designs helps to integrate the two halves of the series formally. In *Il Penseroso* the melancholy poet at this point imagines himself retreating to a lonely tower,

> Where I may oft outwatch the Bear
> With thrice great Hermes or unsphear
> The Spirit of Plato to unfold
> What Worlds or what vast regions hold
> The Immortal Mind that has forsook
> Its Mansion in this Fleshly nook
> And of those Spirits that are found
> In Fire, Air, Flood, & Underground.

Blake's note is again essentially descriptive, except that it draws attention to the three Fates ruling Plato's world, which are not mentioned by Milton: "The Spirit of Plato unfolds his Worlds to Milton in Contemplation. The Three destinies sit on the Circles of Platos Heavens weaving the Thread of Mortal Life these Heavens are Venus Jupiter & Mars. Hermes flies before as attending on the Heaven of Jupiter. The Great Bear is seen in the Sky beneath Hermes & The Spirits of Fire, Air, Water & Earth Surround Miltons Chair" (E 685).

Plato and Milton, portrayed in the relationship of mentor to pupil, provide the focal point of the design—the still-point, one might say, around which all the subordinate figures seem to be revolving. Milton, again in black and seated like the Lady at the Magic Banquet (Figs. 11–12) on a perhaps deliberately rigid upright chair, is seen in a modulation of the traditional reflective pose of Melancholy, and is evidently finding Plato's works before him heavy going.[34] Plato, modelled on Raphael's portrait of him in *The School of Athens* (Fig. 122)—which Blake was again to draw on for his portrayal of Satan in "The First Temptation" (Fig. 68) in the *Paradise Regained* series—is clad appropriately in robes of purest white and standing on a cloud which cushions him from contact with the earth. His gesture is at once expository and admonishing, and leaves no doubt as to his spiritual priorities—priorities echoed in the poem in Milton's allusion to the "Immortal Mind" exiled to "this Fleshly nook." And it is this dualistic attitude to body and soul that Plato bequeathed to Milton and Christian tradition which again seems to be one of Blake's principal targets in his pictorial commentary, for as with the imaginative sun of "The Youthful Poet's Dream," the composition is quite sharply divided into a celestial realm dominated by the spheres and a nether realm inhabited by the elemental spirits. And though there are signs of regeneration, again as so often in Blake coming from below, there is even less actual commerce between heaven and earth than in "A Sunshine Holiday." Blake reiterated his objections to the exaltation of reason and denigration of the senses in the *Marriage* with specific reference to Plato in his annotations to Berkeley's *Siris*, the work of another philosophical idealist:

> Knowledge is not by deduction but Immediate by Perception or Sense at once Christ addresses himself to the Man not to his Reason Plato did not bring Life & Immortality to Light Jesus only did this. . . . Jesus supposes every thing to be Evident to the Child & to the Poor & Unlearned Such is the Gospel The Whole Bible is filled with Imaginations & Visions from End to End & not with Moral virtues that is the baseness of Plato & the Greeks & all Warriors The Moral Virtues are continual Accusers of Sin & promote Eternal Wars & Domineering over others.   (E 664)

In addressing themselves to man's reason, rather than like Christ in this passage to his whole being, both Plato and Milton negated half of life. Blake, it is true, regarded Plato as among the "wisest of the Ancients" (E 702), and some scholars have argued that Thomas Taylor's translations played a seminal role in his development.[35] But one of the fundamental differences between Plato's idealism and Blake's distinction between natural and spiritual man is that in Blake's redemptive scheme the body is not transcended but redeemed. As he insists, again in the annotations to *Siris*, "The Four Senses are the Four Faces of Man & the Four Rivers of the Water of Life" (E 663).

Blake's imaginative point of departure for the heavenly spheres, to which the sage is pointing, appears to have been the myth of Er in the *Republic*, though the three vignettes within the spheres invoke further aspects of Platonic thought. The *Republic* closes with an account of the hereafter as reported by Er, a fallen warrior recruited as a messenger by the gods. This includes visions of the Last Judgment, of the cosmos revolving around the spindle of Necessity, and of the souls drawing lots to determine the order in which they will choose the pattern of their lives. The passage describing the epicyclic movements of the spheres anticipates the fuller accounts in the *Timaeus*, but since it is also echoed in Milton's

Arcades (62 et seq.), it may be the one that is making Milton's head spin here:

> The staff turned as a whole in a circle with the same movement, but within the whole as it revolved the seven inner circles revolved gently in the opposite direction to the whole.... And the spindle turned on the knees of Necessity, and up above on each of the rims of the circles a Siren stood, borne around in its revolution and uttering one sound, one note, and from all the eight there was the concord of a single harmony. And there were three others who sat around about at equal intervals, each one on her throne, the Fates, daughters of Necessity, clad in white vestments with filleted heads, Lachesis and Clotho, and Atropos, who sang in unison with the music of the Sirens, Lachesis singing the things that were, Clotho the things that are, and Atropos the things that are to be. And Clotho with the touch of her right hand helped to turn the outer circumference of the spindle, pausing from time to time. Atropos with her left hand in like manner helped to turn the inner circles, and Lachesis alternately with either hand lent a hand to each.[36]

Though Blake's rendering is essentially emblematic, he does nonetheless attempt to evoke the epicyclic movement of Plato's cosmos. The way Venus and the figure behind Jupiter lean to the right suggests that these spheres are rotating clockwise, which is also the direction in which the factious aerial spirits around Milton's head are flying. The three Fates, who appear to be bracing themselves against this movement, are weaving the thread of mortal life in the opposite direction, and this inclines the eye to see the vaulted sky, which seems to be revolving like a maelstrom, as turning counterclockwise too.

The vignettes within the three spheres are evidently intended to invoke wider aspects of Plato's philosophy. It is probably no accident, in the light of Blake's strictures against "Plato & the Greeks & all Warriors," that Mars and his demonic bat-winged familiar are shown in the exalted and central position traditionally reserved for Jupiter. His elevation, one might say, is the result of Plato's promotion of reason at the expense of sense, represented respectively in the spheres of Jupiter and Venus, which impinge on one another but do not interpenetrate. A rather melancholy Jupiter wields twin compasses as well as his customary scepter, which together associate him with the hegemony of reason as exemplified in Plato's Demiurge. Blake's distrust of this remote inhuman geometrician is again reflected in one of his *Laocoön* inscriptions: "The

Gods of Greece & Egypt were Mathematical Diagrams See Plato's Works" (E 274). Venus's leafy left hand suggests that she has been reduced by the author of the *Symposium*—who seems to have her most directly on his mind in his pedagogic colloquy with Milton—from a potential liberator to a mere nature goddess, like Blake's fallen Vala. And the way she touches her breast with her right hand, like the female Mountain earlier, seems to intimate that she too may in consequence be barren. Classical contempt for women would seem to be implied in the vignette below her on the right, where a female in the grieving attitude of Eve in the Judgment scene from the *Paradise Lost* series (Figs. 37–38) is being banished by her husband. One is tempted therefore to suspect that the couple opposite bound back to back may represent an indictment of Plato's praise of homosexual love. Admittedly their gender is hard to make out, but they are of the same height and the unusual motif of the twin serpents makes identification of them with Adam and Eve quite unsatisfactory.[37] All this makes highly probable Grant's proposal that "the unmentioned man behind [Jupiter] is Vulcan futilely employed (like Sisyphus) with the Shield of Achilles" (I.128). He is the artist as copyist in Plato's system, reduced to "the sordid drudgery of facsimile representations" (E 541) glorifying war.

Milton's "thrice great Hermes" is Hermes Trismegistus, the legendary Egyptian philosopher to whom various mystical, occult, and alchemical writings, including the Emerald Table, were attributed.[38] Blake, however, depicts him as the messenger of the Olympian gods with his traditional winged helmet and caduceus—partly, one suspects, for the convenience of these familiar iconographic attributes. He shows him facing Jupiter and pointing down at Milton, evidently reporting back that they have made a convert. Nevertheless, Blake is unlikely in the context to have misunderstood Milton's reference to the Hermetic philosopher, for he himself mentions him in connection with Plato in *The Song of Los*, where "To Trismegistus, Palamabron gave an abstract Law: / To Pythagoras Socrates & Plato" (*SoL* 3.18, E 67). And he alludes to him again in *Jerusalem* (91.34, E 251), in relation to the Specter's attempts to dehumanize the imagination by drawing Los into admiration of the stellar universe. Since the relative size of Hermes here and his position immediately above Ursa Major seem to imply that he is also an officiating spirit, perhaps we may infer in the three revolving spheres a numerological allusion to his identity as Trismegistus.

The thrust of Blake's attack on Platonic tradition in this design therefore might again be summarized in the dictum, "Attempting to be more than Man We become less" (*FZ* 35.21, E 403). All such rarified systems as Plato and Hermes are promulgating leave man at the mercy of the three Fates in the sense that they diminish his awareness of his own Divine Humanity, and in seeking to repress his elemental spirits, the sources of his creativity, bind him, paradoxically, all the more firmly to the fallen material world. This is the point of the abortive regenerative cycle depicted in the lower foreground. A maternal earth spirit is nurturing the upward aspirations of her root- or worm-encircled offspring next to a second, still-slumbering infant on the left; meanwhile, a larger enrooted female is beginning to blossom under Milton's chair, perhaps in recognition of the first flowering of his poetic genius in poems like *L'Allegro* and *Il Penseroso*, and a third figure is reclining on a leaf as he "struggles into Life" (E 261). But the female fire spirit and her companion engulfed in flames, who are attempting a resurrection from the corpses of a warrior, a long-bearded sage, and a third, possibly bald and bearded, elder (reminiscent of the effigies in *Grave* 7), are making little headway against the demonic figure wielding a scourge in either hand above them. The aerial spirits also seem, like Milton, possessed by "Cloudy Doubts & Reasoning Cares" (E 261), though they come closest to a harmonious relationship with the three spheres. And the abortive final outcome of this incipient resurrection to unity among the elements is portrayed in the vignette representing Water, where a figure plunging headlong like the damned in Blake's *Last Judgment* pictures is caught once more in the sea of time and space by a webbed nymph with a large net—perhaps suggested, given Blake's quick associative mind, by the net in which Vulcan ensnared Mars and Venus.

"The Sun in His Wrath" (Fig. 64) interrupts the pattern of nocturnal scenes maintained so far, and thus corresponds in this respect to "The Goblin" in the *L'Allegro* series. But it is integrated into the sequence formally by the prominent solar orb which Apollo sits astride, much as the Fates had straddled Plato's heavens. Unlike her rival, Melancholy appears in person here a second time to take charge of Milton's spiritual progress, Blake taking his cue from the lines in which the melancholy poet desires that

> when the Sun begins to fling
> His flaring Beams me Goddess bring
> To arched walks of twilight Groves
> And Shadows brown that Sylvan loves.

His again essentially descriptive note also identifies the subordinate figures: "Milton led by Melancholy into the Groves away from
the Suns flaring Beams who is seen in the Heavens throwing his
darts & flames of fire. The Spirits of the Trees on each side are seen
under the domination of Insects raised by the Suns heat" (E 685).

The hermeneutic difficulties of this design center on the status
of Apollo, since whether or not he is again as in "The Sun at His
Eastern Gate" a malevolent figure and one to be shunned deter-
mines how we regard Melancholy's influence at this point, and this
in turn affects how we read Milton's final state of illumination in
his mossy cell. Grant considers these "pestilential 'Apollonian'
arrows (near allied with the arrows of Satan in *Job* 6)," and observes
that Milton "is now of equal stature and a fit companion for haloed
Melancholy" (I.131), whom he regards as a redemptress. And it
would certainly make psychological sense to see this design in
close apposition thematically to the previous one, with Milton
under the sway of melancholy after his Apollonian exertions under
Plato, which here have finally become too much for him. Behrendt
also interprets the moment as a further stage in Milton's progress
toward a supposed higher Innocence, and sees Melancholy as leading him away from "the natural sun of the physical, material world"
(p. 137). There are, however, memorable instances of redemptive
archers in Blake's iconography, such as Hyperion in the illustrations to Gray's "Progress of Poesy," or Christ routing the rebel
angels in the *Paradise Lost* designs (Figs. 31–32). Moreover, when
Blake's un-Miltonic emphasis on the Sun's *wrath* in his title and on
his *heat* (which is only implicit in Milton) in the note are considered,
the thought is bound to suggest itself that, on an analogy with "The
Little Black Boy" from the *Songs* (E 9), where "heat" is used
redemptively in a binary relationship to "light," these arrows may
be "Arrows of desire" (*Mil* 1, E 95) from which Milton is seeking
refuge under chaste Melancholy's aegis.

A number of particulars tend to support this hypothesis, which
Werner (p. 161) also posits, and which is certainly consonant with
Blake's habit of changing the significance of his iconographic
counters to keep us on our toes. Most obviously, the Wrathful Sun
does not have the scepter and spiked crown of the Great Sun in the
L'Allegro series, nor is he confined within his solar orb. Furthermore, his arrows do not emanate directly from the natural sun, and
the way Apollo gazes heavenward, and reaches above his head to
direct them downward, seems to imply that they come from some
higher source. His position astride the sun could therefore betoken

a *subordination* of the natural sun to the power of love, analogous conceptually to its subordination to the brighter sun of imagination in "The Youthful Poet's Dream," or possibly an emblematic marriage of the sun's light and heat. Certainly the Wrathful Sun is one of the more energetic Orc-like figures in the series, his flaming hair rising to a peak like that of the apocalyptic Lark, and the fact that his expression is not actually wrathful may also be propitious, if we remember little Lyca's unfounded fears of the beasts (E 20–22). There is also his remarkable openness about his loins, which is quite conspicuous by virtue of his elevated position, but is rendered even more startling by force of the contrast with the sedate and haloed Melancholy, with her "sable stole of Cypress Lawn / Over her decent shoulders drawn" (35–36). A further argument for seeing a redemptively impassioned Wrathful Sun, counterpointed against Milton's nocturnal reasonings earlier, might be that this would form an aesthetically satisfying parallel with the more obviously irate Goblin's challenge to Enlightenment in the *L'Allegro* series.

All this might seem hard to reconcile with the fact that the Dryads appear to be imprisoned in their grove of "monumental Oak" (135). Both the principal figure with acorn-tipped staff on the left and his serpent-bound (and possibly female) counterpart opposite are clearly somewhat disconsolate. Unlike the revellers in "A Sunshine Holiday," however, they and their dependents are all either looking or aspiring upward or, as in the case of the obeisant spirit on the left, acknowledging the Sun. And if we take propitiously the "domination" of the two insects flying towards him with extended wings, and regard them as emblems not of generation, as does Rose (p. 64), but of regeneration, like the human insects on the *Jerusalem* title page (IB 281), "raised," as Blake's note says, by the sun's heat, it becomes possible to see the general air of expectancy among all the tree spirits as a sign that they regard him as a liberating force. In context, such a reminder of the holiness of generation as the source and image of regeneration would certainly be timely, after Milton's Hermetic nocturnal speculations. He has not relinquished Plato's works, we notice, which will reappear at his side in the final illustration. And it is because of Plato's hold over his imagination that, unlike the innocent Little Black Boy, he has not "learn'd the heat to bear" (*SI*, E 9) and elects to follow pious Melancholy, whose halo associates her with the Wandering Moon, farther into the dark wood of error.

The consequences of this decision and the effects of Melancholy's influence on Milton's subliminal and imaginative life are explored in the ensuing design, "Milton's Mysterious Dream" (Fig. 65), in which Blake amplifies the following lines:

> There in close Covert by some Brook
> Where no profaner Eye may look
> With such concert as they keep
> Entice the dewy featherd Sleep
> And let some strange mysterious Dream
> Wave on his Wings in airy stream
> Of liveliest Portraiture displayd
> On my Sleeping eyelids laid
> And as I wake sweet Music breathe
> Above, about, or underneath:
> Sent by some Spirit to Mortals good
> Or the unseen Genius of the Wood.

Some of the particulars are elucidated further in Blake's note: "Milton sleeping on a Bank. Sleep descending with a Strange Mysterious Dream upon his Wings of Scrolls & Nets & Webs unfolded by Spirits in the Air & in the Brook. Around Milton are Six Spirits of Fairies hovering on the air with Instruments of Music" (E 685). Dominated by the magnificent haloed figure of Sleep, who seems to be at once swooping down and hovering over Milton with his splendid wings extended, this is one of the most exuberantly beautiful—and witty—designs in the entire series. The rainbow sphere surrounding the dream vision on Sleep's upper wing invokes the sphere of the imaginative sun in "The Youthful Poet's Dream," tacitly inviting us to consider whether Milton has fared better under Melancholy than under Mirth. Milton is again dressed in black and is covering his loins, but the six musicians, very plausibly identified by Grant (I.132) with his Sixfold Emanation, who surround him like the Angels of the Divine Presence watching over the sleeping Milton's couch in *Milton* (15.1-7, E 109), are evidently working to restore his psychic harmony. Moreover, the figures struggling out of the waters of Lethe—where Plato's philosophy had plunged them—onto the nether wing of Sleep would seem to indicate that they are being effective.

It is, however, important to consider the dynamic interaction of the particulars more closely, before concluding from the seven eyes in the wings of Sleep that an eighth apocalyptic age is on the point of dawning. One iconographic detail that has not been remarked on is that the cloud trail marking the line of Sleep's descent seems to imply that he hails from a sweet golden clime well above the rainbow sphere, much as the arrows above the wrathful Sun implied that they were emanating from a source higher than the natural sun. The surmise is supported by the fact that the vortex that Sleep initiates—outlined by scrolls and wisps of cloud—ascends his lower wing, past the floating elder and his head-clutching companions, to a point above the rainbow. This suggests that the rainbow cannot be taken as an unqualified symbol of hope, and tends to undermine Werner's identification of the second bearded elder, holding what appears to be a lamb, at the center of its five concentric spheres with the "Divine Humanity" (p. 163). The point about the larger Urizenic figure's gesture, surely, is that he is *refusing* the invitation of the little scroll-bearer he is gazing at to ascend the vortex, which could also account for the distress of his companions. From this vantage it becomes easier to see that Blake has engineered an amusing contrast between the redemptive couple embracing in the scroll and their female attendant on Sleep's nether wing, and this burdensome trio whose combined weight, as Grant (I.133) points out, has cracked his upper wing. The former clearly allude to Milton's passionate responsiveness to the sensory world, reflected in the idyllic scenes in Eden and in his impulsive marriage to Mary Powell; the latter represent the rational and theological censor that prevented him in his visionary flight from uniting Heaven and Hell. And if we suppose the leading elder to be indeed Urizen, it seems likely that his companions would be two of the three remaining Zoas closing off their "all flexible senses" (*Ur* 3.38, E 71), Los to his right covering his ears as on *Urizen* 7 (IB 189) and Luvah opposite shielding his head and burying his nose. "Watry Tharmas" (*FZ* 11.18, E 306), associated with instinct and the tongue, is perhaps implicitly present in the regenerative activities—and the tongue-like scrolls—of Sleep.

In context, therefore, the rainbow sphere becomes a complexly suggestive image, and the presiding deity at its center less—or in a Blakean sense more—mysterious. It is a highly unusual motif which, as Mellor (p. 283) points out, calls to mind the concentric spheres surrounding the Father directing the expulsion of Adam and Eve on the first panel of Ghiberti's *Porta del Paradiso*—a resemblance which is all the more striking in engraved versions (Fig. 86). A primary association of the rainbow here is obviously with Beulah, land of dreams, midway between the world of Generation in which Milton is sleeping and the higher realm of Eternity to which the vortex leads. Blake, as we have seen, envisaged Beulah as a realm of tranquil restoration, but also recognized that it could become a trap, an escape from the mental wars of Eden if remained in overlong. He may therefore have extended the rainbow to form a confining sphere, in order to suggest that this is precisely what is happening to Milton's three contracting Zoas as a result of his unwillingness to face up to the Sun's heat. And when we recall that Blake specifically mentions "webs" in his note as well as the "nets" that Sleep is raising, we can see that the rays emanating through the spheres to the trees also suggest a spider's web. Blake was not overly fond of these predators, though he was prepared to give them their due at the Apocalypse, and he uses them *in malo* both in the *Marriage* (E 91) and in the marginal iconography of *Europe* (IB 170). The bearded replica of Urizen at the center of the rainbow is fairly certainly therefore a parodic image of Milton's Father, in the spirit of Blake's epigram to God:

> If you have formd a Circle to go into
> Go into it yourself & see how you would do.
>
> (E 516)

He is at once a remote and self-sufficient figure—an unmoved First Mover presiding over the "same dull round" (*NNR*, E 2) of an infinitely receding universe—and a victim trapped like Urizen in "The Human Abstract" (IB 89) and *Urizen* 28 (IB 210) in the net of his own system. Even more sinister implications follow if we assume that, on analogy with the similarly isolated Queen Mab in "The Goblin," he is not simply stroking his beard but eating, for his position at the center of the spider's web leads logically to the inference that his sustenance is the sacrificial lamb, the central symbol of Milton's doctrine of atonement. In any event, it seems clear that Milton's mysterious dream is far from being "free of the Urizenic fetters of convention," as Behrendt (p. 136) supposes.

These iconographic progressions within the *Il Penseroso* series are clearly important determinants in how we read "Milton in His Old Age" (Fig. 66), which presents Blake's summary assessment of the spiritual state his prophetic precursor finally attained, and has been interpreted *in bono* and *in malo* by critics in about equal measure. In the lines Blake transcribed, the melancholy poet wishes for a tranquil retirement:

> And may at last my weary Age
> Find out the peaceful Hermitage

> The hairy Gown and mossy Cell
> Where I may sit & rightly spell
> Of every Star that heavn doth shew
> And every Herb that sips the dew
> Till old Experience do attain
> To somewhat like Prophetic strain.

And Blake notes how "Milton in his Old Age sitting in his Mossy Cell Contemplating the Constellations, surrounded by the Spirits of the Herbs & Flowers, bursts forth into a rapturous Prophetic Strain" (E 685). Conceptually his frontal presentation of Milton seated gazing heavenward is probably indebted to the contemporary portrayals of an inspired Milton by, for instance, Fuseli (Fig. 114) and Flaxman (P 69). What is at issue hermeneutically is whether the particulars warrant our taking at face value Blake's use of the term "rapturous," which would tend to support Grant's optimistic reading (I.134), or whether they seem to intimate that Milton attains only to something like prophetic strain, more in line with a literal reading of the poem, as Rose (p. 66) and Kiralis (p. 54) have concluded.

Since many of the particulars can be interpreted either way, the solution seems to depend crucially on whether or not, as Grant (I.134) proposes, the constellations are seen as humanizing. The basic problem with this proposition is that in the iconography of the pictorial planispheres Blake has drawn on, which as David Warrall has shown also influenced the imagery of *America, Europe,* and *The Four Zoas,* the constellations are invariably depicted fighting.[39] A representative map of the northern celestial hemisphere from the 1781 edition of John Flamsteed's *Atlas Coelestis* (Figs. 123–24), for instance, shows Leo attacking Cancer, Gemini brawling, and Orion poised against the charging Taurus in the upper segment. Other prominent scenes of carnage depicted are Bootes with his hounds attacking Ursa Major, Hercules clubbing Cerberus, Ophiuchus wrestling with Serpens, and Perseus decapitating Medusa. In Blake's modulation of this tradition, three of the constellations are actively belligerent: Castor and Pollux, who were sometimes identified with Romulus and Remus, display a true Roman devotion to the sword, while giant Orion, herald of winter storms, who on *Night Thoughts* 502 appears in his more benign aspect as friend of mariners, seems equally determined to quell the charge of that ancient symbol of potency, Taurus.[40] The two remaining constellations appear to be victims of oppression rather than aggression. Cancer is saddled with a backward-looking scholar, and a shepherd, though equipped with a hat and crook like Thyrsis in the *Comus* series, seems to be piously restraining Aries' energetic charge. It is true that in a beautiful passage in *Milton* the constellations are redemptively envisaged as apocalyptic laborers:

> Thou seest the Constellations in the deep & wondrous Night
> They rise in order and continue their immortal courses
> Upon the mountains & in vales with harp & heavenly song
> With flute & clarion; with cups & measures filld with foaming
> wine.
> Glittring the streams reflect the Vision of beatitude,
> And the calm Ocean joys beneath & smooths his awful waves!
> These are the Sons of Los, & these the Labourers of the Vintage.
> (*Mil* 25.66–26.1, E 123)

But the contrast between this happy scene of music-making and the factious constellations above Milton could not be more stark. It might be argued that their martial arts are emblematic of mental rather than corporeal war, but their spectrous appearance, which links them with the violent Goblin rather than the jubilant stars on *Job* 14 (Fig. 112), makes this seem less probable. Moreover, since the factious figures in the pictorial planispheres are all named after the gods and heroes of classical mythology, Blake is likely to have regarded this as a telling vindication of his mistrust of the "Warlike State[s]" (E 270) of Greece and Rome.

The conclusion seems hard to avoid that, as a parting tribute to Milton's prophetic achievement, this too is a vision heavily qualified by irony. The composition is more severely divided into a celestial and terrestrial realm, and there is less intercourse between them than in any of the earlier designs. Milton is depicted alone and root-bound within his mossy hermit's cell, sustained by a "dim religious light" (160), and evidently still dependent on his Plato or his Bible. His arms are extended in a gesture which is closer to the Cherub Contemplation's than to Melancholy's in the opening *Il Penseroso* design, and suggests expansion of his cranial cave. But his countenance is expressive of gloom rather than of rapture, and he is lost in contemplation of the starry universe of Newton's Pantocrator. The mother below suckling her two children, the couple in their bower, and the Easter-lily spirits rising on the side of the redeemed are all unequivocal signs that, as in "The Lark," Mother Earth is awake and an apocalyptic spring is imminent. The lovers who like Milton himself in the previous design are being serenaded in their rose-bower by two pipers and a lyrist, recall Adam and Eve within their bower of bliss and are an undoubted tribute to Milton's genuine knowledge of the human heart. Indeed, in the way their robes fan out to form a lily, they might seem the embodiment of the state in which "the Lilly white, shall in Love delight" (E 25) and relinquish chastity, if one does not pause to ask why they should be so fully clad. But as with the abortive regenerative movement in "The Spirit of Plato," the flight of their aspiring companion spirits seems destined to terminate like that of the seven yearning females, trapped in the breast-like twin hillocks of Mother Earth, divided from their spectrous warring male counterparts in the heavens above. The spirit of true prophecy had been alive in Milton, but he had not seen the restoration of Jerusalem to England's green and pleasant land. This was ultimately because like most of his contemporaries, and like his own sanguine and melancholy poets in *L'Allegro* and *Il Penseroso*, he had failed to see that Mirth and Melancholy, reason and energy, Heaven and Hell are not negations of one another but contraries necessary to fully human existence. This failure, combined with the righteousness of Puritanism, had resulted not in Albion's renewal but in the devastation of the Civil War.

Notes

1 See Paulson, *Emblem and Expression*, p. 81, and Winifred H. Friedman, *Boydell's Shakespeare Gallery* (New York: Garland, 1976), pls. 38, 8, and 34.

2 See Wilson, ed., *Johnson: Prose and Poetry*, p. 832.

3 See Pointon, *Milton and English Art*, pp. 56–57, 64–70, 77–79, 97, and 106–11.

4 Rose, "Blake's Illustrations for *Paradise Lost*, *L'Allegro* and *Il Penseroso*: A Thematic Reading," *Hartford Studies in Literature*, 2 (1970), 61.

5 Anne K. Mellor, *Blake's Human Form Divine* (Berkeley: Univ. of California Press, 1974), pp. 270–85.

6 Grant, "Blake's Designs for *L'Allegro* and *Il Penseroso*, Part I: A Survey of the Designs," *Blake Newsletter*, 16 (1971), 17–34; see "Part II: The Meaning of Mirth and Her Companions," *Blake Newsletter*, 19 (1971–72), 190–202; and "From Fable to Human Vision" in Erdman and Grant, eds., *Blake's Visionary Forms Dramatic*, pp. xi–xiv. Subsequent page references in the text to these three articles are preceded by the appropriate Roman numeral. See also Behrendt, "Bright Pilgrimage: William Blake's Designs for *L'Allegro* and *Il Penseroso*," *Milton Studies*, 8 (1975), 123–47.

7   Kiralis, "Blake's Criticism of Milton's *L'Allegro* and *Il Penseroso* and of Its Author," in *Milton Reconsidered*, ed. Franson (Salzburg: Univ. of Salzburg Press, 1976), pp. 46–77.

8   Werner, *Blake's Vision of the Poetry of Milton*, p. 146.

9   The sheets with Blake's handwritten notes, transcriptions, and numbering are reproduced in Van Sinderen, *Blake: The Mystic Genius*.

10 See Pointon, pp. 56f.

11 See H. J. Todd, ed., *Poetical Works of John Milton* (London: J. Johnson, 1801), V.76.

12 See Bindman, *The Complete Graphic Works of William Blake*, pl. 601b.

13 Grant's identification of the subordinate figures (II.195) has been generally accepted, though Dunbar, *William Blake's Illustrations to the Poetry of Milton*, p. 124, identifies the "dragon-winged" figure below Laughter holding both his sides perhaps more convincingly as a "Quip," and the ass-eared contortionist immediately above her as a "Crank."

14 See Tayler, *Blake's Illustrations to the Poems of Gray*, no. 4 in the series to the "Ode."

15 Todd, V.82.

16 Alternatively, the veil of cloud she lifts can be seen as the string, as it were, to the inverted bow formed by her outstretched arms.

17 Hagstrum, *William Blake, Poet and Painter*, p. 46 and pls. XXVII A & B.

18 Rossetti, "Annotated Lists of Blake's Paintings, Drawings, and Engravings" in Gilchrist, *Life of William Blake*, ed. W. Graham Robertson (London, 1907), p. 243, item 205.

19 See Grant, "The Arlington Court Picture, Part II," *Blake Newsletter*, 13 (1970), 21.

20 See John Adlard, *The Sports of Cruelty* (London: Cecil & Amelia Woolf, 1972), pp. 13–15.

21 Paley, *Continuing City* (Oxford: Clarendon Press, 1983), p. 158 n.5.

22 See Edward A. Maser, ed., *Baroque and Rococo Pictorial Imagery: The 1758–60 Hertel Edition of Ripa's 'Iconologia'* (New York: Dover, 1971), p. 9. Blake had earlier depicted a female with her hair forming a waterfall on *America* 16 (IB 155).

23 Todd, V.94.

24 Warner, *Blake and the Language of Art*, p. 53 and Fig. 87.

25 Todd, V.96.

26 See Hughes, ed., *John Milton: Complete Poems and Major Prose*, p. 1021.

27 Tayler, p. 104, identifies these figures as "Truth severe" and "fairy Fiction." But since prophetic succession is the theme of the Bard's song at this point, and Gray mentions Shakespeare and Milton in his note and alludes to a voice bearing "Gales from blooming Eden," the resemblance of the figures to the standard images of the two poets cannot be coincidental.

28 Todd, V.108.

29 See Rudolf and Margot Wittkower, *Born Under Saturn* (1963; New York: Norton, 1969), pp. 102f.

30 For the connection between Melancholy, Saturn, and geometry, see Panofsky, *The Life and Art of Albrecht Dürer*, pp. 161–67.

31 Todd, V.115.

32 Wittkower, pp. 98f., 106, 109.

33 Pierre Basin, *Dictionnaire des Graveurs*, 2nd ed. (Paris, 1809), II.23.

34 See Wittkower, Figs. 1, 20–21, and Panofsky, pp. 160f. and Figs. 209–21.

35 See Harper, *The Neoplatonism of William Blake* (Chapel Hill: Univ. of North Carolina Press, 1961); and Raine, *Blake and Tradition*.

36 Plato, *Republic*, X.617 in *The Collected Dialogues of Plato*, ed. E. Hamilton and H. Cairns (Princeton: Princeton Univ. Press, 1961), p. 841.

37 Thomas Taylor's 1804 edition of the *Symposium* included a translation of Alcibiades' speech telling of his failure to seduce Socrates, which had been omitted from Sydenham's bowdlerized 1767 translation. See Louis Crompton, *Byron and Greek Love: Homophobia in 19th Century England* (Berkeley: Univ. of California Press, 1985), pp. 89–91.

38 Damon, *A Blake Dictionary*, pp. 182–83.

39 David Warrall, "Blake and the Night Sky, I: The 'Immortal Tent,'" *Bulletin of Research in the Humanities*, 84 (1981), 273–95. See Paul Miner, "Blake and the Night Sky, III: Visionary Astronomy," in the same issue, pp. 305–36; and Basil Brown, *Astronomical Atlases, Maps and Charts: A Historical and General Guide* (London: Search, 1932). There is an extensive collection of pictorial planispheres in the library of the Royal Astronomical Society in London.

40 See Richard Hinckley Allen, *Star Names: Their Lore and Meaning* (1899; New York: Dover, 1963), pp. 225, 305–6, 378–79.

"Embraces are Cominglings":
The *Paradise Regained* Designs

Blake's designs for *Paradise Regained* in the Fitzwilliam Museum are among his most attractive Milton illustrations, yet they have also proved the most elusive and difficult to come to terms with. Three of them are watermarked M & J Lay 1816, and on stylistic grounds too, according to Butlin (I.401), they would seem to emanate from about the same period as the *L'Allegro and Il Penseroso* designs commissioned by Butts. If so, and if Butts ordered them as well to round out his Milton collection, it is curious that they were still in Blake's possession in 1825 when he sold them to Linnell (see BR 589, 604, 607)—so that the possibility remains open that they were done as late as this. Though less intense in color than the *L'Allegro and Il Penseroso* series, they have not faded and appear to be much as they were in 1863 when Gilchrist described them as "of great beauty, refined in execution, especially tender and pure in colour and pervading feeling."[1] Another striking feature of the originals that reproduction obscures is the disparity between Blake's often monumental figure drawing, which seems entirely appropriate to the portrayal of Christ's "deeds / Above Heroic" (I.15–16), and the intimate size of the designs (approx. 17 x 13 cm.)—an effect one is also particularly conscious of in *The Book of Urizen* and *The Song of Los*. The frequency with which echoes of the great Renaissance masters recur is no doubt partly attributable to the comparatively uninspired quality of most commercial illustrations of the poem, a tradition in which, according to Wittreich, five of Blake's subjects do not occur at all.[2] But it also raises delicate questions of interpretation with corresponding persistence. Are we to take for instance the resemblance of Satan in "The Second Temptation" (Fig. 73) to Christ as Judge in Michelangelo's Sistine *Last Judgment* (Fig. 125) as merely formal and perhaps unconscious, or is it, too, charged with subversive iconographic implications?

Undoubtedly, the hallmark of the *Paradise Regained* designs, especially when compared to the delightful exuberance of the *L'Allegro and Il Penseroso* series, is their Raphaelesque simplicity, which on one level is clearly in appreciative response to a four-

Book epic that, as Hayley noticed, seeks to emulate the "sweetness and simplicity of the Evangelists."[3] This and the absence of any obtrusive symbolism or deviance from Milton's text would seem to support the prevailing view, first advanced by Wittreich, that they are executed "not in a spirit of contention but in one of collaboration and celebration" and pay tribute to the "introspective, psychological character" of Milton's epic.[4] And certainly there can be little doubt that Blake found much to admire in a poem which rejected worldly for spiritual values, corporeal for mental warfare, and classical learning for biblical wisdom. But Wittreich's further contention that by attributing man's redemption to Christ's victory over Satan in the wilderness, rather than to his death on the cross, Milton "retracted the terrifying theology of atonement" (p. 144) in *Paradise Lost*, and that Blake's aim is to illuminate the radically Christocentric nature of his precursor's final vision, is more problematic, for reasons already touched on. Leaving aside the issue of whether Milton's choice of subject was governed by theological or aesthetic considerations, it is true that the question of the poem's orthodoxy was raised during the eighteenth century.[5] But the Christocentric hypothesis proceeds on the undeclared assumption that Christ meant the same thing to both poets, and ignores the fact that Blake's age was fundamentally more secular than Milton's. However much Blake may have disagreed with mockers like Voltaire and deists like Tom Paine, their demystified accounts of Christianity are points of departure for his thought. And as early as the *Night Thoughts* series he was using Christ as a symbolic figure with considerable freedom, as Grant has demonstrated.[6] In Milton's age only the radical sectarian fringe approached the uncompromisingly anthropocentric view Blake expresses in the *Marriage* and *Jerusalem* that

> the Worship of God, is honouring his gifts
> In other men: & loving the greatest men best, each according
> To his Genius: which is the Holy Ghost in Man; there is no other
> God, than that God Who is the intellectual fountain of
> Humanity.[7]
>
> (*J* 91.7–10, E 251; see *MHH* 22, E 43)

As in Milton, Christ does not in this series resume the role of emissary from a higher realm that he plays in the *Paradise Lost* designs, but is himself the subject of a human psychodrama—a difference broadly analogous to that between Blake's Jesus as the Imagination in his epics and his more human sketches of him in the

Marriage and the *Everlasting Gospel*. But there is good reason for suspecting that Blake would have been satisfied neither with Milton's account of how Paradise might be regained, nor with his vision of the "perfect man" (I.166), in which he may well have detected an element of idealized self-projection on Milton's part. As we have seen in the *Comus* and *L'Allegro and Il Penseroso* illustrations, he tended to associate his mentor's work quite closely with his personality. Moreover, in view of Milton's acknowledgment of the Book of Job as the model for his brief epic, and his repeated allusions to Job as a type of Christ (I.147, 369, 425; III.64, 67, 95), it would naturally have occurred to Blake to present Milton's Christ as a mental traveler engaged in the same kind of radical self-scrutiny and reappraisal of traditional values as were his protagonists in *Milton* and the *Job* designs. When set against the inspired figure of the Gospels, or the passionate iconoclast he had envisaged in the *Marriage*, the austere Socratic rationalist of *Paradise Regained* seems humanly deficient. His successive victories over Satan are all essentially triumphs of negation, prompting Elizabeth M. Pope to remark on the sense of "the distortion of Christ's character" we feel at "this union of so much reticence with so much denunciation."[8] And his absolute obedience to a rationalist heavenly Father bears the mark of Blake's "Antichrist Creeping Jesus" (*EG* 55, E 519). From this vantage both the general parallel with Milton's struggle to subdue his Urizenic Specter in *Milton*, and the specific resemblance of the bearded Satan in the *Paradise Regained* series to the bearded parody of the Father losing control of the Mosaic tablets on *Milton* 18 (IB 234) would appear to be significant.

As regards Christ's imperviousness to the charms of women that Belial (II.153) proposes he be tried with, an issue in which Milton seems to be compensating for his own weakness over Mary Powell, Edward Le Comte may well be right that he "avoids as a direct subject sensual temptation" simply in deference to biblical authority.[9] But the contrast between Eve's susceptibility to and Christ's control over sensual appetite encapsulated in the immortal lines

> Alas how simple, to these Cates compar'd,
> Was the crude Apple that diverted Eve!
>
> (II.348–49)

is central nonetheless to Milton's entire redemptive scheme. And since this is one of the issues over which Blake has Milton return to confront his emanation Ololon in his epic, one would not expect him to pass up an opportunity to call Milton's ideal of a celibate Christ into question here. A striking feature of the series in this context, considering the predominantly masculine tenor of the poem, is how frequently female figures are introduced (Figs. 67, 70, 72, 75, 78). There is also a suggestive parallel between Mary advancing with extended arms to welcome Jesus in the last design (Fig. 78), and the cruciform Ololon advancing to meet her spouse in the final plate of *Milton* (Fig. 126), which tends to support Dunbar's suspicion (p. 186) that Mary may function as Christ's Emanation. A further, more startling particular that seems to intimate a pattern of spousal symbolism, analogous to those encountered in *Milton* and the *Comus* illustrations, is the decorously formalized phallic configuration formed by the aureole against which Christ is silhouetted on the pinnacle (Fig. 76). This might well appear coincidental, were it not for the fact that a more iconic modulation of the same configuration reappears between the wings of the upper cherubim in the Heavenly Banquet scene that follows (Fig. 77). These particulars have been uniformly ignored or overlooked, doubtless for the same reasons that, until Leo Steinberg's recent study, allusions to the sexuality of Christ in traditional iconography have been ignored, and one wonders whether they had anything to do with Butts's putative rejection of the series.[10]

Both the rationalism and the celibacy of Christ in *Paradise Regained* exemplify the Puritan principle of liberty through repression and restraint which is at the heart of Milton's personality and thought. To Blake this principle constituted a negation of the essential contraries of life, as inimical to his own most deeply held beliefs as the poem's theology, which matches Eve's failings against Christ's triumphs in a legalistic "triple equation" and celebrates his having "aveng'd / Supplanted Adam" (IV.606–7).[11] And perhaps the most fascinating feature of the series is the way he seems to be drawing on the commonplaces of Christian iconography to wrest a more humane and life-affirming counterstatement from Milton's austere and ultimately theocentric poem, and to proclaim that

> The Vision of Christ that thou dost see
> Is my Visions Greatest Enemy.
>
> (*EG*, E 524)

Repeatedly throughout the sequence we seem to encounter displaced allusions to Christ's Passion as represented in pictorial tradition. Among the more prominent are Christ's splayed palms at his Baptism (Fig. 67); Mary seated and grieving like the traditional

Mater Dolorosa (Fig. 70); the darkened sun of Satan's halo in the Storm scene and the echo of the Entombment in the prostrate body of Christ (Fig. 74); the portrayal of Morning with the long flowing locks of Mary Magdalen (Fig. 75); Christ in cruciform position on the pinnacle, invoking both the Crucifixion and the Resurrection (Fig. 76); and the bread and wine of the Last Supper in the Heavenly Banquet scene (Fig. 77). Admittedly there is a risk of overinterpretation here, but the frequency of such allusions seems more than can be ascribed to mere coincidence of subject matter. Moreover, if Blake was indeed concerned to present an answering vision of how Paradise might be regained, it would have been natural for him as a graphic artist to turn not only to the poem but also to the great Passion sequences of Baldung, Dürer, Wierix, and others who had given visual expression to the traditional view of man's redemption.[12]

The series opens with "The Baptism of Christ" (Fig. 67), a design which in its compositional simplicity and lack of affectation resembles such early Italian masters as Mocetto (Fig. 127) and sets the tone for the sequence as a whole.[13] The disposition of the two principal figures, John the Baptist facing inward on the left, Christ confronting the viewer in the center, remains essentially the same as in Blake's earlier tempera of the *Baptism* (Fig. 128), though Christ no longer clasps his hands in prayer but displays his palms in a gesture curiously reminiscent of traditional portrayals of the *Man of Sorrows* (Fig. 129). Dunbar (p. 167) also notes the influence of Michelangelo in the contours of Christ's figure, narrower in the torso than the loins. The muscular foreshortened figure of Satan too with his familiar is distinctly Michelangelesque—his extended arms recalling the Creator congregating the waters on the Sistine ceiling, but seen from behind like the figure at nine o'clock in his *Last Judgment*.[14]

In Milton, as Barbara K. Lewalski observes, "the Baptism is presented as Christ's formal call to enter upon the public exercise of his office."[15] But the interaction of the figures in Blake's inaugural design suggests that it may function rather differently—as a brief pictorial summary of the main theme of the sequence, again analogous to the prose prefaces of *Milton* and *Jerusalem*. This begins to become apparent when one notices that what makes Blake's treatment of St. John seem so distinctive in relation to tradition, as represented here by Mocetto, is that he has emphasized his prophetic as much as his baptismal and prodromic roles. Clad in "raiment of camel's hair" (Matthew 3.4; Mark 1.6), his arms and gaze raised ecstatically toward the Spirit—a symbol for both poets of divine illumination—he is evidently a man inspired, one of a company of visionaries in Blake's pictorial repertory which includes Jacob (B 532), Ezekiel (B 542), Job (B 538), and John of Patmos (B 579). There is of course an epiphanic dimension to the Baptism both in the Gospel accounts and in Milton, where the "Father's voice / From Heav'n pronounc'd him his beloved Son" (I.31–32)—suggested here by the bolts of lightning. But Blake did not believe in the divinity of the historical Jesus in quite the literal sense that Milton did, as is clear from his reply to Crabb Robinson: "'[Christ] is the only God'—but then he added—'And so am I and so are you'" (BR 540). And when we recall that Blake opened his own prophetic career by identifying himself with "The Voice of one crying in the Wilderness" (*AllR* 1, E 2), it requires only a slight imaginative shift of focus to see in St. John here a spiritual portrait of Blake himself, presenting his vision of a more truly human Christ than Milton's.

If we pursue this hypothesis in relation to the way the other figures are presented, the internal dynamics of the design should emerge more clearly. Assessing Milton's convictions in relation to the doctrine of *kenosis*, Lewalski (pp. 133–63) concludes that he did believe the incarnate Christ to have been "emptied" of all knowledge of his own divinity, and to have been subject to temptation and pain like other men. But he also undoubtedly believed that Christ remained sinless; indeed, his whole schema for redemption rests on that assumption, and in *Paradise Regained* he emphasizes that he "was baptiz'd / Not thence to be more pure, but to receive / The testimony of Heaven" (I.76–78). Blake by contrast, again prompted by Crabb Robinson, exclaimed, "Is there any purity in Gods eyes? No! 'He chargeth his angels with folly'" (BR 540). Moreover, both in *Jerusalem* (63.28, E 214) and *A Vision of the Last Judgment* he associates baptism with the casting off of error:

> [Christ] is the Bread & the Wine he is the Water of Life accordingly on Each Side of the opening Heaven appears an Apostle that on the Right Represents Baptism that on the Left Represents the Lords Supper All Life consists of these Two Throwing off Error & Knaves from our company continually & recieving Truth or Wise Men into our Company Continually.   (E 561)

From this vantage it can be surmised that in pouring "laving" (I.280) waters over Jesus from what Werner (p. 181) glosses as a shofar, the ram's horn used to announce the anointing of a new

king over Israel, Blake's prophetic Baptist is proclaiming a vision of
a Christ cleansed of the rationalist errors of Milton and the Churches,
and unself-consciously displaying his (save for a loincloth) "Naked
Human form divine" (E 522). Both Wittreich (p. 136) and Dunbar
(p. 166) suspect that, unlike Milton, Blake would have regarded
Satan as an aspect of Christ himself, his Specter or Selfhood.[16] And
if we consider the startled gesture of the woman to the right of
Christ (her attitude as she raises her arm to ward off Satan closely
resembles that of Goltzius's *Andromeda*), the clear pictorial implication surely is that he and the serpent have just swooped up out of
Jesus.[17] This would also accommodate Christ's gesture, which is
almost identical to that with which he displays his stigmatized
palms in *Christ Appearing to the Apostles After the Resurrection* (Fig.
130). By drawing attention to Christ's palms, Blake seems to be
deliberately invoking the iconographic context this gesture nor-
mally appears in, so as to coax us into reflecting on the difference
between his vision of a living Redeemer and more orthodox portrayals, such as that after Mantegna (Fig. 129), of Christ as victim of
atonement and sacrifice for sin.[18]

If we have followed Blake's thought correctly so far, it is unlikely that the Jordan represents the waters of materialism as in
Milton. Indeed, what the tributary beneath Christ's feet suggests is
that it is from this vision of the living Christ, purified of doctrinal
errors—not, as in the iconographic tradition represented by Hans
Collaert's *The Fountain of Life* (Fig. 131), from Christ's wounds—
that the waters of life proceed.[19] They flow out from the picture as if
to include the spectator in the Divine Family of man surrounding
Jesus, suggested by the bearded elder and the women and children
of different ages. A passage in *Jerusalem* provides a further gloss on
this aspect of the design, and helps us see the difference between
Milton's and Blake's more democratic and human Christ:

> He who would see the Divinity must see him in his Children
> One first, in friendship & love; then a Divine Family, & in the
>   midst
> Jesus will appear.
>
> (J 91.18–20, E 251)

The remainder of the sequence may be envisaged as essentially an
amplification of this opening vision of the true Christ, in which
Blake takes Milton's protagonist on a purgatorial voyage of self-
discovery.

During the Middle Ages, "The First Temptation" (Fig. 68), which in this sense begins Blake's narrative, was related to Adam's gluttony in the triple equation, and more widely to his fleshly concupiscence. But Pope (p. 64) and Lewalski (p. 178) agree that Milton, like many Protestant exegetes, also thought of it as a temptation to doubt God's Providence. And in the broad sense that it exemplified the triumph of spiritual over material values, Blake would have been in substantial accord with Milton and Christian tradition. The episode was fairly popular both among commercial illustrators of the poem and in biblically inspired art.[20] But as Dunbar (p. 171) points out, Blake appears in fact to have modeled his spiritual antagonists on the figures of Plato and Aristotle in Raphael's *The School of Athens* (Fig. 122), a work he had also turned to in "The Spirit of Plato" (Fig. 63) as we have seen. Christ on the left points heavenward (like Plato) and to his lips, intimating to Satan that "Man lives not by bread only" (I.349). But unlike Raphael's sage he is haloed, lightly bearded, and faces inward, intimating that like the figures on the opening plates of *Milton* (IB 217) and *Jerusalem* (IB 280) he is "Into himself descend[ing]" (II.111). The way his stance and gesture are echoed by Satan, who faces outward, suggests that as in the first and third designs to *Paradise Lost* they are mirror images of one another, though with the added implication here that Christ is confronting his own alter ego. Evidently, moreover, he is on the point of entering the pyramid-shaped Druid oak grove, which in outline approximates the contours of the boulder pointed to by Satan, perhaps to establish both as his preserve. Since, therefore, Christ is as yet "untried" (I.177), a further implication of his gesture may well be that he is still paying lip service to traditional pieties, much as Job gives charity to a beggar on *Job* 5, according to Damon, "because it is the correct thing to do."[21]

Satan's heavy beard, though common in traditional engravings of the First Temptation, is usually taken as a sign that here too, as in *Milton*, "Satan is Urizen" (*Mil* 10.1, E 104), and his formidable bulk implies that Milton's Christ will have no easy task in subduing his rationalist specter. Moreover, Blake has invested in his Adversary most of the features adapted from Raphael's philosophers, which if not an accident of formal composition may indicate that he also represents an aggregate of classical culture—also rejected by Milton later in the poem, though primarily on theological grounds.[22] Equally suggestive is the air of uncertainty about Satan—his slight stoop and "curious eye" (I.319)—which reflect Blake's responsiveness to Christ's question, "Why dost thou suggest to me distrust" (I.355). It implies that, again as in *Milton*, he thought of Satan as the "idiot Questioner . . . whose Science is Despair" (*Mil* 41.12–15, E 412) and whom the redeemed Milton finally casts off. These various associations come together and are extended in a passage which specifically alludes to the Stones into Bread temptation in *Jerusalem*, where

> the Spectre like a hoar frost & a Mildew rose over Albion
> Saying, I am God O Sons of Men! I am your Rational Power!
> Am I not Bacon & Newton & Locke who teach Humility to Man!
> Who teach Doubt & Experiment & my two Wings Voltaire:
>   Rousseau.
> Where is that Friend of Sinners! that Rebel against my Laws!
> Who teaches Belief to the Nations, & an unknown Eternal Life
> Come hither into the Desert & turn these stones to bread.
> Vain foolish Man! wilt thou believe without Experiment?
> And build a World of Phantasy upon my Great Abyss!
>
> (*J* 54.15–23, E 203)

In the two subsequent biblical temptations (Figs. 73, 76), Blake portrays Satan successively more hunched and less fully clad, suggesting both the consolidation and exposure of error within Christ—essentially a more subtle and dynamic alternative to the traditional iconographic device for exposing Satan used by Lucas van Leyden (Fig. 132), Martin de Vos (Fig. 133), and others of giving him bat wings, horns, hoof, or tail.[23]

The next three designs, "Andrew and Simon Peter Searching for Christ" (Fig. 69), "Mary at Her Distaff Watched Over by Two Angels" (Fig. 70), and "Satan in Council" (Fig. 71), depict scenes which in *Paradise Regained* occur early in Book II and play a subordinate role in Jesus' meditative combat. According to Wittreich, only the second of these was chosen by commercial illustrators of the poem. What makes one suspect that their function in the series is more central and symbolic is the recurrence of what may be described as a heart-shaped configuration, linking them structurally in a sort of triptych. In the first design it is suggested by the outer contours of the hovering female angels attending the two disciples and introduced without Miltonic authority. In the second it is perhaps more distinctly conveyed by the upward movement of the two male cherubim, also not mentioned by Milton, and by the curve of their wings, the palms behind, and the tip of Mary's hut. In "Satan in Council" it reappears, but inverted, the apex of the heart being suggested by the bent knee of the devil holding a barbed spear or arrow on the right. The heart as a motif is of course a commonplace of devotional iconography, and was deployed with considerable inventiveness by such artists as Wierix or in emblem books such as Hawkins's *The Devout Hart*.[24] Often, as in the elder Cranach's *Four Saints Adoring Christ Crucified on the Sacred Heart* (Fig. 134), it is specifically associated with Mary's suffering, providing an inverse precedent for Blake's deployment of it in "Mary at Her Distaff" (Fig. 70). Evidence that Blake knew and made use of the tradition elsewhere is provided by his watercolor of *The Great Red Dragon and the Woman Clothed with the Sun* (Fig. 135), where the Woman has beautiful heart-shaped wings which, with her hair fanning out between them, recall the flaming hearts of Catholic tradition. In the context of *Paradise Regained*, the motif might well have been suggested to him by Christ's earlier observation to Satan that "henceforth the Oracles are ceast . . . at Delphos," and that

> God hath now sent his living Oracle
> Into the World to teach his final will,
> And sends his spirit of Truth henceforth to dwell
> In Pious Hearts, an inward Oracle.

> (I.456–63)

Since the motif's recurrence is clearly deliberate, and since these are the only designs in which Christ himself does not appear and they occur immediately after his initial confrontation with Satan, it seems reasonable to propose that they represent allegorical explorations of psychological states within his heart. They may, that is, amplify the consequences of taking Milton's satanically Urizenic, heavily platonized form of Christianity to heart. The common denominator in the poem linking the disciples' fears lest the Messiah not return, Mary's concern for his welfare, and Satan's uncertainty as to how to proceed is doubt. And the golden string that arguably gives narrative coherence to the three designs is as follows. The rationalist religion to which Christ pays lip service leads in "Andrew and Simon Peter" to doubt at all levels, but particularly to sexual doubts; this in turn leads to repression and the exaltation of "Virgin purity" (*Comus* 427) as an ideal; and the inevitable result is the inverted sexuality of violence represented by Satan and his cohorts mustering to war. Blake's intuitive understanding of these causal connections is given especially memorable expression in *Jerusalem*, where the warriors cry out "I am drunk with unsatiated love / I must rush again to War: for the Virgin has frownd & refusd" (*J* 68.62–63, E 222).

In *Paradise Regained* Andrew and his younger brother Peter speak in chorus, and the "fears" and "hopes" (I.52–58) they express summarize the collective doubts of Jesus' disciples in the Gospels concerning his Messianic identity. And it was perhaps the parallel with Christ's own uncertainties that first suggested to Blake the idea of using them as projections of his psyche. Visual continuity with the previous design is maintained by their medial position, again like Christ and Satan facing in opposite directions. Peter facing inward on the left is depicted in the traditional manner in a yellow gown and with short hair and trim beard.[25] And if Blake has allegorized them as Fear and Hope, Andrew with longer hair and dressed in mauve looks arguably more fearful, while Peter, who looks up and (in terms of the unfolding sequence) toward the future, could therefore be construed as Hope. Their different hair lengths also give them a marked resemblance to Rintrah and Palamabron, Blake's two "witnesses," as they are portrayed on *Milton* 10 (IB 226), which perhaps provides a further clue to their function in the series. Werner makes the plausible suggestion that the two guardian angels flanking them serve "as reminders of Divine Providence, to which the disciples decide finally to surrender their cares" (p. 187). But this does not explain why they should be female angels, surely no accident since Mary's guardians in the next design are both distinctly male. Also remarkable is the way they seem to shy away from the disciples—the *noli me tangere* gesture of Peter's guardian in relation to his left hand is particularly clear. It would appear therefore that this may be yet another variant on the theme of man's fall into division and that the brothers are having trouble with their Emanations. Distrust between the sexes is also perhaps suggested by the contrast between the angels' spiked or "thorny" halos—somewhat resembling that of Satan in "The Second Temptation" (Fig. 73)—and the more globular nimbuses in which Andrew and Peter seem almost imprisoned. Peter's evident interest in Andrew's Emanation and Andrew's undecided gesture may be intended to hint at psychic confusion within Christ of the same order that we encounter in *Milton* in the Bard's Song. A more harmonious norm is perhaps suggested by the twin palms flanking "Jericho / The City of Palms" (II.20–21), since as Piloo Nanavutty points out in another context, they were considered emblems of marital concord because they were thought to grow and fructify in pairs.[26] They reappear in the next design behind Mary's hut and again in the final illustration, this time bearing fruit. But the color of the sky behind the city indicates that the sun has just set, as it is seen setting on *Job* 1, intimating that Christ's long night of the soul has just begun, and as in the *Comus* (Figs. 17–18) and *Job* series it will not rise again until the closing illustration.

In "Mary at Her Distaff Watched Over by Two Angels" (Fig. 70), Mary's figure robed in white, the angle at which she sits, the way she looks up and even her halo—which like that of Morning later on (Fig. 75) is colored blue—are all remarkably close to those of Michelangelo's Madonna in his *Lamentation of the Virgin Beneath the Cross* (Fig. 110). Echoes of this work were also encountered in "Michael Foretells the Crucifixion" (Figs. 39–40, 81), it will be recalled, so that we may here be faced with a comparatively rare instance of a specific source.[27] Though simple, Blake's design is iconographically among the most suggestive in the series, the more so since elsewhere he used Mary, as he used the Crucifixion, in both fallen and redemptive contexts. As icons worshipped by the Churches,

> A Vegetated Christ & a Virgin Eve, are the Hermaphroditic
> Blasphemy, by his Maternal Birth he is that Evil-One
> And his Maternal Humanity must be put off Eternally
> Lest the Sexual Generation swallow up Regeneration.
>
> (J 90.34–37, E 250)

But earlier in *Jerusalem* Mary is presented as a free spirit, who finds herself "with Child by the Holy Ghost" (J 61.27, E 211) because like her son she "acted from impulse: not from rules" (*MHH* 23, E 43). She challenges the Law which would condemn her as "a Harlot & an Adulteress," demanding "Doth he Forgive Pollution only on conditions of Purity / That debt is not Forgiven!" And she becomes both an advocate for, and in her reconciliation with Joseph an example of, "Forgiveness & Pity & Compassion!" (J 61 et seq., E 211).

In the present context Mary's distaff and the resemblance of her hut to the stable in the *Nativity Ode* series—prompted no doubt initially by Mary's meditation on the Annunciation and the circumstances of Christ's birth (II.66 et seq.)—might seem to support Dunbar's conjecture that she is being presented *in malo* as "spinner of Christ's mortal body" (p. 174). The difficulty is that in the last design (Fig. 78) she is clearly not "put off Eternally" but rather reunited with her son. Therefore, if the heart configuration does indeed have the psychological significance we have suggested, the idea that she might represent Christ's Emanation would seem more plausible. One thing that supports this with a simplicity that is often characteristic of Blake's art is that, by comparison with Michelangelo's *Lamentation,* for instance, Mary and Christ are clearly of an age. But the resemblance of Mary's distracted gesture and forlorn appearance to those of Jerusalem, Albion's exiled Emanation on *Jerusalem* 92 (Fig. 136), is also striking. And about the same period, Blake again used the same basic formula in his third illustration to the *Divine Comedy* to depict Dante's emanation Beatrice, ensconced with spinning wheel and distaff in an arbor of conspicuously fruitless vines—like those struggling up the front of Mary's hut.[28] This recurrent gesture of despair is essentially a more forceful modulation of that by which the Lady reveals her virgin fears in *Comus* 2 (Figs. 5–6). It is true that distaffs frequently have sinister connotations in Blake's iconography, but spinning apparatus and sewing baskets are also frequently present in traditional Annunciation scenes.[29] So here too he may simply have intended it as an emblem of Mary's spinster status, and it is important to notice that on her second appearance, in the last design, it is no longer there.

From this vantage it seems reasonable to propose that Mary be understood here as a vision of Milton's ideal of woman as chaste enshrined in the heart of Christ—a reading which from another point of view would imply a rather different cause for her distress than Milton had in mind. She leans against a stone altar (also absent in the last design), in token perhaps of her bondage to the law of conventional morality, while her niche-like hut invokes the centuries of patriarchal worship of virginity that have held her captive and which, though no friend of Catholic Mariolatry, the sage and serious Milton had succumbed to. The two angels are not mentioned in Milton, but perhaps we can infer from the looks of disapproval on their faces—the one on the left seems positively inquisitorial—that they are intended to represent the masculine distrust of the feminine within Christ's heart, the obverse side as it were of the Emanations' feminine coyness in the previous design. Perhaps too Blake made their halos obscure the fruit on the twin palms revealed in the final illustration, to suggest that they are also Covering Cherubim, and the hut, therefore, as in the *Nativity Ode* designs, an ark. If so, then Mary's typological association with the Ark of the Covenant in which the deity resides would appear to have been displaced, in order to suggest that *she* as Christ's anima or Emanation represents a divine element within *him*.[30] The tradition Bryant outlines of arks—sometimes emblematically associated with the moon—as places of refuge and rebirth also seems pertinent in view of the parallel between Mary and Ololon, who descends "as a

Moony Ark" (*Mil* 42.7, E 143), and Mary's final emergence from her hut.[31] And if we take her blue halo as a lunar emblem, then in terms of Christ's inner quest we may envisage him as descending from Beulah here to "Ulro, Seat of Satan" (*Mil* 27.45, E 125) in the next design.

"Satan in Council" (Fig. 71), so much more violent and factious than either of Milton's infernal council scenes (I.44 et seq.; II.121 et seq.), seems to fall into place as a vision amplifying the ultimate consequences of the process of doubt that Satan set in motion in "The First Temptation." When in *Paradise Regained* Christ responds to Satan with "Why dost thou then suggest to me distrust" (I.355), the clear implication is that he refuses to doubt God's Providence. But here Satan's exalted position, as he sits with his staff of authority on a three-tiered throne within the inverted heart configuration, is a modulation of his stance in the opening *Paradise Lost* design (Figs. 19–20). This suggests that what we are witnessing in Blake's more secular and psychologically penetrating account is indeed the temporary triumph of the reasoning Specter over Christ, as a direct result of his distrust and implicit rejection of his Emanation. Satan's resemblance surrounded by his flaming minions to "Fire" in the *Gates of Paradise* (E 262) is also pertinent, and Blake's "Keys" to his four emblematic Elements (or fallen Zoas) contending within natural man provides a suggestive gloss—particularly to such minutiae as the horn-like tips of Satan's wings and his ambivalent and scaly loins:

> Blind in Fire with shield & spear
> Two Horn'd Reasoning Cloven Fiction
> In doubt which is Self contradiction
> A dark Hermaphrodite We stood
> Rational Truth Root of Evil & Good.
>
> (*GP* 12–16, E 268)

The way Satan's followers fall apart into two main factions on either side of his throne is also consistent with the notion that Christ's fall into division has now reached its nadir. It is tempting therefore to identify the four leading devils with the four fallen Zoas as they are described in a familiar passage in *Milton*:

> These are the Gods of the Kingdoms of the Earth: in contrarious
> And cruel opposition: Element against Element, opposed in War
> Not Mental, as the Wars of Eternity, but a Corporeal Strife.
>
> (*Mil* 31.23–25, E 130)

At all events, their gestures and expressions suggest a complex and emotional interchange between them, recalling that between Andrew, Peter, and their Emanations earlier. On analogy with the patriarchal opening design to *Paradise Lost* (Figs. 19–20), moreover, one suspects that the entire assembly (including the scaly figure with long hair) may be male, and therefore to Blake hermaphroditic. The moment in Christ's introspective voyage is thus comparable to that presented in *Job* 4, where a triumphant Satan is seen smiting the repressed Job with boils. From the spectator's point of view it is literally a revelation of Satan as he really is, whereas Christ himself only gradually strips away the "rotten rags" (*Mil* 41.4, E 142) of his innocent-seeming pastoral disguise, and does not perceive him as the naked epitome of error until the pinnacle design (Fig. 76).

There has been considerable debate among Miltonists as to precisely how the Banquet and Storm scenes in *Paradise Regained* are related to the three Gospel temptations, which during the Middle Ages were glossed as temptations of the World, the Flesh, and the Devil, and which form the core of the triple equation in Milton:

> His weakness shall o'ercome Satanic strength
> And all the world, and mass of sinful flesh.[32]

(I.161–62)

Blake, however, having used the First Temptation to inaugurate Christ's descent into self-doubt, and with other plans in mind for the Third Temptation, seems to have resolved the problem to his own artistic advantage by making his Banquet Temptation (Fig. 72) represent the Flesh, condensing Milton's panoramic vision of the World into "The Second Temptation" (Fig. 73) and using "Christ's Troubled Dream" (Fig. 74) as an emblem of "Satanic strength." This slight displacement is doubly felicitous because, while highlighting matters over which Blake up to a point agreed with his precursor, it also clusters the core of the system of virtues and vices that had bedevilled Milton and the Churches at the exact center of the sequence. And it allows Blake to suggest that Christ's successive rejections of them, though laudable, are nonetheless all triumphs of negation, by leaving him space to present four contrasting scenes (Figs. 75–78) of affirmation and renewal.

In "Christ Refusing the Banquet Offered by Satan" (Fig. 72) Christ is now deep in the wood of error toward which he was seen advancing in the second design, and he is shown turning away from Satan's enticements in an attitude quite closely modeled on that of Michelangelo's Adam fleeing before Michael on the Sistine ceiling (Fig. 137). Blake has remained true to his text in the general sense that this too is a Banquet of Sense, but it is clearly more overtly sexual than Milton's, with overtones of Roman or more contemporary orgies among the rich and powerful, and places no emphasis on culinary delights. A more fundamental difference is that Satan, the power responsible for such excess, is evidently a parodic image of Milton's Father, hovering with arms outstretched in the traditional position of dominion. His dualistically bifurcated beard (both here and in his subsequent appearances), and the large cog wheel against which he is silhouetted, also point to the causal connection Blake perceived between oppressive rationalism and lust. The crown in his left hand above Christ's halo makes a Republican point of which Milton would doubtless have approved, but it also perhaps serves as a reminder that the divine right of kings was still being upheld by Burke and others in the name of Milton's God.

As Satan's succubi, the three temptresses are evidently pagan counterparts of the Great Whore—as depicted, for instance, in Blake's 1809 watercolor (B 584), where she wears a pompom-fringed garment similar to that of the leading figure, or in "The Harlot and the Giant" from the Dante series, where the martial and reptilian associations of such scaly bodices are particularly clear.[33] Moreover, they are introduced at the same approximate point in the sequence as the Whore in Revelation. As Dunbar (p. 177) points out, however, they are grouped like the three Graces of antiquity, which partly accounts for the predominantly classical mood of the whole scene, and the curve of their floating bodies is beautifully expressive of their insidious allure. As a threefold sexual emblem of love perverted in a fallen world, the two naked Graces perhaps represent woman as coy or courtly mistress, while the central figure, whose invitation is more blatant—significantly in terms of Blake's directional symbolism, she points downward—represents woman as camp whore. Together with the two amorous revelers at the table, they may represent all empirical philosophies that would confine man to what he can perceive with his five senses—a numerological interpretation which could also account for the two five-branched candelabra.

It is hard to know in this context how much to make of Christ's resemblance to Michelangelo's Adam, though it seems unlikely that the allusion was unconscious on Blake's part. It may be no more than an acknowledgment of Milton's portrayal of Jesus as the Second Adam. But it would certainly be consistent with the iconographic progressions we have so far traced to suggest that this represents a turning point in Christ's spiritual development. Having descended into the Ulro state of doubt and self-division represented by "Satan in Council," here he begins his ascent through Generation, like all of us, as Adamic natural man. The six guardian spirits in the background doubtless function like the seven Angels of the Divine Presence who watch over Milton's sleeping humanity in *Milton*. In the *Paradise Lost* designs we saw them organized around the fully integrated Christ in the act of casting out the rebel angels (Figs. 31–32).

"The Second Temptation" (Fig. 73) is the third design in the series devoted to a subject not previously chosen by illustrators of the poem. In sacred art it is generally subordinated to representations of the First Temptation, where it is often introduced in the background, sometimes together with the temptation on the Temple.[34] It is, however, the main subject in Sadeler's engraving after Martin de Vos (Fig. 133), a precedent with which Blake may have been familiar. As in "The First Temptation," he again juxtaposes Christ and Satan in a way that underlines the basic contrast between spiritual values and the values of Caesar which he shared with Milton and Christian tradition. But the fact that Milton had devoted over a third of *Paradise Regained* to the Kingdoms/Power/Glory sequence brings to mind Blake's observation to Crabb Robinson that like Dante he had been too much "a mere politician busied about this world."[35] As Michael Fixler observes, "Puritanism had dwelt on no aspect" of "Christ's threefold nature" as Prophet, Priest, and King "more intensely than his Kingship."[36] Blake's compression of all this into one design seems intended to redress the balance.

Christ is shown in left profile, haloed and standing very upright on the rock, and has apparently overcome much of his self-doubt. By contrast, Satan, who though still wearing a loincloth is now more fully exposed, looks the epitome of uncertainty as he hangs precariously over the abyss. His raised left arm makes him appear almost to cower before Christ, as though he already anticipates his eventual casting off. They are less obviously mirror images of one another than in "The First Temptation," but a bond between them is again established by the similarity of their gestures. Whereas Satan points heavenward with his left forefinger and to the Kingdoms with his right, Christ reverses this, thus appearing to correct his antagonist's priorities. The Kingdoms are emblematically represented within an oval configuration, clearly a version of the "Mundane Egg" (*Mil* 19.15, E 112) depicted diagrammatically on *Milton* 36 (IB 252), and perhaps also of the triple tiara of the Pope on *Europe* 11 (IB 169), imbued with deceptive sanctity by the surrounding aureole. The individual scenes within it may well represent Parthia, Rome, and Athens as Dunbar (p. 179) suggests, but they also seem to function as synecdoche for all idolatry, worldly hierarchies, and tyranny. Here too it is difficult to assess whether Satan's resemblance, suggested earlier, to Michelangelo's Christ as Judge (Fig. 125) is iconographically significant, particularly since Blake has reversed the position of Satan's arms and redirected his gaze upward. But the case could be argued that he is making the best of an opportunity to discriminate between the false spectrous traditional image of Christ and his own, by identifying one of the most celebrated representations of him as Accuser, Judge, and Executioner with the "God of This World" (E 269). Certainly Satan's spiked halo, which on a literal level echoes Christ's reflection that a "Crown / Golden in show, is but a wreath of thorns" (II.459–60), is suggestive and could be a badge of this identity which Blake's protagonist is here relinquishing.

In the last five designs, which are all based on episodes in Book IV and bring the series to a more climactic resolution than *Paradise Regained*, the apocalyptic overtones and allusions to Christ's Passion seem to increase in frequency. "Christ's Troubled Dream" (Fig. 74) represents the darkest hour in his spiritual quest, immediately preceding the dawn of "Morning Chasing Away the Phantoms" (Fig. 75)—contrasting scenes in the poem which one eighteenth-century critic described as "exquisitely sublime and beautiful."[37] Conceptually the design is indebted to the iconography of the *Temptation of St. Anthony* (Fig. 138), a tradition which Roland M. Frye has suggested might also have inspired the original episode in *Paradise Regained*.[38] Satan is again as in the Banquet scene in the ascendant, but he has relinquished guile for a show of his "Satanic strength" (I.161), and classical hedonism has been replaced by Hebraic wrath. Indeed, with his bat wings, goggle-eyes, and unruly beard he is here more obviously than in the Banquet scene a parodic image of Jehovah, in the spirit of Blake's Nobodaddy, "Father of Jealousy" (E 471), or the presiding figure in *The House of Death* (B 397–99). As the substance of what the sleeping Christ is dreaming, this is again a revelation of the false image of the Father worshipped by Milton and the Churches. As such, the moment is closely analogous to Job's nightmare vision in *Job* 11 (Fig. 91), where he perceives the cloven hoof of his Mosaic God.

It is also thematically related to the Fall in the *Paradise Lost* series (Figs. 35–36), where Adam is intimidated by the thunderings of the Father against following his impulses, and like Albion in *Jerusalem* turns his back on his Emanation Eve. Christ, however, seems unimpressed by the "Fierce rain with lightning mixt, water with fire / In ruin reconcil'd" (IV.412–13) that Satan pours on him—recalling the plagues in the Old Testament and the "hail and fire mingled with blood" of Revelation 8.7. Though hard-pressed by the five serpents and two lions, emblems again perhaps of Urizen's "Seven deadly Sins of the soul" (E 72), his slightly rigid but impassive figure is turned away from them, and in the next design he awakens to a vision of Woman in the guise of Morning.

Additional resonances suggest themselves when the design is contemplated in relation to the traditional iconography of the suffering Christ. While it is true that one recumbent figure is bound to resemble another more or less, in an age still conscious of the Bible as the great code of art, an image of *Christ* reclining at this angle would surely have evoked the broken body of Christ in innumerable pious Deposition, *Pietà*, and Entombment scenes. The image, which Kenneth Clark has traced back to classical reliefs commemorating fallen heroes, constitutes one of the great *pathos* formulae of Western art, and· Blake used it twice in his *Job* series to depict Job's sufferings.[39] Though the formula was modified in a wide variety of ways, Christ's body was perhaps most commonly depicted limp as in Raphael's *Bearing of the Body* or Michelangelo's *Pietà*.[40] But it was also common, as in Marcantonio's *Lamentation of the Virgin* (Fig. 139) after Raphael, or in several engravings by the Wierix brothers, to present a fairly rigid Christ, as if to convey that *rigor mortis* had set in.[41] The possibility that Blake did indeed intend us to recall these traditional images of Christ's "Dead Corpse" (*GP* 7, E 259) is strengthened by the fact that almost immediately he portrays him on the pinnacle (Fig. 76) in the position of the resurrected Christ. The logic behind the iconography in the Nightmare scene is clarified if we again turn to the *Not Gottes* tradition represented by Dürer's woodcut of the *Trinity* (Fig. 93), in which the dead Christ and the Father, often with arms (like Satan's) extended to support the cross, appear together in the same design. From Blake's point of view, of course, as we have seen in relation to the *Paradise Lost* designs, the whole doctrine of atonement it encapsulates provided the rationale for the irrational behavior of Milton's Father, which is being exposed here as satanic. In this context Satan's cruciform position and his darkened halo would appear to be deliberate allusions to the Crucifixion. And one wonders whether the triple serpent is meant by association to recall the scourge and their companions the lance and cock, three of the traditional *Arma Christi*.

"Morning Chasing Away the Phantoms" (Fig. 75), Blake's fourth design on a subject not illustrated previously, is both formally and thematically a mirror image of "Christ's Troubled Dream," which reverses its life-denying implications. It represents a second turning point in the symbolic action, analogous to that in which Milton— rather earlier in Blake's epic—asks himself, "What do I here before the Judgment? without my Emanation?" (*Mil* 14.28, E 108). Christ is still seen reclining, now on his right side, but he is awake and gazes up at Morning, who advances toward him "with Pilgrim steps in amice gray" (IV.427), replacing Satan in the position of dominion over him—her staff is identical to that held by Satan in the Council scene—and driving out the specters of the night. The scene, we may surmise, represents an epiphanic moment in Christ's quest, a revelation of the redemptive power of woman and the affective side of life that dispels the errors of Milton's patriarchal Puritan religion. Part of the evidence that Morning here assumes Mary's role as Christ's Emanation is contextual, and depends on the fact that the next two designs amplify the "moment of desire!" (*VDA* 7.3, E 50). But the idea that she and Christ are indeed contraries is conveyed by their resemblance in scale and dress, by the way they gaze at each other enrapt, and by their halos, which are identical save that Christ's is yellow and Morning's blue—like Mary's earlier—suggesting humanized sun and complementary Beulaic moon. Their relationship thus reverses that established between Christ and Satan as his Urizenic double in "The First Temptation."

A further particular which is especially tantalizing in relation to traditional iconography of the Passion is that Morning has the long flowing locks of Mary Magdalen as she was frequently portrayed—for instance by Duvet (Fig. 140)—ardently embracing the foot of the cross or the body of Christ, or meditating over a crucifix with a quasi-erotic fervor Blake would have recognized as symptomatic of the whole cycle of dualism, sublimation, and guilt perpetuated by the Churches. The Virgin by contrast was usually presented with her head covered, and several of Blake's Bible illustrations (B 600, 601, 606) indicate that he was familiar with this traditional distinction. Commenting on Blake's rhetorical question, "Was Jesus Chaste?" in the *Everlasting Gospel*, Hagstrum considers it probable Blake meant to imply that "one who selected publicans and harlots . . . for his company literally entered the Magdalen's 'dark Hell' and literally dwelled in her 'burning bosom.'"[42] And in *Jerusalem* Blake associates the Magdalen, who beheld the "Spiritual Risen Body" (*J* 62.14, E 213) of the resurrected Christ, with Jerusalem herself. Here, moreover, Morning makes her appearance immediately after Christ's darkest hour, so that the circumstantial evidence in support of the Magdalen parallel seems quite strong. The way Christ half rises to meet her therefore implicitly reverses the Gospel account of how Jesus bade Mary "Touch me not, for I am not yet ascended to my Father" (John 20.17)—another popular subject in devotional art. Christ's imminent restoration to unity is also signalled by the insect Morning points to, which resembles the one seen departing in the engraved version of *Glad Day*.[43] A youthful version of the Goblin in *L'Allegro and Il Penseroso* 5 (Fig. 59) is prominent among the routed specters. Most have assumed grotesque human faces, perhaps to remind us that all along they were not plagues from on high but reptiles of the human mind.

The last three designs (Figs. 76–78), two of them among the most visually impressive in the series, form an organic unit which appears to be intended to amplify the consequences of Christ's epiphanic vision of the redemptive power of woman and "an improvement of sensual enjoyment" (*MHH* 14, E 39). They may be envisaged as successive frames in Blake's "visionary cinema"— again analogous to the expanded moment in the poem to Butts (E 712f.) or to the more complex apocalyptic close of *Milton*.[44] Thus Christ ascends through Beulah and—considering the three angels against the blue sky—threefold vision on the pinnacle (Fig. 76), to the fourfold ecstasy of the Edenic Banquet (Fig. 77), where for the first time appropriately he is shown suspended in midair and the sky becomes suffused with the glow of sunrise. And in the last design (Fig. 78), like Blake himself at the end of *Milton*, he returns home to Mary's humble cottage, behind which the sun is rising.

In *Paradise Regained* the Third Temptation, with its threat of physical danger, is a temptation to vainglorious presumption, and in terms of the triple equation Christ stands firm where Eve and Adam fell. As Pope (pp. 94f.) and Lewalski (pp. 303f.) have pointed out, moreover, Christ's reply to Satan, "Tempt not the Lord thy God" (IV.561), when interpreted as an assertion of his own divinity, also resolves the doubt motif. So here again there is considerable common ground between the two poets, and one would be disposed to accept Wittreich's conclusion that for Blake too this represents the "moment of [Christ's] triumph and complete self-realization" without qualification, were it not for the phallic aureole surrounding Christ.[45] If this is not too explicit, it is surely as much on aesthetic grounds as out of respect for conventional pieties, since the erotic side of human experience is notoriously difficult to handle with artistic tact. Moreover, Blake may have been uncomfortably aware that some of his fellow engravers supplemented their income by contributing to the brisk underground trade in pornographic art.[46]

Acceptance of passion, as opposed to Milton's restraint, is so fundamental to Blake's vision of psychic health and Christian liberty that pictorial analogues and precedents are in a sense beside the point. Hagstrum and others have pointed to various antiquarian sources for his use of phallic symbolism elsewhere, however, and a thematically relevant image he may also have been familiar with occurs in Payne Knight's *Discourse on the Worship of Priapus* (1786), where a phallic rooster is characterized in the Greek inscription as the "Saviour of the World" (Fig. 141).[47] In the Christian context, Steinberg has recently drawn attention to a number of paintings and engravings by Heemskerck, Krug (Fig. 142), Cranach, and others, in which pre-Christian notions of phallic power seem to resurface in the context of the *Man of Sorrows* and the *Crucifixion* as proleptic allusions to the Resurrection.[48] Steinberg summarizes what appears to be the typological thinking behind these remarkable anticipations of Blake's image as follows:

> To justify his conception, [the artist] could have said, or thought, something like this: if it was in the organ of generation and lust that Christ initiated his Passion; and if, in the exegetic tradition, its circumcision on the eighth day prefigures the Resurrection, the final putting away of corruption; then what is that organ's status in the risen body? Or more simply: if the truth of the Incarnation was proved in the mortification of the penis, would not the truth of the Anastasis, the resuscitation, be proved by its erection? Would not this be the body's best show of power?   (p. 91)

One can only speculate whether, given his professional interest in old prints, Blake might have come across rare engravings such as Krug's, impressions of which as Steinberg points out "can have survived only by being locked away in print cabinets seldom disturbed" (p. 86). An engraving on a related theme he undoubtedly did know, since it is echoed on *America* 6 (IB 144), the *Grave* title page, *Nativity Ode* 1 (Figs. 43–44), and *Jerusalem* 6 (IB 285), is Michelangelo's *Dream of Human Life* (Fig. 143). But there, explicit phallic imagery is introduced in antithesis to the spiritual resurrection of the central figure, as one of a series of vignettes depicting the Seven Deadly Sins.

But in "The Third Temptation" (Fig. 76) Blake's most immediate source of inspiration may not in fact have been visual at all. Conceptually it seems more probable that he had Satan's seduction of Eve "erect / Amidst his circling Spires" (IX.501–2) in mind. By depicting Christ on the pinnacle in cruciform position, again with palms displayed as at his Baptism, he seems to be signalling that this is a moment of self-surrender and rejection of selfhood—in the guise of the now naked Satan—altogether different from that symbolized by the Crucifixion in traditional Passion sequences. As might be inferred from Satan's cloven appearance, it is analogous to the moment in which the redeemed hero of *Milton* turns to his bride Ololon and says:

> There is a Negation, & there is a Contrary
> The Negation must be destroyd to redeem the Contraries
> The Negation is the Spectre; the Reasoning Power in Man
> This is a false Body: an Incrustation over my Immortal
> Spirit; a Selfhood, which must be put off & annihilated alway
> To cleanse the Face of my Spirit by Self-examination.
>
> (*Mil* 40.32–37, E 142)

By depicting Christ in an attitude identical to that he used in his watercolor of *The Resurrection* (Fig. 94), and endorsing this association by presenting him poised on the highest of a row of gothic pinnacles, suggestive both of an ornamental tomb and of a veritable field of "Living Form" (E 270), Blake implies that Christ's dark night of "Self-examination" is now over, and that his resurrection to unity and restoration to life through acceptance of its contraries is under way. And by depicting him against an aureole which appears to revive the erection/resurrection equation that Steinberg has detected in an earlier tradition, he may be understood to be presenting a redemptive modulation of Milton's demonic symbolism, which implicitly undermines his vision of the Fall as an abandonment of rational self-control and an unlawful increase in sensual enjoyment.

In what is essentially an audacious raid on the ineffable, the configuration is delicately etherealized to suggest the state in which "Embraces are Cominglings: from the Head even to the Feet; / And not a pompous High Priest entering by a Secret Place" (*J* 69.43–44, E 223). This state constitutes the antithesis of the phallic power psychology exemplified by Comus in the "Magic Banquet" (Figs. 11–12), or by "Apollyon" (Fig. 88) in the *Pilgrim's Progress* series. Milton himself had recognized this syndrome and dramatized it brilliantly in Satan's seduction of Eve, but from Blake's point of view he had diagnosed its causes incorrectly by attributing it to Satan's willful, irrational revolt rather than to God's repressive law of freedom through rational restraint. The aureole around Christ is "circumcised" to emphasize that "Establishment of Truth depends on destruction of Falshood continually / On Circumcision: not on Virginity" (*J* 55.65–66, E 205), and the plummeting Satan is shown accordingly enveloped in an apocalyptic vortex of flame. As an emblem of the Tree of Life, this composite image of a risen Christ in cruciform position represents a life-affirming alternative to Adam's vision of the "Dead Corpse" on the cross in the penultimate design to *Paradise Lost* (Figs. 39–40, 81). The presence of the three short-haired ministering angels, therefore, though in broad compliance with the poem, also perhaps bears witness to the holiness of this moment of regeneration, for as Blake believed, "everything that lives is Holy" (*MHH* 27, E 45).

"Christ Ministered to by Angels" (Fig. 77) may thus be seen as a sequel, amplifying the moment of desire in a way which also accommodates the contrary feminine response. Werner suggests that Blake has "arranged the figures of the design to represent the symbols *alpha* and *omega*" (p. 206), with which Christ is identified in Revelation. But this risks attributing an orthodox teleology to Blake's conception of Christ which seems hard to reconcile with his humanist vision of him as "a brother and friend" (*J* 4.18, E 146). The design is more iconic and stylized than any of the others in the series except "Satan in Council," the two spiritual poles of Christ's quest being appropriately removed from local time and space. And when it is contemplated as part of an iconographic continuum, it does not seem too farfetched to propose that Blake has here trans-figured Milton's "table of Celestial Food, Divine" with its "Fruit fetcht from the tree of life, / And from the fount of life Ambrosial drink" (IV.588–90) in such a way as to suggest the life-renewing moment of ecstatic, self-transcendent sexual consummation. In another daring raid on the ineffable, he has achieved a brilliant visual analogue to his poetic account in *Jerusalem* of how "In Beulah the Female lets down her beautiful Tabernacle; / Which the Male enters magnificent between her Cherubim: / And becomes One with her" (*J* 44.34–36, E 193). The notion of an androgynous union in which sexual difference is forgotten is perhaps suggested by the presence of angels of both sexes; and that there are now four of them implies that the moment is "fourfold in [their] supreme delight" (E 722). Having cast off the satanic errors of Milton's religion in the previous design, Christ here blesses the bread and wine of life held up to him, in acknowledgment of the truth of this experience. That the sacraments no longer carry their traditional association with the body and blood of the crucified Christ is implied by the fact that they emanate from the place of seed, suggested by the lower angels' halos. As food from the Tree and Fountain of Life in this vision of the marriage of contraries, they should be thought of rather as emblems of the apocalyptic "Supper of the Lamb & his Bride" (*Mil* 25.60–61, E 122). We may therefore be confident that the two harp-playing cherubim are not praising Christ for having "aveng'd / Supplanted Adam" (IV.606–7), but like the "harpers harping with their harps" in Revelation are indeed singing "a new song" (14.2–3).

In harmony with the final lines of *Paradise Regained*, "Christ Returns to His Mother" (Fig. 78) brings the sequence to a subdued domestic close. Though it is hard to credit Blake with a desire to bring out Christ's humility in this scene, he may nonetheless have detected a redeemingly human touch in Milton's vision of him returning to "begin to save mankind" (IV.635). But the symbolic significance of this reunion is surely very much wider than in Milton, for with great economy Blake has managed to gather together a number of earlier iconographic strands, so as to ratify and formalize, as it were, the spousal implications of the three designs depicting Christ's resurrection to unity. In keeping with the restrained decorum of the sequence on the literal level, Mary is still veiled of course, but now that Christ has rent the veil of moral law she is released from the protective ark or tomb of her virginity. And like bridal Ololon between what Erdman glosses as "the male and female human forms of . . . two deep rows of wheat" (IB 266) on *Milton* 50 (Fig. 126), she advances with arms extended to reciprocate Christ's eager embrace. Her distaff has vanished with her spinsterish fears and the altar of the law has been replaced by what, in view of her association with forgiveness in *Jerusalem*, might possibly be intended as a Mercy Seat. Now that the cherubim have indeed left their "guard at the tree of life" (*MHH* 14, E 39), the twin palms have brought forth clusters of dates. Moreover, they now lean toward each other in sympathy with the spousal reunion, and perhaps also to recall the heart configuration earlier, as a reminder that all is to be "Spiritually Discerned." Andrew and Simon Peter are reintroduced without Miltonic authority, partly no doubt to sustain the notion numerologically that this is an extension of the fourfold vision of the Heavenly Banquet, an interpretation endorsed by the squared circle suggested by the rising sun. But they are also present surely both as witnesses and disciples of Blake's vision of a Christ freed from the negations inherent in Milton and Puritanism, restored to unity by acceptance of the "Two Contrary States of the Human Soul" (*SI*, E 7), and humanized by marriage.

Notes

1   Gilchrist, *Life of William Blake*, introd. Ruthven Todd (London: Dutton, 1942), p. 330.

2   Wittreich, *Calm of Mind* (Cleveland: Case Western Reserve Univ. Press, 1971), Appendix A, pp. 326–28.

3   Hayley, *The Life of Milton*, ed. Wittreich, p. 219.

4   Wittreich, *Angel of Apocalypse*, pp. 139, 120, 75f.; see Werner, *Blake's Vision of the Poetry of Milton*, pp. 176f.

5   See Todd, ed., *Poetical Works of John Milton*, IV.330, 335.

6   Grant, "Jesus and the Powers That Be in Blake's Designs for Young's *Night Thoughts*" in Erdman, ed., *Blake and His Bibles*, pp. 71–115.

7   See Hill, *The World Turned Upside Down* (Harmondsworth: Penguin, 1975), pp. 87f. and 314f.; and Winstanley, *The Law of Freedom and Other Writings*, ed. Hill (Harmondsworth: Penguin, 1973), pp. 45f.

8   Elizabeth M. Pope, *Paradise Regained: The Tradition and the Poem* (1947; New York: Russell, 1962), pp. 39–40. Hill, *Milton and the English Renaissance*, p. 421, observes that "Milton's concept of liberty was itself rather negative"; while William Kerrigan, *The Prophetic Milton* (Charlottesville: Univ. of Virginia Press, 1974), p. 180, remarks that Milton "glories in the negative construction."

9   Edward Le Comte, *Milton and Sex* (London: Macmillan, 1978), p. 101.

10 Leo Steinberg, *The Sexuality of Christ in Renaissance Art and in Modern Oblivion* (New York: Pantheon, 1983), pp. 82f.

11 See Pope, pp. 51–69.

12 See F. W. H. Hollstein, *German Engravings, Etchings and Woodcuts ca. 1400–1700* (Amsterdam: Van Gendt & Co., 1980), VI.pls. 10–23; W. Kurth, ed., *The Complete Woodcuts of Albrecht Dürer* (1927; rpt. New York: Dover, 1963), pls. 228–58; Walter L. Strauss, ed., *The Complete Engravings, Etchings & Drypoints of Albrecht Dürer* (New York: Dover, 1972), pls. 47–67; and Marie Mauquoy-Hendrickx, *Les Estampes des Wierix* (Brussels: Bibliothèque Royale Albert Iᵉʳ, 1978), I.pls. 145–62.

13 Samuel Palmer recalled that "he fervently loved the early Christian art, and dwelt with peculiar affection on the memory of Fra Angelico, often speaking of him as an inspired inventor and as a saint." See Gilchrist, p. 302.

14 See Frye, *Milton's Imagery and the Visual Arts*, pls. 106 and 60.

15 Barbara K. Lewalski, *Milton's Brief Epic: The Genre, Meaning and Art of Paradise Regained* (Providence: Brown Univ. Press, 1966), p. 186.

16 Neither scholar, however, pursues the implications of this insight in relation to Blake's total orchestration of particulars.

17 See Strauss, ed., *Hendrik Goltzius: The Complete Engravings and Woodcuts* (New York: Abaris, 1977), I.pl. 170. Goltzius gave the same gesture (though in reverse) to the female figure of Hope in his *Seven Virtues* series; see I.pl. 68.

18 The alternative gesture of palms displayed at chest or head level, which occurs in Raphael's *Transfiguration* and Marcantonio's engraving of *Five Saints* is undoubtedly more common, but if Blake had used it here he would have created semiotic confusion at the literal level. See Heinrich Wölfflin, *Classic Art* (1898; Ithaca: Cornell Univ. Press, 1980), pls. 90, 157, and further pls. 89, 97. Both gestures occur in the work of the Wierix brothers; see Hendrickx, II.pls. 1019, 1497, 1989.

19 In the King James version, the Latin inscriptions beneath Collaert's design read "I will give unto him that is athirst of the fountain of the water of life freely" (Revelation 21.6); and "Come unto me, all ye that labour and are heavy laden, and I will give you rest" (Matthew 11.28). The traditional connection between the Fountain of Life and baptismal symbolism is discussed in Schiller, *Iconography of Christian Art*, I.130–31. See further Strauss, *The German Single-Leaf Woodcut 1550–1600* (New York: Abaris, 1975), I.1393; Dorothy Alexander, *The German Single-Leaf Woodcut 1600–1700* (New York: Abaris, 1977), I.227; and Henry Hawkins, *The Devout Hart* (1634; rpt. London: Scholar Press, 1975), p. 83.

20 See Wittreich, *Calm of Mind*, p. 327; Pope, pp. 42–50 and pls. I–IX; and Frye, pp. 319f. and pls. 234–36, 240–45, 248, 251–52, and 259.

21 Damon, *Blake's Job*, p. 20.

22 See Lewalski, pp. 241–49.

23 See Frye, pls. 234 et seq.

24 Goltzius uses the heart motif in two emblematic designs in his series on the *Life of Christ*. In one he depicts Christ the Healer holding up a heart-shaped glass vessel containing a toad and pig, as might a physician. In another a woman representing "Imitatio Christi" is seated at her easel copying a heart—inscribed with a wayfaring Infant Jesus

accompanied by a lamb—which is held out to her by Christ; see Strauss, *Hendrik Goltzius*, I.pls. 25–26. One emblem in Hawkins's *The Devout Hart*, p. 45, which is particularly suggestive in relation to the frontispiece to *Jerusalem* (IB 280), depicts Christ knocking on a large wooden door inscribed within a heart. For further examples see, for instance, Strauss, *The German Single-Leaf Woodcut*, I.pls. 19, 20, 58 and Hendrickx, II.pls. 1564–73.

25 Ferguson, *Signs and Symbols in Christian Art*, p. 139, writes that St. Peter's yellow gown is "symbolic of Revealed Faith."

26 Piloo Nanavutty, "A Title-Page in Blake's Illustrated Genesis Manuscript," in Essick, ed., *The Visionary Hand*, p. 136. Bryant in *A New System*, I.321–22, records the association of the palm with Jewish nuptial festivities, and also with the phoenix as an emblem of immortality.

27 See Chayes, "Fallen Earth and Man in Nature: William Blake in Iconographic Tradition," *Studies in Iconography*, 10 (1984–86), 179. Chayes points out that Hans Sebald Beham's "The Penance of St. John Chrysostom" provides a probable model both for the reclining female on *Marriage* 11 (IB 108) and for the *Nebuchadnezzar* (B 393, 406, 407) prototype on *Marriage* 24 (IB 121). And she raises an interesting methodological point when she concludes that "if we make the reasonable assumption that, when he could, Blake would have used one source rather than two for the same work," the presence of two figures in the *Marriage* from Beham's print "is all but conclusive evidence that Blake adapted both from the version of 'The Penance of St. John Chrysostom' not by Dürer but by Hans Sebald Beham." It would certainly seem that such multiple echoes increase the likelihood that Blake knew the work in question, though the quest for specific sources, as distinct from *topoi*, has always to reckon with the possibility of fortuitous resemblance. What is harder to assess is whether Blake worked in quite the way that is implied in Chayes's conclusion, directly consulting a specific source, or whether he drew on a well-stocked repository of visual memories, as both his training and his supposed eidetic faculty would seem to argue.

28 Roe, *Blake's Illustrations to the Divine Comedy*, p. 53 and pl. 3.

29 The motif has its origin in the *Apocrypha* apparently: see Schiller, I.34–37, and Figs. 66, 68, 70–74, 90, 93, 95, 120, 124.

30 Attention is drawn to this typology in Raine, *The Human Face of God* (London: Thames & Hudson, 1982), p. 73.

31 Bryant, *A New System*, II.59f., 198f., 328f.

32 See Walter MacKellar, ed., *Paradise Regained* in *Variorum Commentary on the Poems of John Milton* (New York: Columbia Univ. Press, 1975), IV.25–29, 124 et seq., 226 et seq.

33 Roe, pp. 171–74 and pl. 89.

34 See Frye, *Milton's Imagery and the Visual Arts*, pls. 234, 240–42, 248.

35 Morley, ed., *Henry Crabb Robinson on Books and Their Writers*, I.329.

36 Michael Fixler, *Milton and the Kingdoms of God* (London: Faber & Faber, 1964), p. 224.

37 See Todd, IV.330–31, 335.

38 Frye, pp. 339–41 and pls. 254–58.

39 Kenneth Clark, *The Nude* (Princeton: Princeton Univ. Press, 1956), pp. 496–97; Damon, pls. 6–7. See Lindberg, *William Blake's Illustrations to the Book of Job*, pp. 119, 129–30.

40 See Wölfflin, pls. 21, 53, and 54.

41 Hendrickxs, I.pls. 157, 403, and 653. See Panofsky, *Early Netherlandish Painting*, II.pls. 264–65, 286, 299. Geoffrey M. Down, Head of the Baillieu Library Print Room, University of Melbourne, informs me that "it was Raphael's practice to supply Marcantonio with only the basics of the design, viz. the figures, and he allowed considerable freedom with the engraved versions. Marcantonio was left to devise most of the scenery and settings himself."

42 Hagstrum, "Christ's Body" in Paley and Michael Phillips, eds., *William Blake: Essays in Honour of Sir Geoffrey Keynes* (Oxford: Clarendon Press, 1973), p. 140.

43 See David Bindman, *The Complete Graphic Works of William Blake*, pl. 400.

44 See Howard, *Blake's Milton*, pp. 247–56; and Harold Bloom, "The Visionary Cinema of Romantic Poetry" in Alvin H. Rosenfeld, ed., *William Blake: Essays for S. Foster Damon* (Providence: Brown Univ. Press, 1969), pp. 18–35.

45 Wittreich, *Angel of Apocalypse*, p. 140.

46 See Iain McCalman, *Radical Underworld: Prophets, Revolutionaries and Pornographers in London, 1795–1840* (Cambridge: Cambridge Univ. Press, 1988), pp. 204–31.

47 Hagstrum, *William Blake, Poet and Painter*, p. 89 and pls. XLIXA–B. See Ashley Montagu, ed., *Sexual Symbolism: A History of Phallic Worship* (New York: Julian Press, 1956), where Payne Knight's treatise is reprinted.

48 Steinberg, pp. 82f.

Select Bibliography

Abrams, M. H. *Natural Supernaturalism: Tradition and Revolution in Romantic Literature*. New York: Norton, 1971.

Adams, Hazard. *William Blake: A Reading of the Shorter Poems*. Seattle: Univ. of Washington Press, 1963.

Adlard, John. *The Sports of Cruelty*. London: Woolf, 1972.

Alexander, Dorothy. *The German Single-Leaf Woodcut 1600–1700*. 2 vols. New York: Abaris, 1978.

Altizer, Thomas J. J. *The New Apocalypse: The Radical Christian Vision of William Blake*. Michigan State Univ. Press, 1967.

Ault, Donald D. *Visionary Physics: Blake's Response to Newton*. Chicago: Univ. of Chicago Press, 1974.

Babb, Lawrence. *The Moral Cosmos of Paradise Lost*. East Lansing: Michigan State Univ. Press, 1970.

Banks, Theodore H. "The Banquet Scene in *Paradise Regained*." *PMLA*, 55 (1940), 773–76.

Barrell, John. *The Political Theory of Painting from Reynolds to Hazlitt*. New Haven: Yale Univ. Press, 1986.

Baxandall, Michael. *Painting and Experience in Fifteenth Century Italy*. Oxford: Oxford Univ. Press, 1972.

Becker, Carl L. *The Heavenly City of the Eighteenth-Century Philosophers*. New Haven: Yale Univ. Press, 1932.

Behrendt, Stephen C. "Bright Pilgrimage: William Blake's Designs for *L'Allegro* and *Il Penseroso*." *Milton Studies*, 8 (1975), 123–47.

———. "Blake's Illustrations to Milton's *Nativity Ode*." *Philological Quarterly*, 55 (1976), 65–95.

———. "*Comus* and *Paradise Regained*: Blake's View of Trial in the Wilderness." *Milton and the Romantics*, 3 (1977), 8–13.

———. "The Mental Contest: Blake's *Comus* Designs." *Blake Studies*, 8 (1978), 65–68.

———. *The Moment of Explosion: Blake and the Illustration of Milton*. Lincoln: Univ. of Nebraska Press, 1983.

Bell, John. *New Pantheon; or, Historical Dictionary of the Gods, Demi-Gods, Heroes and Fabulous Personages of Antiquity*. 2 vols. London, 1790.

Belsey, Catherine. *John Milton: Language, Gender, Power*. Oxford: Blackwell, 1988.

Bentley, G. E., Jr. *Blake Records*. Oxford: Clarendon Press, 1969.

———. *Blake Records Supplement*. Oxford: Clarendon Press, 1988.

———. *Blake Books*. Oxford: Clarendon Press, 1977.

Bindman, David. *Blake as an Artist*. Oxford: Phaidon, 1977.

———. *The Shadow of the Guillotine: Britain and the French Revolution*. London: British Museum, 1989.

———, ed. *William Blake: Catalogue of the Collection in the Fitzwilliam Museum, Cambridge*. Cambridge: Heffer, 1970.

———, ed. *The Complete Graphic Works of William Blake*. London: Thames & Hudson, 1978.

———, ed. *John Flaxman*. London: Thames & Hudson, 1979.

Bloom, Harold. *Blake's Apocalypse: A Study in Poetic Argument*. Ithaca: Cornell Univ. Press, 1963.

———. "Dialectic of *The Marriage of Heaven and Hell*." In *The Ringers in the Tower: Studies in Romantic Tradition*. Chicago: Univ. of Chicago Press, 1971.

———. *The Anxiety of Influence: A Theory of Poetry*. New York: Oxford Univ. Press, 1973.

Blunt, Anthony. *The Art of William Blake*. New York: Columbia Univ. Press, 1959.

Brisman, Leslie. *Milton's Poetry of Choice and Its Romantic Heirs*. Ithaca: Cornell Univ. Press, 1973.

Bryant, Jacob. *A New System; or an Analysis of Ancient Mythology*. 5 vols. London, 1775.

Burke, Edmund. *A Philosophical Enquiry into the Origins of Our Ideas of the Sublime and Beautiful*. Ed. J. T. Boulton. London: Routledge, 1958.

Burke, Joseph. "The Eidetic and the Borrowed Image: An Interpretation of Blake's Theory and Practice of Art." In *The Visionary Hand*, ed. Robert N. Essick. Los Angeles: Hennessy & Ingalls, 1973.

Butlin, Martin. "Cataloguing William Blake." In *Blake in His Time*, ed. Robert N. Essick and Donald Pearce. Bloomington: Indiana Univ. Press, 1978.

———. "A Newly Discovered Watermark and a Visionary's Way with His Dates." *Blake: An Illustrated Quarterly*, 15 (1981–82), 101–3.

———. *The Paintings and Drawings of William Blake*. 2 vols. New Haven: Yale Univ. Press, 1981.

————, and Ted Gott. *William Blake in the Collection of the National Gallery of Victoria*. Melbourne: National Gallery of Victoria, 1989.

Cantor, Paul A. *Creature and Creator: Myth-making and English Romanticism*. Cambridge: Cambridge Univ. Press, 1984.

Chayes, Irene H. "The Presence of Cupid and Psyche." In *Blake's Visionary Forms Dramatic*, ed. David V. Erdman and John E. Grant. Princeton: Princeton Univ. Press, 1970.

————. "Blake's Ways with Art Sources: Michelangelo's *Last Judgment*." *Colby Library Quarterly*, 20 (1984), 60–89.

————. "Fallen Earth and Man in Nature: William Blake in Iconographic Tradition." *Studies in Iconography*, 10 (1984–86), 169–94.

Clark, Kenneth. *The Nude: A Study of Ideal Art*. Princeton: Princeton Univ. Press, 1956.

Coleman, Deirdre, and Peter Otto, eds. *Imagining Romanticism: Essays on English and Australian Romanticisms*. West Cornwall: Locust Hill Press, 1992.

Cook, B. F. *The Elgin Marbles*. London: British Museum, 1984.

————. *The Townley Marbles*. London: British Museum, 1985.

Crompton, Louis. *Byron and Greek Love: Homophobia in 19th Century England*. Berkeley: Univ. of California Press, 1985.

Curran, Stuart, and Joseph A. Wittreich, Jr., eds. *Blake's Sublime Allegory: Essays on The Four Zoas, Milton and Jerusalem*. Madison: Univ. of Wisconsin Press, 1973.

Damon, S. Foster. *William Blake: His Philosophy and Symbols*. 1924; rpt. Gloucester: Peter Smith, 1958.

————. *Blake's Grave: William Blake's Illustrations for Robert Blair's The Grave*. Providence: Brown Univ. Press, 1963.

————. *A Blake Dictionary*. Providence: Brown Univ. Press, 1965.

————. *Blake's Job: William Blake's Illustrations of the Book of Job*. Providence: Brown Univ. Press, 1966.

Damrosch, Leopold, Jr. *Symbol and Truth in Blake's Myth*. Princeton: Princeton Univ. Press, 1980.

Davies, Edward. *Celtic Researches*. London, 1804.

————. *The Mythology and Rites of the British Druids*. London, 1809.

Davies, J. G. *The Theology of William Blake*. Oxford: Clarendon Press, 1948.

Di Salvo, Jackie. *War of Titans*. Pittsburgh: Univ. of Pittsburgh Press, 1983.

Dunbar, Pamela. *William Blake's Illustrations to the Poetry of Milton*. Oxford: Clarendon Press, 1980.

Easson, Roger, and Robert N. Essick, eds. *William Blake Book Illustrator: A Bibliography and Catalogue of the Commercial Engravings*. 2 vols. Normal: American Blake Foundation, 1972; Memphis: American Blake Foundation, 1979.

Eaves, Morris. *William Blake's Theory of Art*. Princeton: Princeton Univ. Press, 1982.

Eisler, Colin. *The Master of the Unicorn: The Life and Work of Jean Duvet*. New York: Abaris, 1979.

Erdman, David V. *Blake: Prophet Against Empire*. Rev. ed. Princeton: Princeton Univ. Press, 1969.

———. *The Illuminated Blake*. New York: Doubleday, 1974.

———, ed. *The Notebook of William Blake: A Photographic Facsimile*. Oxford: Clarendon Press, 1973.

———, ed. *Blake and His Bibles*. West Cornwall: Locust Hill Press, 1990.

———, and Harold Bloom, eds. *The Complete Poetry and Prose of William Blake*. New York: Doubleday, 1982.

———, and John E. Grant, eds. *Blake's Visionary Forms Dramatic*. Princeton: Princeton Univ. Press, 1970.

Essick, Robert N. "Blake's Newton." *Blake Studies*, 3 (1971), 149–62.

———. *William Blake, Printmaker*. Princeton: Princeton Univ. Press, 1980.

———. *The Works of William Blake in the Huntington Collections: A Complete Catalogue*. San Marino: Huntington Library, 1985.

———. *William Blake and the Language of Adam*. Oxford: Clarendon Press, 1989.

———, ed. *The Visionary Hand: Essays for the Study of William Blake's Art and Aesthetics*. Los Angeles: Hennessy & Ingalls, 1973.

———, and Donald Pearce, eds. *Blake in His Time*. Bloomington: Indiana Univ. Press, 1978.

Ferguson, George. *Signs and Symbols in Christian Art*. 1954; London: Oxford Univ. Press, 1961.

Fish, Stanley Eugene. *Surprised by Sin: The Reader in Paradise Lost*. New York: St. Martin's Press, 1967.

Fisher, Peter F. "Blake and the Druids." *Journal of English and Germanic Philology*, 58 (1959), 589–612.

———. "Blake's Attacks on the Classical Tradition." *Philological Quarterly*, 40 (1961), 1–18.

Fixler, Michael. *Milton and the Kingdoms of God*. London: Faber & Faber, 1964.

———. "The Apocalypse Within *Paradise Lost.*" In *New Essays on Paradise Lost,* ed. Thomas Kranidas. Berkeley: Univ. of California Press, 1969.

Fox, Susan. *Poetic Form in Blake's Milton.* Princeton: Princeton Univ. Press, 1976.

———. "The Female as Metaphor in William Blake's Poetry." *Critical Inquiry,* 3 (1977), 507–19.

Franson, John Karl. "Christ on the Pinnacle: Interpretive Illustrations of the Crisis in *Paradise Regained.*" *Milton Quarterly* 10 (1976), 48–53.

———. "The Serpent Driving Females in Blake's *Comus* 4." *Blake: An Illustrated Quarterly,* 12 (1978–79), 164–77.

Freeman, Rosemary. *English Emblem Books.* London: Chatto & Windus, 1948.

Friedman, Winifred H. *Boydell's Shakespeare Gallery.* New York: Garland, 1976.

Frye, Northrop. *Fearful Symmetry: A Study of William Blake.* Princeton: Princeton Univ. Press, 1947.

———. *The Return of Eden: Five Essays on Milton's Epics.* Toronto: Univ. of Toronto Press, 1965.

Frye, Roland Mushat. *Milton's Imagery and the Visual Arts: Iconographic Tradition in the Epic Poems.* Princeton: Princeton Univ. Press, 1978.

Gardner, Helen. "Milton's First Illustrator." *Essays and Studies,* 9 (1956), 27–38.

Gilbert, Sandra M., and Susan Gubar. *The Madwoman in the Attic: The Woman Writer and the Nineteenth Century Literary Imagination.* New Haven: Yale Univ. Press, 1979.

Gilchrist, Alexander. *Life of William Blake.* 2nd ed. London: Macmillan, 1880.

Gleckner, Robert F. *Blake and Spenser.* Baltimore: Johns Hopkins Univ. Press, 1985.

Gombrich, E. H. *Norm and Form: Studies in the Art of the Renaissance.* London: Phaidon, 1966.

———. *Symbolic Images: Studies in the Art of the Renaissance.* London: Phaidon, 1972.

Gourlay, Alexander S. "'Idolatry or Politics': Blake's Chaucer, the Gods of Priam, and the Powers of 1809." In *Historicizing Blake,* ed. Stephen Clark and David Worrall. London: Macmillan, 1992.

Grant, John E. "The Arlington Court Picture, Part I." *Blake Newsletter,* 3 (1970), 96–105.

——. "The Arlington Court Picture, Part II." *Blake Newsletter*, 4 (1970), 12–25.

——. "Blake's Designs for *L'Allegro* and *Il Penseroso*, Part I: A Survey of the Designs." *Blake Newsletter*, 4 (1971), 117–34.

——. "Blake's Designs for *L'Allegro* and *Il Penseroso*, Part II: The Meaning of Mirth and Her Companions." *Blake Newsletter*, 5 (1972), 190–202.

——. "The Female Awakening at the End of Blake's *Milton*: A Picture Story, with Questions." In *Milton Reconsidered: Essays in Honor of Arthur R. Barker*, ed. John Karl Franson. Salzburg Studies in English Literature, 49. Salzburg: Univ. of Salzburg Press, 1976.

——. "Blake's Title Pages for *Songs of Innocence and of Experience* and other Visions of the Expulsion from Eden." In *Examining the Sister Arts: Essays on English Art and Literature 1700–1850*, ed. Richard Weydorf. Minneapolis: Univ. of Minnesota Press, 1982.

——. "Jesus and the Powers That Be in Blake's Designs for Young's *Night Thoughts*." In *Blake and His Bibles*, ed. David V. Erdman. West Cornwall: Locust Hill Press, 1990.

——, Edward J. Rose, and Michael J. Tolley. *William Blake's Designs for Edward Young's Night Thoughts*. 2 vols. Oxford: Clarendon Press, 1980.

Hagstrum, Jean H. *The Sister Arts: The Tradition of Literary Pictorialism and English Poetry from Dryden to Gray*. Chicago: Univ. of Chicago Press, 1958.

——. *William Blake, Poet and Painter: An Introduction to the Illuminated Verse*. Chicago: Univ. of Chicago Press, 1964.

——. "Christ's Body." In *William Blake: Essays in Honour of Sir Geoffrey Keynes*, ed. Morton D. Paley and Michael Phillips. Oxford: Clarendon Press, 1973.

——. *Sex and Sensibility: Ideal and Erotic Love from Milton to Mozart*. Chicago: Univ. of Chicago Press, 1980.

——. *The Romantic Body: Love and Sexuality in Keats, Wordsworth and Blake*. Knoxville: Univ. of Tennessee Press, 1985.

——. *Eros and Vision: The Restoration to Romanticism*. Evanston: Northwestern Univ. Press, 1989.

Harper, George Mills. *The Neoplatonism of William Blake*. Chapel Hill: Univ. of North Carolina Press, 1961.

Haskell, Francis, and Nicholas Penny. *Taste and the Antique: The Lure of Classical Sculpture 1500–1900*. New Haven: Yale Univ. Press, 1981.

Havens, R. D. *The Influence of Milton on English Poetry*. Cambridge: Harvard Univ. Press, 1922.

Hayley, William. *The Life of Milton*. Ed. Joseph A. Wittreich, Jr. Gainesville: Scholars' Facsimiles, 1970.

Helmstadter, Thomas H. "'Bright Visions of Eternity': Blake's Designs for Blair's *Grave*." *Blake Studies*, 8 (1978), 37–64.

Hill, Christopher. *Milton and the English Revolution*. London: Faber & Faber, 1977.

Hilton, Nelson. *Literary Imagination: Blake's Vision of Words*. Berkeley: Univ. of California Press, 1983.

Hirsch, E. D., Jr. *Validity in Interpretation*. New Haven: Yale Univ. Press, 1967.

Howard, John. *Blake's Milton: A Study in the Selfhood*. Cranbury: Associated Univ. Presses, 1976.

Hughes, Merritt Y., ed. *The Complete Poems and Major Prose of John Milton*. New York: Odyssey Press, 1957.

———. *The Variorum Commentary on the Poems of John Milton*. New York: Columbia Univ. Press, 1970–75.

Irwin, David. *English Neoclassical Art: Studies in Inspiration and Taste*. London: Faber & Faber, 1966.

———. *John Flaxman 1755–1826: Sculptor, Illustrator, Designer*. London: Studio Vista, 1979.

Johnson, Mary Lynn. "'Separating what has been Mixed': A Suggestion for a Perspective on *Milton*." *Blake Studies*, 6 (1973), 11–17.

———. "Emblem and Symbol in Blake." *Huntington Library Quarterly* 37 (1974), 151–70.

———. "David's Recognition of the Human Face of God in Blake's Designs for the Book of Psalms." In *Blake and His Bibles*, ed. David V. Erdman. West Cornwall: Locust Hill Press, 1990.

Jones, Roger, and Nicholas Penny. *Raphael*. New Haven: Yale Univ. Press, 1983.

Jordan, Richard D. "*Paradise Regained* and the Second Adam." *Milton Studies*, 9 (1976), 261–75.

Katzenellenbogen, Adolf. *Allegories of the Virtues and Vices of Medieval Art*. 1939; rpt. Toronto: Univ. of Toronto Press, 1989.

Kerrigan, William. *The Prophetic Milton*. Charlottesville: Univ. of Virginia Press, 1974.

Keynes, Geoffrey. *Blake Studies: Essays on His Life and Work*. 1949; rev. ed., Oxford: Clarendon Press, 1971.

Kiralis, Karl. "William Blake as an Intellectual and Spiritual Guide to Chaucer's Canterbury Pilgrims." *Blake Studies*, 1 (1969), 139–90.

————. "Blake's Criticism of Milton's *L'Allegro* and *Il Penseroso* and of Its Author." In *Milton Reconsidered: Essays in Honor of Arthur R. Barker*, ed. John Karl Franson. Salzburg Studies in English Literature, 49. Salzburg: Univ. of Salzburg Press, 1976.

Klonsky, Milton. *William Blake: The Seer and His Vision*. London: Orbis, 1977.

————. *Blake's Dante: The Complete Illustrations to the Divine Comedy*. New York: Harmony Books, 1980.

Knight, Richard Payne. *Discourse on the Worship of Priapus*. 1786; rpt. in *Sexual Symbolism: A History of Phallic Worship*, ed. Ashley Montagu. New York: Julian Press, 1956.

La Belle, Jenijoy. "Michelangelo's Sistine Frescoes and Blake's 1795 Color-Printed Drawings: A Study in Structural Relationships." *Blake: An Illustrated Quarterly*, 54 (1980), 66–84.

Labriola, Albert C., and Edward Sichi, Jr., eds. *Milton's Legacy in the Arts*. University Park: Pennsylvania State Univ. Press, 1988.

Lawner, Lynne, ed. *I Mondi. The Sixteen Pleasures: An Erotic Album of the Italian Renaissance*. Evanston: Northwestern Univ. Press, 1988.

Le Brun, Charles. *A Method to Learn to Design the Passions*. Trans. John Williams, London, 1734.

Le Comte, Edward. *Milton and Sex*. London: Macmillan, 1978.

Lee, Rensselaer W. *Ut Pictura Poesis: The Humanistic Theory of Painting*. New York: Norton, 1967.

Lewalski, Barbara K. *Milton's Brief Epic: The Genre, Meaning, and Art of Paradise Regained*. Providence: Brown Univ. Press, 1966.

Lindberg, Bo. *William Blake's Illustrations to the Book of Job*. Åbo, Finland: Åbo Akademi, 1973.

Lipking, Lawrence. *The Ordering of the Arts in Eighteenth-Century England*. Princeton: Princeton Univ. Press, 1970.

Lister, Raymond. *The Paintings of William Blake*. Cambridge: Cambridge Univ. Press, 1986.

Lowth, Robert. *Lectures on the Sacred Poetry of the Hebrews*. Trans. G. Gregory. London, 1787.

McCalman, Iain. *Radical Underworld: Prophets, Revolutionaries and Pornographers in London, 1795–1840*. Cambridge: Cambridge Univ. Press, 1988.

Malekin, Peter. *Liberty and Love: English Literature and Society, 1640–88*. London: Hutchinson, 1981.

Mallet, Paul Henri. *Northern Antiquities*. Trans. Thomas Percy. 1770; rpt. London, 1847.

Manuel, Frank E. *The Eighteenth Century Confronts the Gods.* Cambridge: Harvard Univ. Press, 1959.

Mason, Endo C. *The Mind of Henry Fuseli: Selections from His Writings with an Introductory Study.* London: Routledge, 1951.

Mauquoy-Hendrickx, Marie. *Les Estampes des Wierix conservées au Cabinet des Estampes de la Bibliothèque Royal Albert Ier: Catalogue Raisonné.* 3 vols. Brussels: Bibliothèque Royale Albert Ier, 1978.

Mellor, Anne K. *Blake's Human Form Divine.* Berkeley: Univ. of California Press, 1974.

Miner, Paul. "Blake and the Night Sky III: Visionary Astronomy." *Bulletin of Research in the Humanities,* 84 (1981): 305–35.

Mitchell, W. J. T. "Style and Iconography in the Illustrations of Blake's *Milton.*" *Blake Studies,* 6 (1973), 47–72.

———. *Blake's Composite Art: A Study of the Illuminated Poetry.* Princeton: Princeton Univ. Press, 1978.

Monk, Samuel H. *The Sublime: A Study of Critical Theories in Eighteenth-Century England.* Ann Arbor: Univ. of Michigan Press, 1960.

Montfaucon, Bernard de. *Antiquity Explained.* Trans. David Humphreys. 4 vols. London, 1721–22.

Moor, Edward. *The Hindu Pantheon.* 1810; rpt. Los Angeles: Philosophical Research Society, 1976.

Morley, Edith J., ed. *Henry Crabb Robinson on Books and Their Writers.* 3 vols. London: Dent, 1938.

Ostriker, Alicia. "Desire Gratified and Ungratified: William Blake and Sexuality." *Blake: An Illustrated Quarterly,* 16 (1982), 136–65.

Otto, Peter. *Constructive Vision and Visionary Deconstruction.* London: Oxford Univ. Press, 1991.

Paine, Thomas. *Common Sense and Other Political Writings.* Ed. Nelson F. Adkins. New York: Bobbs-Merrill, 1953.

———. *Rights of Man.* Ed. Henry Collins. Harmondsworth: Penguin, 1969.

Paley, Morton D. *Energy and Imagination: A Study of the Development of Blake's Thought.* Oxford: Clarendon Press, 1970.

———. "The Truchsessian Gallery Revisited." *Studies in Romanticism,* 16 (1977), 165–77.

———. "'Wonderful Originals': Blake and Ancient Sculpture." In *Blake in His Time,* ed. Robert N. Essick and Donald Pearce. Bloomington: Indiana Univ. Press, 1978.

———. *The Continuing City: William Blake's Jerusalem.* Oxford: Clarendon Press, 1983.

————, and Michael Phillips, eds. *William Blake: Essays in Honour of Sir Geoffrey Keynes*. Oxford: Clarendon Press, 1973.

Panofsky, Erwin. *Hercules am Scheidewege und andere antike Bildstoffe in der neueren Kunst*. Leipzig: Teubner, 1930.

————. *The Life and Art of Albrecht Dürer*. Princeton: Princeton Univ. Press, 1955.

Parker, William Riley. *Milton: A Biography*. 2 vols. Oxford: Clarendon Press, 1968.

Patrides, C. A. *Milton and the Christian Tradition*. Oxford: Clarendon Press, 1966.

————, ed. *Approaches to Paradise Lost*. Toronto: Univ. of Toronto Press, 1968.

Paulson, Ronald. *Hogarth: His Life, Art and Times*. Abridged ed. New Haven: Yale Univ. Press, 1974.

————. *Emblem and Expression: Meaning in English Art of the Eighteenth Century*. London: Thames & Hudson, 1975.

————. *Book and Painting: Shakespeare, Milton and the Bible*. Knoxville: Univ. of Tennessee Press, 1982.

————. *Representations of Revolution 1789–1820*. New Haven: Yale Univ. Press, 1983.

Peckham, Morse. "Blake, Milton, and Edward Burney." *Princeton University Library Chronicle*, 11 (1950), 107–26.

Pecorino, Jessica P. "Eve Imparadised: Milton's Expulsion and Iconographic Tradition." *Milton Quarterly*, 15 (1981), 1–10.

Pinto, Vivian de Sola, ed. *The Divine Vision: Studies in the Poetry and Art of William Blake*. London: Victor Gollancz, 1957.

Pointon, Marcia R. *Milton and English Art*. Toronto: Univ. of Toronto Press, 1970.

Pope, Elizabeth M. *Paradise Regained: The Tradition and the Poem*. Baltimore: Johns Hopkins Univ. Press, 1947.

Priestley, Joseph. *A Discourse on the Resurrection of Jesus*. Birmingham, 1801.

Raine, Kathleen. *Blake and Tradition*. 2 vols. Princeton: Princeton Univ. Press, 1968.

————. *The Human Face of God: William Blake and the Book of Job*. London: Thames & Hudson, 1982.

————, and George Mills Harper, eds. *Thomas Taylor Platonist: Selected Writings*. London: Routledge, 1969.

Reynolds, Joshua. *Discourses on Art.* Ed. Stephen O. Mitchell. New York: Bobbs-Merrill, 1965.

Ripa, Cesare. *Baroque and Rococo Pictorial Imagery: The 1758–60 Hertel Edition of Ripa's Iconologia.* Ed. Edward A. Maser. New York: Dover Publications, 1971.

Roe, Albert S. *Blake's Illustrations to the Divine Comedy.* Princeton: Princeton Univ. Press, 1953.

Rose, Edward J. "Mental Forms Creating: 'Fourfold Vision' and the Poet as Prophet in Blake's Designs and Verse." *Journal of Aesthetics and Art Criticism,* 23 (1964), 173–83.

———. "Blake's Milton: The Poet as Poem." *Blake Studies,* 1 (1968), 16–38.

———. "Blake's Illustrations for *Paradise Lost, L'Allegro* and *Il Penseroso*: A Thematic Reading." *Hartford Studies in Literature,* 2 (1970), 40–67.

Rosenbloom, Robert. *Transformations in Late Eighteenth Century Art.* Princeton: Princeton Univ. Press, 1967.

Rosenfeld, Alvin H., ed. *William Blake: Essays for S. Foster Damon.* Providence: Brown Univ. Press, 1969.

Rousseau, Jean Jacques. *The Social Contract.* Trans. Maurice Cranston. Harmondsworth: Penguin, 1968.

Samuel, Irene. *Plato and Milton.* Ithaca: Cornell Univ. Press, 1947.

Sandler, Florence. "The Iconoclastic Enterprise: Blake's Critique of 'Milton's Religion.'" *Blake Studies,* 5 (1972), 13–57.

———. "'Defending the Bible': Blake, Paine, and the Bishop on the Atonement." In *Blake and His Bibles,* ed. David V. Erdman. West Cornwall: Locust Hill Press, 1990.

Saxl, F., and R. Wittkower. *British Art and the Mediterranean.* London: Oxford Univ. Press, 1948.

Schama, Simon. *Citizens: A Chronicle of the French Revolution.* New York: Knopf, 1989.

Schiff, Gert. *Johann Heinrich Füsslis Milton-Galerie.* Zürich: Fretz & Wasmuth, 1963.

Schiller, Friedrich. *On the Naive and Sentimental in Literature.* Trans. Helen Watanabe-O'Kelly. Manchester: Carcanet New Press, 1981.

Schiller, Gertrud. *Iconography of Christian Art.* 2 vols. Trans. Janet Seligman. Greenwich: New York Graphic Society, 1971.

Schneewind, J. B. *Moral Philosophy from Montaigne to Kant: An Anthology.* 2 vols. Cambridge: Cambridge Univ. Press, 1990.

Seymour, Charles, Jr. *Michelangelo: The Sistine Chapel Ceiling.* New York: Norton, 1972.

Shaftesbury, Earl of. *Characteristics of Men, Manners, Opinions, Times*. 3 vols. London, 1723.

Steinberg, Leo. *The Sexuality of Christ in Renaissance Art and in Modern Oblivion*. New York: Pantheon, 1983.

Strauss, Walter L., ed. *The German Single-Leaf Woodcut 1550–1600*. 2 vols. New York: Abaris, 1975.

———, ed. *Hendrik Goltzius: The Complete Engravings and Woodcuts*. 2 vols. New York: Abaris, 1977.

Stuart, James, and Nicholas Revett. *The Antiquities of Athens Measured and Delineated*. 4 vols. London, 1762–1816.

Stukeley, William. *Stonehenge, A Temple Restor'd to the British Druids*. London, 1740.

———. *Abury, A Temple of the British Druids*. London, 1743.

Sutherland, John. "Blake: A Crisis of Love and Jealousy." *PMLA*, 87 (1972), 424–31.

Svendsen, Kester. "John Martin and the Expulsion Scene of *Paradise Lost*." *Studies in English Literature*, 1 (1961), 63–73.

Tannenbaum, Leslie. *Biblical Tradition in Blake's Early Prophecies: The Great Code of Art*. Princeton: Princeton Univ. Press, 1982.

Tayler, Irene. *Blake's Illustrations to the Poems of Gray*. Princeton: Princeton Univ. Press, 1971.

———. "Say First! What Mov'd Blake? Blake's *Comus* Designs and *Milton*." In *Blake's Sublime Allegory: Essays on the Four Zoas, Milton and Jerusalem*, ed. Stuart Curran and Joseph A. Wittreich, Jr. Madison: Univ. of Wisconsin Press, 1973.

Taylor, Dick, Jr. "The Storm Scene in *Paradise Regained*: A Reinterpretation." *University of Toronto Quarterly*, 24 (1955), 359–76.

Thompson, E. P. *The Making of the English Working Class*. London: Victor Gollancz, 1963.

Todd, H. J., ed. *Poetical Works of John Milton*. 5 vols. London, 1801.

Todd, Ruthven. *Tracks in the Snow: Studies in English Science and Art*. London: Grey Wall Press, 1946.

Tolley, Michael J. "*Europe*: 'to those ychain'd in sleep.'" In *Blake's Visionary Forms Dramatic*, ed. David V. Erdman and John E. Grant. Princeton: Princeton Univ. Press, 1970.

———. "Blake's Songs of Spring." In *William Blake: Essays in Honour of Sir Geoffrey Keynes*, ed. Morton D. Paley and Michael Phillips. Oxford: Clarendon Press, 1973.

———. "Marriages in Heaven and Hell: Blake's Enigmatic Title Page." In *Symposium on Romanticism*, ed. Deirdre Coleman and Peter Otto. Adelaide: Univ. of Adelaide. Centre for British Studies, 1990.

———. "'Words Standing in Chariots': The Literalism of Blake's Imagination." In *Imagining Romanticism: Essays on English and Australian Romanticisms*, ed. Deirdre Coleman and Peter Otto. West Cornwall: Locust Hill Press, 1991.

Trapp, Joseph B. "The Iconography of the Fall of Man." In *Approaches to Paradise Lost*, ed. C. A. Patrides. Toronto: Univ. of Toronto Press, 1968.

Tuve, Rosemond. *Images and Themes in Five Poems by Milton*. Cambridge: Harvard Univ. Press, 1957.

Van Sinderen, Adrian. *Blake: The Mystic Genius*. Syracuse: Syracuse Univ. Press, 1949.

Voltaire, François Marie Arouet. *Philosophical Dictionary*. Trans. Theodore Besterman. Harmondsworth: Penguin, 1972.

Wardle, Judith. "Satan not having the Science of Wrath but only of Pity." *Studies in Romanticism*, 13 (1974), 147–54.

Warner, Janet A. *Blake and the Language of Art*. Kingston: McGill–Queens Univ. Press, 1982.

Warner, Nicholas O. "Blake's Moon-Ark Symbolism." *Blake: An Illustrated Quarterly*, 54 (1980), 44–59.

Welch, Dennis M. "Blake's Critique of Election: *Milton* and the *Comus* Illustrations." *Philological Quarterly*, 64 (1985), 509–22.

Wells, William. *William Blake's Heads of the Poets*. Manchester: Manchester City Art Gallery, 1969.

Werner, Bette Charlene. *Blake's Vision of the Poetry of Milton: Illustrations to Six Poems*. Lewisburg: Bucknell Univ. Press, 1986.

Willey, Basil. *The English Moralists*. London: Chatto & Windus, 1964.

Wilson, Mona. *The Life of William Blake*. 1927; rev. ed. London: Oxford Univ. Press, 1971.

———, ed. *Johnson: Prose and Poetry*. London: Hart-Davis, 1957.

Wind, Edgar. *Pagan Mysteries in the Renaissance*. New York: Norton, 1968.

Winkelmann, Johann Joachim. *Reflections on the Imitation of Greek Works in Painting and Sculpture*. Trans. Elfriede Heyer and Roger C. Norton. La Salle: Open Court, 1987.

Wittkower, Rudolf and Margot. *Born Under Saturn: The Character and Conduct of Artists*. New York: Norton, 1963.

Wittreich, Joseph A., Jr. "William Blake: Illustrator-Interpreter of *Paradise Regained*." In *Calm of Mind*, ed. Joseph A. Wittreich, Jr. Cleveland: Case Western Reserve Univ. Press, 1971.

———. "Domes of Mental Pleasure: Blake's Epics and Hayley's Epic Theory." *Studies in Philology*, 4 (1971), 101–19.

———. *Angel of Apocalypse: Blake's Idea of Milton*. Madison: Univ. of Wisconsin Press, 1975.

———. *Visionary Poetics: Milton's Tradition and His Legacy*. San Marino: Huntington Library, 1979.

Wölfflin, Heinrich. *Classic Art*. 1898; Ithaca: Cornell Univ. Press, 1980.

Wollheim, Richard, ed. *Hume on Religion*. New York: Collins, 1963.

Worrall, David. "Blake and the Night Sky I: The 'Immortal Tent.'" *Bulletin of Research in the Humanities*, 84 (1981), 273–95.

Illustrations

Fig. 1   *Head of Milton*. Manchester City Art Gallery, Manchester.

Fig. 2   William Faithorne, *John Milton, Aged 62*. National Library of Australia, Canberra.

Fig. 3   *Comus with His Revellers*. Huntington Library, San Marino.

Fig. 4   *Comus with His Revellers*. Museum of Fine Arts, Boston.

Fig. 5 *Comus, Disguised as a Rustic, Addresses the Lady in the Wood.* Huntington Library, San Marino.

Fig. 6   *Comus, Disguised as a Rustic, Addresses the Lady in the Wood*. Museum of Fine Arts, Boston.

Fig. 7   *The Brothers Seen by Comus Plucking Grapes.* Huntington Library, San Marino.

Fig. 8   *The Brothers Seen by Comus Plucking Grapes.* Museum of Fine Arts,
          Boston.

Fig. 9   *The Brothers Meet the Attendant Spirit in the Wood.* Huntington Library, San Marino.

Fig. 10   *The Brothers Meet the Attendant Spirit in the Wood.* Museum of Fine Arts, Boston.

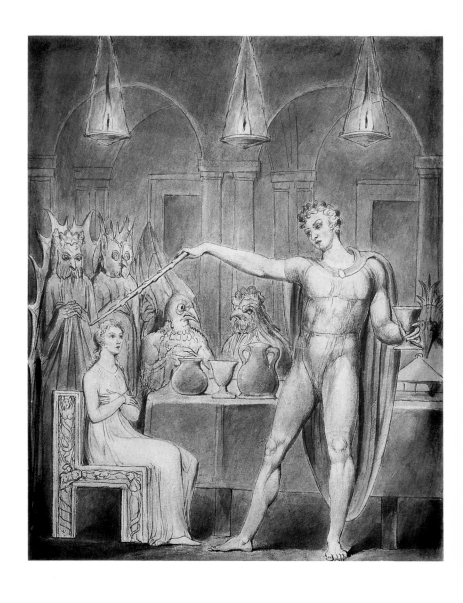

Fig. 11 *The Magic Banquet with the Lady Spell-Bound.* Huntington Library, San Marino.

Fig. 12   *The Magic Banquet with the Lady Spell-Bound*. Museum of Fine Arts, Boston.

Fig. 13 *The Brothers Driving Out Comus*. Huntington Library, San Marino.

Fig. 14   *The Brothers Driving Out Comus*. Museum of Fine Arts, Boston.

Fig. 15 *Sabrina Disenchanting the Lady*. Huntington Library, San Marino.

Fig. 16 *Sabrina Disenchanting the Lady*. Museum of Fine Arts, Boston.

Fig. 17 *The Lady Restored to Her Parents.* Huntington Library, San Marino.

Fig. 18 *The Lady Restored to Her Parents.* Museum of Fine Arts, Boston.

215

Fig. 19 *Satan Arousing the Rebel Angels.* Huntington Library, San Marino.

Fig. 20 *Satan Arousing the Rebel Angels*. Victoria and Albert Museum, London.

Fig. 21 *Satan, Sin and Death: Satan Comes to the Gates of Hell.* Huntington Library, San Marino.

Fig. 22   *Satan, Sin and Death: Satan Comes to the Gates of Hell.* Huntington Library, San Marino.

Fig. 23 *Christ Offers to Redeem Man*. Huntington Library, San Marino.

Fig. 24 *Christ Offers to Redeem Man*. Museum of Fine Arts, Boston.

Fig. 25 *Satan Watching the Endearments of Adam and Eve.* Huntington Library, San Marino.

Fig. 26 *Satan Watching the Endearments of Adam and Eve.* Museum of Fine Arts, Boston.

Fig. 27   *Satan Spying on Adam and Eve, and Raphael's Descent into Paradise.*
Huntington Library, San Marino.

Fig. 28 *Adam and Eve Asleep*. Museum of Fine Arts, Boston.

Fig. 29 *Raphael Warns Adam and Eve*. Huntington Library, San Marino.

Fig. 30   *Raphael Warns Adam and Eve*. Museum of Fine Arts, Boston.

Fig. 31 *The Rout of the Rebel Angels.* Huntington Library, San Marino.

Fig. 32 *The Rout of the Rebel Angels*. Museum of Fine Arts, Boston.

Fig. 33 *The Creation of Eve*. Huntington Library, San Marino.

Fig. 34 *The Creation of Eve.* Museum of Fine Arts, Boston.

Fig. 35 *The Temptation and Fall of Eve.* Huntington Library, San Marino.

Fig. 36 *The Temptation and Fall of Eve*. Museum of Fine Arts, Boston.

Fig. 37 *The Judgment of Adam and Eve*. Huntington Library, San Marino.

Fig. 38 *The Judgment of Adam and Eve.* Houghton Library, Harvard University, Cambridge.

Fig. 39 *Michael Foretells the Crucifixion*. Huntington Library, San Marino.

Fig. 40 *Michael Foretells the Crucifixion*. Museum of Fine Arts, Boston.

Fig. 41 *The Expulsion of Adam and Eve from the Garden of Eden.* Huntington Library, San Marino.

Fig. 42 *The Expulsion of Adam and Eve from the Garden of Eden.* Museum of Fine Arts, Boston.

Fig. 43 *The Descent of Peace*. Whitworth Art Gallery, Manchester.

Fig. 44 *The Descent of Peace.* Huntington Library, San Marino.

Fig. 45 *The Annunciation to the Shepherds.* Whitworth Art Gallery, Manchester.

Fig. 46   *The Annunciation to the Shepherds.* Huntington Library, San Marino.

Fig. 47 *The Old Dragon*. Whitworth Art Gallery, Manchester.

Fig. 48 *The Old Dragon*. Huntington Library, San Marino.

Fig. 49   *The Overthrow of Apollo and the Pagan Gods*. Whitworth Art Gallery, Manchester.

Fig. 50 *The Overthrow of Apollo and the Pagan Gods.* Huntington Library, San Marino.

Fig. 51 *The Flight of Moloch*. Whitworth Art Gallery, Manchester.

Fig. 52   *The Flight of Moloch.* Huntington Library, San Marino.

Fig. 53 *The Night of Peace*. Whitworth Art Gallery, Manchester.

Fig. 54 *The Night of Peace*. Huntington Library, San Marino.

Fig. 55 *Mirth*. Pierpont Morgan Library, New York.

Fig. 56   *Night Startled by the Lark*. Pierpont Morgan Library, New York.

Fig. 57 *The Sun at His Eastern Gate*. Pierpont Morgan Library, New York.

Fig. 58 *A Sunshine Holiday.* Pierpont Morgan Library, New York.

Fig. 59 *The Goblin*. Pierpont Morgan Library, New York.

Fig. 60　*The Youthful Poet's Dream*. Pierpont Morgan Library, New York.

Fig. 61 *Melancholy*. Pierpont Morgan Library, New York.

Fig. 62 *The Wandering Moon*. Pierpont Morgan Library, New York.

Fig. 63 *The Spirit of Plato*. Pierpont Morgan Library, New York.

Fig. 64 *The Sun in His Wrath*. Pierpont Morgan Library, New York.

Fig. 65   *Milton's Mysterious Dream.* Pierpont Morgan Library, New York.

Fig. 66 *Milton in His Old Age*. Pierpont Morgan Library, New York.

Fig. 67 *The Baptism of Christ*. Fitzwilliam Museum, Cambridge.

Fig. 68 *The First Temptation*. Fitzwilliam Museum, Cambridge.

Fig. 69 *Andrew and Simon Peter Searching for Christ*. Fitzwilliam Museum, Cambridge.

Fig. 70 *Mary at Her Distaff Watched Over by Two Angels.* Fitzwilliam Museum, Cambridge.

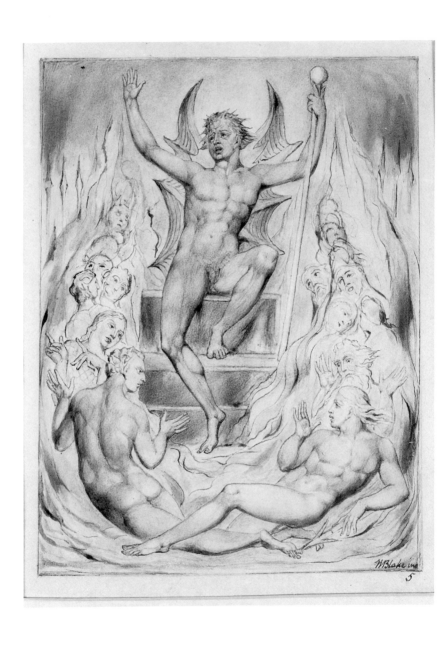

Fig. 71 *Satan in Council*. Fitzwilliam Museum, Cambridge.

Fig. 72   *Christ Refusing the Banquet Offered by Satan*. Fitzwilliam Museum, Cambridge.

Fig. 73 *The Second Temptation*. Fitzwilliam Museum, Cambridge.

Fig. 74 *Christ's Troubled Dream*. Fitzwilliam Museum, Cambridge.

Fig. 75 *Morning Chasing Away the Phantoms.* Fitzwilliam Museum, Cambridge.

Fig. 76 *The Third Temptation*. Fitzwilliam Museum, Cambridge.

Fig. 77 *Christ Ministered to by Angels*. Fitzwilliam Museum, Cambridge.

Fig. 78 *Christ Returns to His Mother.* Fitzwilliam Museum, Cambridge.

Fig. 79   *Satan Watching the Endearments of Adam and Eve.* Felton Bequest, National Gallery of Victoria, Melbourne.

Fig. 80 *The Creation of Adam and Eve*. Felton Bequest, National Gallery of Victoria, Melbourne.

Fig. 81   *Michael Foretells the Crucifixion*. Fitzwilliam Museum, Cambridge.

Fig. 82 *Europe: A Prophecy*, Frontispiece. British Museum, London.

The terror answerd: I am Orc, wreath'd round the accursed tree:
The times are ended; shadows pass the morning gins to break;
The fiery joy, that Urizen perverted to ten commands.
What night he led the starry hosts thro' the wide wilderness:
That stony law I stamp to dust: and scatter religion abroad
To the four winds as a torn book, & none shall gather the leaves;
But they shall rot on desart sands, & consume in bottomless deeps;
To make the desarts blossom, & the deeps shrink to their fountains,
And to renew the fiery joy, and burst the stony roof.
That pale religious letchery, seeking Virginity.
May find it in a harlot, and in coarse-clad honesty
The undefil'd tho' ravish'd in her cradle night and morn:
For every thing that lives is holy, life delights in life;
Because the soul of sweet delight can never be defil'd.
Fires inwrap the earthly globe, yet man is not consumd;
Amidst the lustful fires he walks; his feet become like brass,
His knees and thighs like silver, & his breast and head like gold.

Fig. 83 *America: A Prophecy*, pl. 8. Paul Mellon Collection, Yale Center for British Art, New Haven.

Fig. 84   *America: A Prophecy*, pl. 10. Paul Mellon Collection, Yale Center for British Art, New Haven.

281

Fig. 85   *Jerusalem: The Emanation of the Giant Albion*, pl. 99. Paul Mellon
Collection, Yale Center for British Art, New Haven.

Fig. 86 Engraving after Lorenzo Ghiberti, *The Creation of Eve*. State Library of Victoria, Melbourne.

Fig. 87 Engraving by Johann Sadeler after Friedrich Sustris, *Hercules at the Crossroads*. British Museum, London.

Fig. 88   *Illustrations to John Bunyan's The Pilgrim's Progress:* Christian Beaten Down by Apollyon. Frick Collection, New York.

Fig. 89 *The Vision of the Last Judgment*. Petworth House, Sussex.

Fig. 90   Richard Westall, *Satan Calling Up His Legions*. University of Illinois
Library, Champaign.

Fig. 91 *Illustrations to the Book of Job,* pl. 11. Felton Bequest, National Gallery of Victoria, Melbourne.

Fig. 92 James Barry, *Satan, Sin and Death*. British Museum, London.

Fig. 93   Albrecht Dürer, *The Trinity*. British Museum, London.

Fig. 94   *The Resurrection.* Winthrop Bequest, Fogg Art Museum, Harvard University, Cambridge.

Fig. 95   W. H. Brown, *Satan Watching Adam and Eve*. University of Illinois
Library, Champaign.

The Soul hovering over the Body reluctantly parting with Life.

----------------------------------- *How wistfully she looks*
On all she's leaving, now no longer hers.'

Fig. 96   *Illustrations for Robert Blair's The Grave*, pl. 6: The Soul Hovering Over
the Body Reluctantly Parting with Life. State Library of Victoria,
Melbourne.

The Reunion of the Soul & the Body

Fig. 97 *Illustrations for Robert Blair's The Grave*, pl. 10: The Reunion of the Soul & the Body. State Library of Victoria, Melbourne.

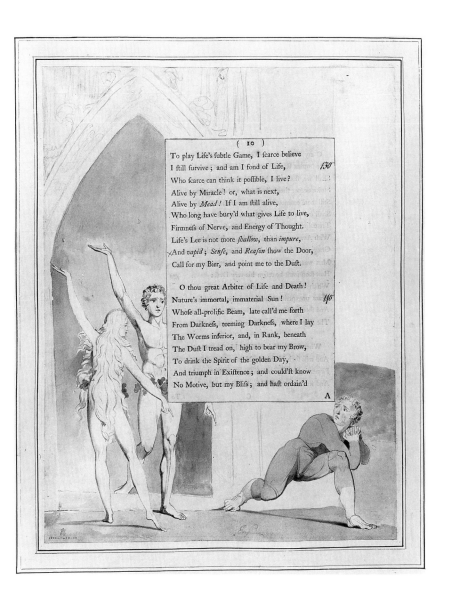

Fig. 98   *Illustrations to Edward Young's Night Thoughts*, No. 119. British Museum,
London.

Fig. 99   Engraving by Marcantonio Raimondi after Raphael, *Mercury Descending from Heaven*. British Museum, London.

Fig. 100 Richard Westall, *Unawak'n'd Eve*. University of Illinois Library,
Champaign.

(12)

With Joy,---with Grief, that *healing Hand* I see;
Ah! too confpicuous! It is fix'd on high?
On high?--What means my Frenzy? I blafpheme;
Alas! how low? how far beneath the Skies?
The Skies it form'd; and now it bleeds for me---
But bleeds the Balm I want---yet ftill it *bleeds*;
Draw the dire Steel---Ah no!--- the dreadful Bleffing
What Heart, or can fuftain? or dares forego?
There hangs all human Hope: That Nail fupports
Our falling Univerfe: That gone, we drop;
Horror receives us, and the difmal Wifh
Creation had been fmother'd in her Birth---
Darknefs His Curtain, and His Bed the Duft;
When Stars and Sun are Duft beneath his Throne!
In Heaven itfelf can fuch Indulgence dwell?
O what a Groan was there? A Groan *not His*,
He feiz'd our dreadful Right, the Load fuftain'd;
And heav'd the Mountain from a guilty World.

A

Fig. 101 *Illustrations to Edward Young's Night Thoughts,* No. 121. British Museum, London.

298

Fig. 102 *Milton: A Poem*, pl. 42. British Museum, London.

Fig. 103 Edward Burney, *Raphael Conversing with Adam and Eve*. University of Illinois Library, Champaign.

Fig. 104 *The Garden of Eden*, attributed to Lucas Cranach. Scheide Collection,
Princeton University Library, Princeton.

Fig. 105 *The Fall of Man*. Victoria and Albert Museum, London.

Fig. 106 Albrecht Dürer, *The Fall*. Felton Bequest, National Gallery of Victoria, Melbourne.

Fig. 107 Grinling Gibbons, Font in St. James's Church, Piccadilly.

Quos connectit amor verus, castumq; cubile,
Auspice unguntur Christo, remanentq; fideles.

Fig. 108 Hendrick Goltzius, *Marriage Founded Solely on Pure and Chaste Love,
Which Is Blessed by Christ*. British Museum, London.

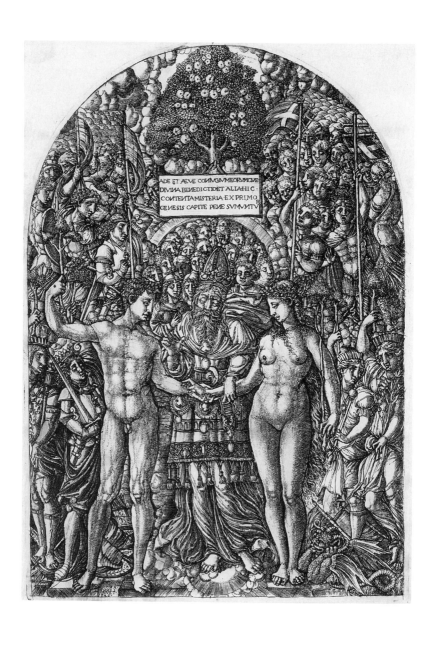

Fig. 109 Jean Duvet, *The Marriage of Adam and Eve*. British Museum, London.

Fig. 110 Engraving by Mario Cartaro after Michelangelo, *The Lamentation of the Virgin Beneath the Cross*. British Museum, London.

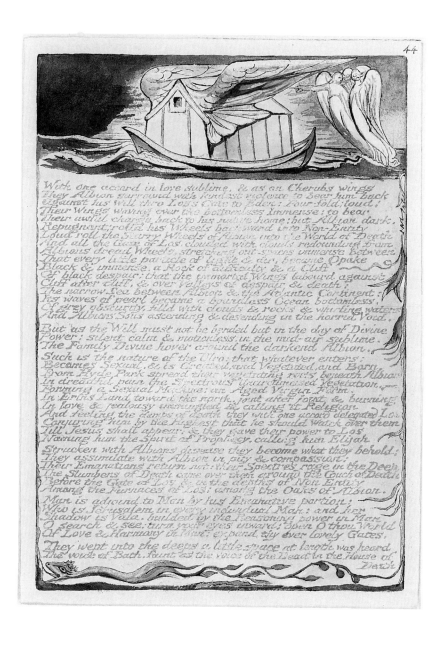

With one accord in love sublime, & as on Cherubs wings
They Albion surround with kindest violence to bear him back
Against his will thro Los's Gate to Eden: Four-fold: loud!
Their Wings waving over the bottomless Immense: to bear
Their awful charge back to his native home; but Albion dark,
Repugnant; rolld his Wheels backward into Non-Entity
Loud roll the Starry Wheels of Albion into the World of Death
And all the Gate of Los, clouded with clouds redounding from
Albions dread Wheels, stretching out spaces immense between
That every little particle of light & air, became Opake
Black & immense, a Rock of difficulty & a Cliff
Of black despair; that the immortal Wings labourd against
Cliff after cliff, & over Valleys of despair & death:
The narrow Sea between Albion & the Atlantic Continent:
Its waves of pearl became a boundless Ocean bottomless,
Of grey obscurity, filld with clouds & rocks & whirling waters
And Albions Sons ascending & descending in the horrid Void.

But as the Will must not be bended but in the day of Divine
Power: silent calm & motionless, in the mid-air sublime,
The Family Divine hover around the darkend Albion.

Such is the nature of the Ulro; that whatever enters:
Becomes Sexual, & is Created, and Vegetated, and Born,
From Hyde Park spread their vegetating roots beneath Albion
In dreadful pain the Spectrous Uncircumcised Vegetation,
Forming a Sexual Machine: an Aged Virgin Form,
In Erins Land toward the north, joint after joint & burning
In love & jealousy immingled & calling it Religion
And feeling the damps of death they with one accord delegated Los
Conjuring him by the Highest that he should Watch over them
Till Jesus shall appear: & they gave their power to Los
Naming him the Spirit of Prophecy, calling him Elijah.

Strucken with Albions disease they become what they behold;
They assimilate with Albion in pity & compassion;
Their Emanations return not: their Spectres rage in the Deep
The Slumbers of Death came over them around the Couch of Death
Before the Gate of Los & in the depths of Non Entity
Among the Furnaces of Los: among the Oaks of Albion.

Man is adjoind to Man by his Emanative portion:
Who is Jerusalem in every individual Man: and her
Shadow is Vala, builded by the Reasoning power in Man
O search & see: turn your eyes inward: open O thou World
Of Love & Harmony in Man: expand thy ever lovely Gates.

They went into the deeps a little space at length was heard
The voice of Bath, faint as the voice of the Dead in the House of
Death.

Fig. 111 *Jerusalem: The Emanation of the Giant Albion*, pl. 44. Paul Mellon Collection, Yale Center for British Art, New Haven.

Fig. 112 *Illustrations to the Book of Job*, pl. 14. Felton Bequest, National Gallery of Victoria, Melbourne.

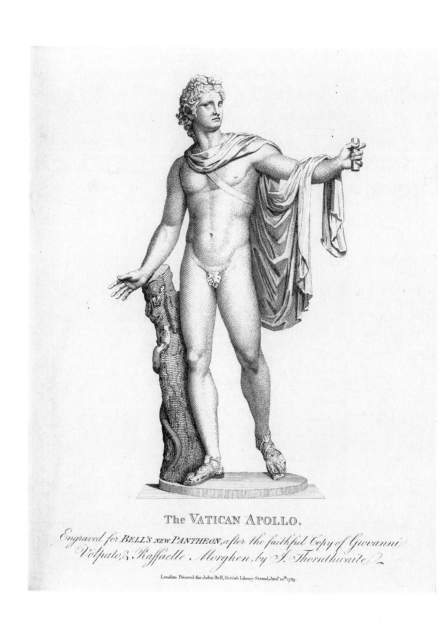

The VATICAN APOLLO.

Engraved for BELL'S NEW PANTHEON, *after the faithful Copy of Giovanni
Volpato,*& *Raffaelle Morghen, by J. Thornthwaite.*

London Printed for John Bell, British Library Strand, Jan.ʸ 10ᵗʰ 1789.

Fig. 113 Engraving of the *Apollo Belvedere*, from John Bell's *New Pantheon*.
Huntington Library, San Marino.

Fig. 114 Henry Fuseli, *Milton Dictating to His Daughter*. British Museum, London.

Fig. 115 Mezzotint by R. Dunkerton after George Romney, *Mirth*. British
Museum, London.

Fig. 116 *Illustrations to John Bunyan's The Pilgrim's Progress:* Vanity Fair. Frick Collection, New York.

Fig. 117 *Satan in His Original Glory: 'Thou wast perfect till iniquity was found in thee.'* Tate Gallery, London.

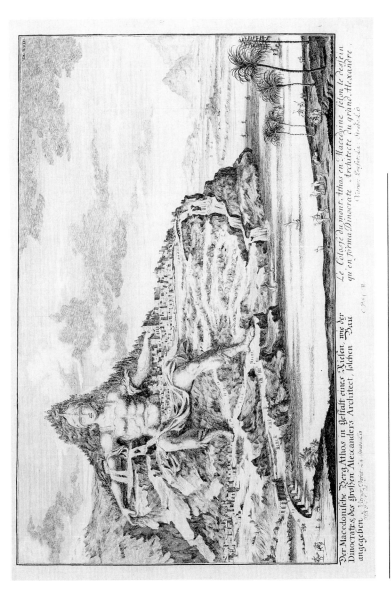

Fig. 118 *Mount Athos*, from J. B. Fischer von Erlach, *Entwurf einer historischen Architektur*. British Library, London.

Fig. 119 *Earth*, from the 1758–60 edition of Cesare Ripa, *Iconologia*, illustrated by Gottfried Eichler, published by Georg Hertel. British Library, London.

Fig. 120 Mezzotint by R. Dunkerton after George Romney, *Melancholy*. British Museum, London.

Fig. 121 *Diana*, from P. Basin, *Dictionnaire des Graveurs*. State Library of Victoria, Melbourne.

Fig. 122 Detail of Plato and Aristotle from Raphael, *The School of Athens*. Stanza della Segnatura, Vatican Palace, Rome.

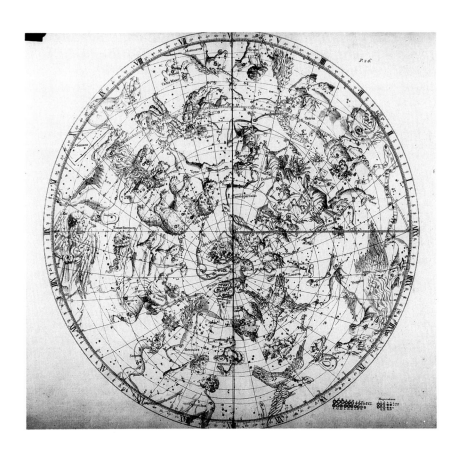

Fig. 123 John Flamsteed, *Atlas Coelestis*, pl. 26. State Library of Victoria, Melbourne.

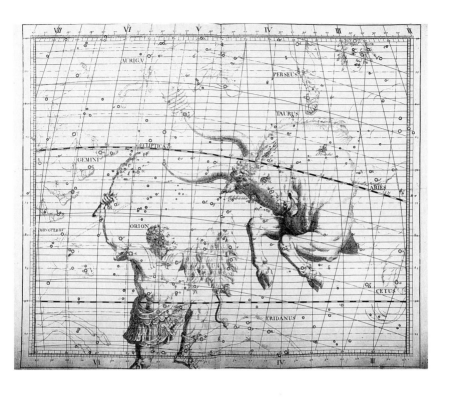

Fig. 124 John Flamsteed, *Atlas Coelestis*, pl. 34. State Library of Victoria, Melbourne.

Fig. 125 Detail of Christ as Judge from Michelangelo, *The Last Judgment*. Sistine Chapel, Vatican Palace, Rome.

Fig. 126 *Milton: A Poem*, pl. 50. Library of Congress, Washington.

Fig. 127 Girolamo Mocetto, *The Baptism of Christ*. British Museum, London.

Fig. 128 *The Baptism of Christ*. Museum of Art, Rhode Island School of Design, Providence.

Fig. 129 School of Mantegna, *The Man of Sorrows*. British Museum, London.

Fig. 130 *Christ Appearing to the Apostles After the Resurrection*. Yale Center for British Art, New Haven.

EGO SITIENTI DABO DE FONTE AQVÆ VITÆ GRATIS. *Apocalip. 21.*
VENITE AD ME OMNES QVI LABORATIS, ET ONERATI ESTIS, ET EGO REFICIAM VOS.

Hans. Collaert

Fig. 131 Hans Collaert, *The Fountain of Life*. Kitto Bible, Huntington Library, San Marino.

Fig. 132 Lucas van Leyden, *The First Temptation*. British Museum, London.

Fig. 133 Martin de Vos, *The Temptation of Christ*. Kitto Bible, Huntington Library, San Marino.

Fig. 134 Lucas Cranach the Elder, *Four Saints Adoring Christ Crucified on the Sacred Heart*. British Museum, London.

Fig. 135 *The Great Red Dragon and the Woman Clothed with the Sun.* Rosenwald
Collection, National Gallery of Art, Washington.

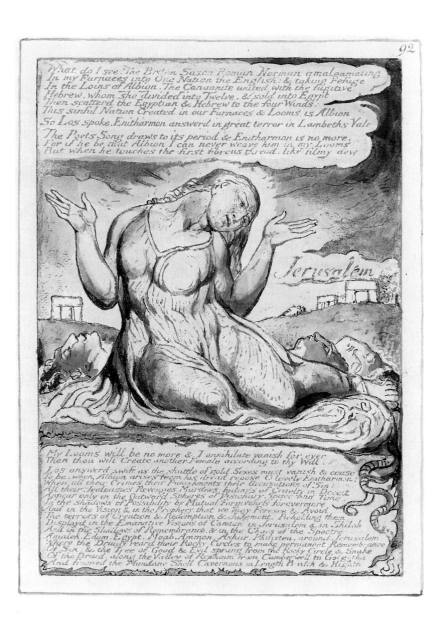

Fig. 136 *Jerusalem: The Emanation of the Giant Albion*, pl. 92. Paul Mellon Collection, Yale Center for British Art, New Haven.

Fig. 137 Detail from Michelangelo, *The Fall and Expulsion*. Sistine Chapel Ceiling, Vatican Palace, Rome.

Fig. 138 Antonio Tempesta, *The Temptation of St. Anthony*. British Museum, London.

Fig. 139 Engraving by Marcantonio Raimondi after Raphael, *The Lamentation of the Virgin*. British Museum, London.

Fig. 140 Jean Duvet, *The Crucifixion*. British Museum, London.

Fig. 141 Richard Payne Knight, *Discourse on the Worship of Priapus*, pl. 3.
Huntington Library, San Marino.

Fig. 142 Ludwig Krug, *Man of Sorrows*. British Museum, London.

Fig. 143 Engraving after Michelangelo, *A Dream of Human Life*. Kitto Bible, Huntington Library, San Marino.

Index

Index

Index

The Locust Hill
Literary Studies Series